CW00672831

THE WOUNDED ANIMAL

THE WOUNDED ANIMAL

J. M. COETZEE AND THE DIFFICULTY OF REALITY
IN LITERATURE AND PHILOSOPHY

STEPHEN MULHALL

PRINCETON UNIVERSITY PRESS

PRINCETON AND OXFORD

Copyright © 2009 by Princeton University Press
Published by Princeton University Press, 41 William Street,
Princeton, New Jersey 08540
In the United Kingdom: Princeton University Press, 6 Oxford Street,
Woodstock, Oxfordshire OX20 1TW

All Rights Reserved

Library of Congress Cataloging-in-Publication Data

Mulhall, Stephen, 1962–
The wounded animal : J. M. Coetzee and the difficulty of reality in
literature and philosophy / Stephen Mulhall.
p. cm.
Includes bibliographical references and index.
ISBN 978-0-691-13736-0 (cloth : alk. paper)
ISBN 978-0-691-13737-7 (pbk. : alk. paper)
1. Coetzee, J. M., 1940—Criticism and interpretation.
2. Coetzee, J. M., 1940—Philosophy. 3. Philosophy in literature.
4. Animals (Philosophy) 5. Literature—Philosophy. I. Title.
PR9369.3.C58Z86 2009
823′14—dc 22   2008015470

British Library Cataloging-in-Publication Data is available

This book has been composed in Sabon

Printed on acid-free paper. ∞

press.princeton.edu

Printed in the United States of America

10 9 8 7 6 5 4 3 2 1

I still believe that no good joke is ever racist. And I believe it for the same reasons that I believe no good play or novel is ever racist, regardless of the politics of its author. The discourse of racism is bald, monotonous, unquestioning, single-voiced and desolate. Art, when it is good . . . is none of those things. Art is dramatic, and by dramatic I mean that it holds everything in opposition and suspense.

The moment art forgets it is dramatic and grows tendentious, the moment it begins to formulate a programme for the amelioration of mankind, or for spreading faith or disbelief, or for promoting racial disquiet or racial harmony, it ceases to be art. And a good joke belongs to art. Call it a little novel, comprising voices at intellectual and moral odds with one another, taking you by surprise and told, vertiginously, by a narrator it would not be wise of you to trust.

Thus in art, do matters of morality wait upon aesthetics.
Howard Jacobson

The wounded is the wounding heart.
Richard Crashaw

CONTENTS

ABBREVIATIONS

AA C. Diamond, "Anything but Argument," in *The Realistic Spirit* (Cambridge: MIT Press, 1991).

AT V. Hearne, *Adam's Task: Calling Animals by Name* (New York: Harper Perennial, 1994).

AAT M. Fried, *Absorption and Theatricality: Painting and Beholder in the Age of Diderot* (Chicago: University of Chicago Press, 1980).

CR O. O'Neill, "Critical Review of Clark, *The Moral Status of Animals,*" *Journal of Philosophy* 77 (1980).

DP J. M. Coetzee, *Doubling the Point*, ed. D. Attwell (Cambridge: Harvard University Press, 1992).

DR A. Crary and S. Shieh, eds., *Reading Cavell* (London: Routledge, 2006).

E S. Mitchell, *Erotikon* (New York: HarperCollins, 2000).

EC J. M. Coetzee, *Elizabeth Costello: Eight Lessons* (London: Secker and Warburg, 2003).

EK J. McMahan, *The Ethics of Killing* (Oxford: Oxford University Press, 2002).

EM C. Diamond, "Eating Meat and Eating People" in *The Realistic Spirit* (Cambridge: MIT Press, 1991).

EN T. Eagleton, *The English Novel: An Introduction* (Oxford: Blackwell, 2005).

FCM M. Heidegger, *Fundamental Concepts of Metaphysics*, trans. W. McNeill and N. Walker (Bloomington: Indiana University Press, 1995).

LA J. M. Coetzee, *The Lives of Animals* (Princeton: Princeton University Press, 1999).

LC H. von Hofmannsthal, *The Lord Chandos Letter and Other Writings*, trans. J. Rotenberg (New York: New York Review Books, 2005).

MSA S. Clark, *The Moral Status of Animals* (New York: Oxford University Press, 1977).

PAL S. Cavell et al., *Philosophy and Animal Life* (New York: Columbia University Press, 2008).

PD R. Gaita, *The Philosopher's Dog* (Melbourne: Text Publishing, 2002).

PE O. O'Neill, "The Power of Example," *Philosophy* 61 (1986).

PI   L. Wittgenstein, *Philosophical Investigations*, trans.
G.E.M. Anscombe (Oxford: Blackwell, 1958).
RA   F. Kafka, "A Report to an Academy," in *The Complete
Short Stories of Franz Kafka*, trans. W. and E. Muir, ed.
N. N. Glatzer (London: Vintage, 1983).
RN   I. Watt, *The Rise of the Novel* (London: Pimlico, 1957).
RS   C. Diamond, *The Realistic Spirit* (Cambridge: MIT Press, 1991).
SM   J. M. Coetzee, *Slow Man* (London: Secker and Warburg, 2005).
WGO J. M. Coetzee, "As a Woman Grows Older," *New York Review
of Books*, January 15, 2004.
WLB T. Nagel, "What Is It Like to Be a Bat?" in *Mortal Questions*
(Cambridge: Cambridge University Press, 1979).
WML A. Crary, *Wittgenstein and the Moral Life: Essays in Honour
of Cora Diamond* (Boston: MIT Press, 2007).
WV   S. Cavell, *The World Viewed* (Cambridge: Harvard
University Press, 1971).

THE WOUNDED ANIMAL

Chapter One

INTRODUCTION: THE ANCIENT QUARREL

IN 1997, THE EMINENT novelist and critic J. M. Coetzee (later to be awarded the Nobel Prize for Literature) gave two Tanner Lectures on Human Values at Princeton University, under the general title "The Lives of Animals." They took the form of two fictions—two linked short stories about the visit of the eminent novelist Elizabeth Costello to Appleton College to deliver the annual Gates Lecture (together with a seminar in the literature department), in which she chooses to speak about animals, and in particular the ways in which animals have been and are treated not only by human beings in general, but by philosophers and poets in particular. Since the Tanner Lectures generally take the form of philosophical essays or addresses, and an invitation to give them is seen as a mark of real distinction in the philosophical world, it is hard to see Coetzee's way of responding to that invitation as anything other than a deliberate attempt to reopen an issue that has marked—indeed, defined—philosophy from its inception among the ancient Greeks: the quarrel between philosophy and poetry, described by Plato as ancient even though his invocation of it (epitomised in his notorious claim that the poets must be banished from the just city, the philosophical republic) is in fact the means by which philosophy distinguishes itself for the first time as an autonomous form of intellectual inquiry.

Plato offers a bewildering number of interrelated justifications for his expulsion order, outlined both within the precincts of the *Republic* and elsewhere. Some appear to depend heavily upon specific epistemological and metaphysical doctrines that hold little appeal for many contemporary philosophers; but all can be formulated in ways that are likely to resonate with anyone capable of identifying with philosophy's highest aspirations for itself, and so for us. Plato fears what he sees as literature's capacity to engage and incite our emotions while bypassing our rational faculties. He distrusts its ability to construct simulacra of real persons and events, in whose purely imaginary vicissitudes we can effortlessly lose ourselves, thereby distracting ourselves from the genuinely real and the slow, hard struggle to comprehend what lies behind its often-misleading presentations of itself. He takes very seriously the poet's interpretation of himself as subject to divine inspiration, a mere channel for the muses—a self-image that reveals poetry to be an essentially nonrational activity, lacking any secure, transmissible, and impersonal body of knowledge or expertise that might ground a claim to any depth of understanding; and he despises the poet's ability to construct convincing representations of those possessed of genuine knowledge and understanding (generals, kings, even philosophers) without himself being in possession of the comprehension he counterfeits. He sees the poet's imaginative capacities as essentially amoral—entirely unconstrained not only by truthfulness (even when the nature of the divine is at stake), but also by the demands made on all comprehending creatures by the nature and reality of good and evil; indeed, the poet is often more attracted to the representation of interesting, vivid evil than banal and boring good. Taken together, Plato sees a fundamental threat of corruption that literature poses to the soul of the poet as well as that of his readers and listeners, the obstacles it creates for their distinctively human attempts to achieve self-knowledge and live a good life through a lucid grasp of reality—the task to which philosophy distinctively devotes itself.

Against this background, merely banishing the poet might seem like an excessively charitable response. And yet: quite apart from certain hesitations or qualifications to the universality of the anathema Plato pronounces (as when he excepts certain kinds of music from his ban, or allows certain kinds of artistic tools and techniques to be deployed in the education of the republic's young), and setting aside the broader question this raises of whether he might usefully distinguish between vices that are inseparable from the literary enterprise as such and those that happen to infest its contemporary manifestations (as in Homeric misrepresentations of the nature of the gods), the form of his pronouncements seems in deep contradiction with their content. For the Socrates of the *Republic* and elsewhere is not only willing to, but adept in, employing striking quasi-poetic imagery in conveying his message of the superiority of philosophy to literature: such figures as the divided line and the cave, not to mention the utopian allegory of the just republic (with its political structures further functioning as a figure for the internal articulation proper to the just soul), have become part of the philosophical canon. Moreover, Plato's favoured medium for presenting Socrates's message and method is that of the dialogue: he stages his condemnation of theatre in the form of dramatized conversations between idealized characters whose shape and orientation make manifest what Plato's Socrates sees as the essential core of philosophical investigation as such—the dialectical examination of one soul by another.

Is this best understood as an essentially dispensable or ornamental feature of his enterprise? Or as an adroit attempt to turn the resources of poetry against itself, addressing philosophy's audience in the terms most likely to motivate them in their presently benighted, cave-dwelling state, possibly be a way of establishing rational conviction. It could only be mere persuasion—an essentially causal matter.

O'Neill never exactly asserts (let alone argues) that rationality, so conceived, is the peculiar province of the human animal; but she has never hidden her allegiance to a broadly Kantian conception of human moral worth as residing in the rationality that distinguishes our mode of animality, and there is evidently an internal relation between her resistance to Clark's vision of kinship between human and nonhuman animals and her sense of the essential unrelatedness of mind and heart in the human being. By the same token, Clark's conception of a peaceable animal kingdom patently concerns not only the relation between human and nonhuman animals, but also the relation within human animals between heart and mind, body and intellect. And from Clark's point of view, O'Neill's Kantian conception of reason and her Kantian resistance to the moral claims of animals both give expression to the same phenomenon—the fateful vulnerability of humans to paranoid fantasies about their own animality, and hence their relation to other animals.

But my primary concern at present is not to follow out these very real hints that this specific topic in moral philosophy and more general conceptions of moral thinking and of thinking as such are nonaccidentally related. The key point for our purposes is rather that the conception of moral thinking, and of thinking as such, that O'Neill invokes in her critique of Clark's book is not itself philosophically uncontentious; hence it cannot provide an Archimedean point from which to achieve objective leverage on Clark's specific moral claims. There simply is no account of rationality, and so of moral reasoning, available to us here that is not itself essentially open to question, and more specifically open to moral evaluation. For what is to count as a legitimate instance of moral reasoning is itself partly determined by one's conception of morality, as well as by one's more general philosophical commitments and preconceptions. Philosophers can no more call upon a universally accepted conception of rationality than they can call upon an essentially uncontroversial conception of morality in their deliberations about moral thinking, and so in their deliberations about philosophy and literature.

This last matter is relevant here precisely because Diamond clearly expresses her temptation to regard the moral force of literature as a decisive piece of evidence against O'Neill's stance, since that stance makes the self-evident relevance of literature to moral thinking essentially incomprehensible. A central example in her paper of this relevance comes from Charles Dickens, and his attempts (in such novels as *Great Expectations* and *David Copperfield*) to convince those whose hearts are inclined against it that prevailing Victorian attitudes towards children and those classified as mad are morally objectionable. These novels are, in Diamond's view, attempts to enlarge the moral imagination of his readers; they do not assume that his readers' hearts are already inclined in the way Dickens would like, but rather work to change their prevailing inclinations and assumptions, to lead them to a more sympathetic way of looking at children. By presenting his readers with the world as viewed from a child's perspective, even (even particularly) when this does not involve the child being treated badly or generously, he aims to get them and us to attend to a child *as* a centre of a distinctive view of the world, and so to attend to children in their own right. By this kind of imaginative exercise, itself internally related to the engendering of pleasure of a distinctive kind, Dickens can succeed not only in altering our affections, but in enhancing our understanding—or rather, he enhances our understanding by engaging with and altering our affections and sensibility.

O'Neill might naturally respond as follows. If what Dickens aims to do is to redirect our attention, then the relevance of his enterprise to our moral thinking will turn on what we can find out, not on how we did so; and the moral relevance of whatever facts were thereby brought to our attention would then be demonstrable purely in the terms of the model of reasoning that we have apparently left behind (that of providing a rational ground for the assignment of a particular kind of moral significance). Diamond finds this response to be not so much mistaken as ludicrous. For what are "the facts" about children such that the kind of interest in them that Dickens takes and advocates is fitting? "Are we to describe children, their perceptions, emotions and thoughts, and then find some principle for directing emotional attitudes towards things of any sort whatever (small sentient Martians included) having such-and-such properties? This is sheer comedy" (AA, 301). And what the comedy reveals is that, for Dickens, it is not that the point of the kind of attention we give lies in what we find out; it is rather that what we can find out is conditioned by the kind of attention we give.

There are, after all, many ways of attending to things. There is Gradgrind's way, which is cold and even insolent; what we could possibly find out through such a chillingly presumptuous approach to the world can feed no adequate moral thought, or show us what we need to respond well to the world. And there is Dickens's way, the characteristic emotional colouring of which derives from its combination of great warmth, concentration of energy, and humour. It gives expression to a particular style of affectionate interest in and imaginative engagement with human affairs of exactly the kind that it aims to create in us, precisely by virtue of the capacity of that mode of attention to engage and reorient our own present interests and engagements.

There are many other such modes of attention; and, because they give expression to a certain conception of what is worth attending to and why, they are all necessarily subject to critical evaluation. But the one way in which that cannot be done is by asking which is most appropriate to the way things really are. For which way is that? Can it be seen except through the adoption of a particular mode of attention, or specified except through the adoption of a particular style of expression? There is no evaluatively neutral way of justifying any such adoption or rejection—no way of using the facts to determine which response to them is morally appropriate or fitting. To think otherwise is to commit oneself to a rather crude version of the all-too-familiar philosophical fantasy of an abyssal distinction between the domain of value-neutral facts and the evaluative systems we superimpose upon it.

Of course, to say this is not to deny that there are other ways of critically evaluating modes of attention, and so what they reveal. Dickens's mode of attention is, for example, inherently vulnerable to the threat of sentimentality and sometimes succumbs to that threat. By this I do not mean that it fails to reveal what is there to be seen as a consequence of Dickens's being in the grip of an excessively sentimental mood; I mean rather that sentimentality is the distinctive form or mode of its failure—that it constitutes one particular respect in which his moral thinking can show itself to be deficient. Such a form of criticism is not a hypothesis about the author's emotional state, but a judgement about the intellectual and moral texture of his writing and his thought. Failures of moral thinking are not exclusively matters of invalid inference or distorting external conditions. Our moral thinking (and our thinking more generally) can also be sentimental, shallow, cheap, or brutal in itself, as such; and we cannot identify such failures of thinking except by utilizing our own affective responses to them—responses that might at first be unreflective, but which we can, and must, reflect upon and submit to critical evaluation in exactly the kinds of terms that they make it possible for us to apply to the thoughts and emotions of others.

The point here is not to deny that more familiar forms of critical reflection, of the kind associated with philosophy in general and analytical philosophy in particular, and which tend to focus on questions of inferential validity in the context of assertion and argument, are real and important elements in the human rational armoury. It is simply to point out that there are other forms of critical reflection as well—ones with which we are perhaps more familiar in extraphilosophical contexts, but which are no less concerned to deepen our understanding and enrich our thought by embodying certain kinds of affective response to things, and inviting us to share those responses, as well as to critically evaluate them (perhaps by placing them next to very different modes of response, as Dickens's work invites us to reflect upon the differing moral sensibilities of Gradgrind and Betsy Trotwood).

If these really are forms of critical reflection, and hence amount to legitimate ways in which we can respond to the claims of reason upon us, it cannot be right to conceive of the domain of moral thought in such a way as to exclude them. And the further question arises: why couldn't a philosophical text—a text that aims not so much correctly to characterize the legitimate forms of moral thought evinced elsewhere but rather itself to contribute to distinctively philosophical debates about some range of moral issues—draw upon such modes of critical reflection, and so reasonably expect its readers to be willing and able to respond in similar ways? On Diamond's view, this is precisely what Stephen Clark is aiming to do in his book.

> If Clark's aim is that his readers acknowledge something in themselves which habits of thought and response overlay and keep hidden, it is essential that he invite us to set our imagination and sensibility and intelligence to work; only that exercise can put us in a position properly to judge the view of animals he invites us to take up. Like any judgements worth bothering with, it will draw on more than just the capacities of the head. (AA, 303–4)

That last sentence may go a little too far: questions about valid inference in the domain of assertion and argument are surely worth bothering with. But in the end, Diamond is not primarily interested in claiming that philosophers such as O'Neill should be compelled to recognize either the validity of Clark's vision of animals or the deep human value of the modes of attention and response through which he gives it expression, and in terms of which he invites us to respond. Both embody views about the natural world, about moral understanding, and about reason, that are eminently disputable. But what is not legitimate is for philosophers to bring their own, equally disputable, opposing views about these matters to bear in such a way as to imply that their view is the only conceivable one.

O'Neill's assumptions about the heart and the mind, and about assertion and argument, operate unquestioningly in her thinking in such a way as to exclude the very possibility that Clark might be attempting to address her, and our, capacities for rational reflection at all. And in so doing, she reproduces Plato's exclusionary gesture: in O'Neill's philosophical republic of letters, it is not only literature, but any form of critical reflection that employs those modes of attention and thought best exemplified in much literature, that suffers banishment. But of course, precisely because her assumptions exclude those modes of attention and reflection from the domain of genuine moral thinking even as a possibility, they can hardly be overturned by the citation of cases that exemplify those modes; every such apparent counterexample will simply fail to meet O'Neill's criteria for relevance, counting for her as persuasion, not argument. Hence, Diamond concludes by acknowledging that the exemplary

A moral philosophy that restricts itself to such examples risks reducing itself to mere aestheticism, to a form of moral connoisseurship that fails even to address the real problems we actually face.

It is evident that O'Neill's countercritique of Diamond rests on a number of presuppositions: some concern what she calls "the Wittgensteinian method in philosophy," others concern literature. To take the former first: even if some moral philosophers who would describe their work as Wittgensteinian might fit the description O'Neill constructs, is there any reason to think that Diamond does? It is true that Diamond's defence of Clark is in part a defence of his claim to be inviting his readers to acknowledge something in themselves that is overlain or hidden by unthinking habits of thought and response; so she plainly recognizes that one way of convincing another to alter their moral views is to remind them of something that they already know or acknowledge, something that is already common to author and reader. But it is also true that Diamond repeatedly emphasizes the capacity of literature, and so of literary examples, to enlarge our moral imagination, to educate the heart towards enlarged and deepened moral sympathies. Does this not show that she cannot accept the putative "definitively Wittgensteinian" idea that the only alternative to speaking to the converted is not to be able to speak to them at all?

O'Neill does note this apparently recalcitrant aspect of Wittgensteinian work such as Diamond's, and she responds as follows:

> This [idea of enlarging sympathies] seems empirically dubious—plenty of people have been converted (or corrupted) to mean or violent or racist moral practice and outlook—and in any case assumes a standpoint from which distinct moral traditions can be compared, which is not obviously available within the Wittgensteinian approach. We have to remember that within a position which sees all justification as relative to locally accepted practice any reason for converting those beyond the pale of one's own current practices would be matched by others' reasons for undertaking a counter-conversion. (PE, 15)

The inadequacy of this response is striking. First, why should the fact that sympathies can sometimes be contracted by modes of address to the convictions of the heart show that they cannot also be enlarged thereby? One might as well argue that the fact that such corruption can equally well be engendered by logically valid arguments shows that argument is a morally dubious mode of addressing one's reflective capacities. Beyond this patently invalid inference, we have only the assertion that enlargement of sympathies is not obviously consistent with a central assumption of the Wittgensteinian approach. But if Diamond's paper explicitly emphasizes the possibility of critical reflection of a kind that enlarges sympathies, surely that gives us reason to reconsider the assumption that she believes that all justification is relative to locally accepted practice. The fact that she underlines Dickens's capacity to lead his readers beyond the pale of their current practices suggests on the contrary that she does not in fact belong in O'Neill's artificially constructed category of "Wittgensteinian moral philosophers." Indeed, it raises the possibility that O'Neill's idea of a single, Wittgensteinian approach to moral philosophy united around such views of justification might itself be a fantasy. And here we reach a more fundamental philosophical disagreement between Diamond and O'Neill.

O'Neill simply takes it for granted that Wittgensteinian moral philosophers can and must be distinguished from other kinds of moral philosopher by virtue of the specific account they offer of such things as the nature of moral justification; the only question for her is what that distinctively Wittgensteinian account might be—what particular requirements it lays down for something to count as a moral justification, for example. We might disagree about what those Wittgensteinian requirements are, but there must be some; otherwise, there would be no distinctively Wittgensteinian position to analyse. In effect, then, O'Neill imposes particular requirements for what is to count as a Wittgensteinian account of ethics, and does so in terms of the particular requirements such accounts imposes on their subject matter.

But Diamond's Wittgenstein is precisely someone who sees the original sin of philosophy as that of attempting to lay down requirements on the reality it aims to contemplate, and who accordingly sees its possibility for redemption as lying in the attempt simply to attend to what is there to be seen, in all its variety and complexity. So one cannot properly appreciate the nature of the misunderstanding manifest in O'Neill's critique of Diamond if one restricts oneself to pointing out that Diamond's critique of O'Neill does not in fact presuppose that all moral justification must be relative to a practice; for one might then go on to ask: "Well, if that isn't what Diamond thinks about ethics, what *are* her distinctive commitments and theses?" But Diamond is not even attempting to argue that it is a requirement on all competent moral beings that they acknowledge the reality of convictions of the heart, or the relevance and importance of literature to philosophy; she is not trying to—she is in fact trying not to—lay down any requirements at all. Her aim is simply to remind us that it is perfectly intelligible to talk of convictions of the heart, and to regard literature as having moral force because of its ability to address them—that these ways of conceiving morality and rationality exist, and can be explained, and even rendered convincing (although not, of course, to everyone). But all that follows from such reminders is that philosophers can have no business laying down requirements on the nature of moral thought such that these possibilities entirely disappear from sight. To argue against their cogency or plausibility is one thing; to write as if their of literary examples: she sees the authority of literary texts as something that "imposes a largely shared interpretation of examples" and so helps to occlude the depth and ubiquity of disagreement in moral life. But to accept her point about textual warrant does not in any way establish the claim that interpretations of literary examples are largely shared or agreed upon; and this is evident even with respect to the work of authors who most plausibly fit her earlier content claim—those whose work focuses primarily upon inwardness and personal relations.

The novels and tales of Henry James are certainly "distinctive, nuanced and well-articulated . . . each is *sui generis* and in itself a complete example of moral thinking" (PE, 12). It is hard to think of literary texts that are more dense, substantial, and closely textured; but this has not ensured agreement upon how they are to be interpreted. On the contrary, the literary criticism of Henry James by now constitutes a literary critical tradition in its own right, with its epochs and revolutions, its conflicting paradigms and topics of unending debate. One might well define the canonicity of such texts as manifest in their capacity indefinitely to sustain productive critical attention; and what is thereby produced is not a monolith of self-reinforcing and inherently conservative agreement but rather an extended conversation between a variety of different voices and perspectives, none of which could be said entirely to lack textual warrant or to depend solely upon extratextual hunches (as if there is any way of rendering that distinction at once exhaustive and informative). The point here is not to contest the thought that interpretation requires textual warrant; it is to contest the assumption that the need for textual warrant makes determining the content and significance of a literary text any less complex, exploratory, and inherently open-ended a business than that of understanding the moral significance of a real-life situation.

O'Neill claims that the action of stories such as those of Henry James is essentially or inherently completed, something that she opposes to what she describes as less complete situations in real life that raise moral problems or dilemmas; but this is multiply misleading. For first, the relevant actions are not confronted by the characters as always already completed; rather, they find themselves in situations of necessarily partial knowledge in which their problem is precisely to decide what to do. Furthermore, it is characteristic of a James story that even when the action of the plot is complete, its moral significance remains a matter of debate and conflict among the characters, as well as among his readers; what that meaning is typically remains an unresolved problem, and so to the same extent does the question of what precisely was done (by Maggie Verver, or Isabel Archer). Accordingly, O'Neill's initial, guiding opposition between passing judgement on what has been done and deciding between possible actions simply does not have any direct application to the situations of

James's characters, and it might even be argued that that is an important part of their moral significance for the author himself.[4] In which case O'Neill's earlier point that guidance for real-life action cannot simply be read off from concrete literary examples would not count against the moral relevance of attention to literature. For those propounding that view could simply agree, suggesting instead that both the vicissitudes of literary characters in such texts and the vicissitudes of readers attempting to understand them might exemplify exactly the kind of attentiveness to particularity, the priority of right judgement to the application of general principle, that is needed to find one's moral way in real life, and indeed to find guidance in finding that way from literature. O'Neill's further idea that such guidance could result only from the application of principle or theory would then appear as yet another a priori requirement imposed on the reality of moral reflection.

The key point here, however, is not whether we accept or reject this way of understanding the moral force and relevance of James's writing in particular or of literature in general; it is whether we acknowledge that this is at least a possibility that the genre of the novel is capable of realising and hence acknowledge that O'Neill is once again laying down requirements on the nature of her subject matter that reveal themselves to be illegitimate as soon as we pay properly close attention to that subject matter in all its protean variety. If so, then her sense of the exiguous relevance of literature to philosophy rests as much on her highly restrictive conception of what literature may be as on her equally restrictive sense of the possible ways in which philosophy might acknowledge the claims of reason. And the shape of those restrictions—with their preference for theoretical principle over the exercise of right judgement from case to case, their relegation of the heart's concerns to the realm of mere persuasion, their conception of literary characters and situations not only as mere simulacra of the real but also as directing us away from moral reality rather than closer to its true nature—matches those originally imposed by Plato to such an extent that we can plausibly regard this conversation between O'Neill and Diamond as one more episode in what by now truly has become the ancient quarrel between philosophy and poetry. Coetzee's intervention is thus not in any sense an attempt to revive a philosophically moribund debate; it is rather a contribution to an utterly contemporary controversy.

---

[4] Cf. Robert Pippin, *Henry James and Modern Moral Life* (Cambridge: Cambridge University Press, 2000).

PART ONE

THE LIVES OF ANIMALS

Chapter Two

ELIZABETH COSTELLO'S LECTURE:
STORIES, THOUGHT-EXPERIMENTS,
AND LITERAL-MINDEDNESS

BEFORE TAKING SERIOUSLY the ways in which Costello and Coetzee variously contextualize it, we need to acknowledge that it is one fundamental purpose of Costello's first lecture to engage as directly as she can with the claims and assumptions of a number of philosophers who have pronounced (for very different reasons) upon the nature of nonhuman animal life, and in particular on the ways in which human beings can understand and should treat such animals. When discussing the particular case of Thomas Nagel and his famous article "What Is It Like to Be a Bat?"[1] she specifies the nature of her general approach as follows:

> I know that Nagel is only using bats . . . as aids in order to pose questions of his own about the nature of consciousness. But like most writers, I have a literal cast of mind, so I would like to stop with the bat. . . . [W]hen Nagel writes about a bat, I take him to be writing, in the first place, about a bat.[2]

It is worth noting that not only does she describe some of her remarks as "scholarly speculations, backed up with footnotes" (LA, 26), she (or rather, her author) actually provides some. Suppose that this formal gesture is Coetzee's modernist way of questioning the boundary between character and author by blurring their supposedly distinct lines of accountability for the words that issue at once from Costello's mouth and from Coetzee's keyboard; even so, its effect is necessarily to entangle Costello in Coetzee's admittedly partial and undeniably ironic, but nevertheless real, acknowledgment of scholarly responsibilities when addressing an academic audience.[3] Thus encouraged, I want to propose that, just as

---

[1] "What Is It Like to Be a Bat?," in *Mortal Questions* (Cambridge: Cambridge University Press, 1979), 169 (hereafter WLB).

[2] J. M. Coetzee, *The Lives of Animals* (Princeton: Princeton University Press, 1999), hereafter LA.

[3] All of these footnotes were eliminated when the text was reprinted as part of the later book, *Elizabeth Costello: Eight Lessons* (London: Secker and Warburg, 2003)—perhaps because of that book's rather different envisaged audience.

Costello does her philosophers the credit of taking it that, when they are writing about an animal, they are writing, in the first place, about an animal, so we should do her the credit of taking it that, when she is writing about philosophy and its arguments, she is writing, in the first place, about philosophy and its arguments.

It is perhaps worth acknowledging at the outset that this proposal, or at least my way of taking it, will hardly be uncontroversial from the point of view of philosophical readers of the lecture (and of the lecture containing it). And two such readers provide an unavoidable preliminary orientation to Costello's first lecture—unavoidable in that any other readers of that lecture on its first appearance in print will encounter both on the way to and through it. One of these philosophers is to be found within the fiction and the other beyond or rather before it, assigned the responsibility of introducing Coetzee's two Tanner Lectures, together with the four invited responses to them, to their first readers. Neither exactly shares my sense of where to begin.

The external reader is the political philosopher Amy Gutmann. Her introduction isolates and emphasizes two main elements that she finds in Costello's lecture: a general critique of philosophy's supposed tendency to privilege the mind over the heart, and a specific, extremely controversial argument by analogy—Costello's repeated comparison of contemporary human ways of treating nonhuman animals with the Nazis' treatment of Jews in the Holocaust. Gutmann is not exactly wrong to see such elements in the lecture, and to assign them a central role in its thrust; but I have two reasons for nevertheless declining her invitation to begin with them.

The first is that she decontextualizes, or more exactly recontextualizes, them in accordance with her general understanding of the nature and purpose of Coetzee's lectures. That understanding is summarized as follows: "In the frame of fiction, Coetzee's story of Elizabeth Costello's visit to Appleton College contains empirical and philosophical arguments that are relevant to the ethical issue of how human beings should treat animals" (LA, 4). This image of Coetzee's fiction as a frame or container for philosophical arguments implies that its relevance for philosophy can be at once demonstrated and exhausted by identifying and abstracting from it a sequence of self-contained elements that uncontroversially fall under an essentially uncontroversial category called "arguments." I hope that the introductory chapter of this study provides enough reason to hesitate before accepting any such mode of presentation of literature's relation to philosophy as essentially beyond question.

My second reason for not beginning with these two elements is that neither counts as one of the many ways in which Costello does (according to my understanding) directly engage with specific philosophical arguments and texts advanced by others. The second element is (or at least appears to be) an argument itself, of a familiar kind, rather than a response to one; whereas the first invites us to abstract from the particular manner or mode of Costello's confrontation with the more or less distinctive ways in which particular philosophers have actually found themselves defending such an assignment of privilege.

Putting these two concerns together, then, I am inclined to say that Gutmann's introduction actually directs us away from both the literariness and the concrete responsiveness that are jointly essential to Costello's stance towards philosophy, however critical or uncomprehending it may turn out to be—from her willingness to engage in dialogue, and in detail, with her opponents, without ever ceding her right in so doing to draw upon the distinctive powers of literature.

The internal reader is Costello's daughter-in-law, Norma Bernard, who possesses a Ph.D. degree in the philosophy of mind, although at present she lacks an academic post. She is shown to be driven to a public expression of her deep exasperation with her mother-in-law specifically when she declares her general attitude towards philosophers (her proposal to take them literally) as part of her response to Nagel, despite her simultaneous acknowledgment that, for Nagel himself, his bats are essentially characters in a thought-experiment in the philosophy of mind (cf. LA, 32). Coetzee never spells out the reason for Norma's exasperation; but given the exact occasion of its expression, there are two fairly obvious candidates for that role—one having to do with the form of Nagel's enterprise, the other having to do with its specific content or purpose.

The point about content is this. Given her Ph.D. specialization, Norma will be well aware that Nagel's bat is intended to be relevant only to a question about the human capacity to comprehend forms of consciousness other than its own, and not (certainly not directly) to questions in the domain of ethics. If Costello properly understood that internal relation between Nagel's bat and the philosophy of mind, as she claims to do, then (Norma might well think) she would not be dragging it into a lecture on the moral status of nonhuman animals—at least not without providing an elaborate justification of some kind. And yet Costello gives no indication that she sees herself as having any such responsibility.

But Norma's carefully calibrated sigh of disdain might also derive from a more formal concern—her familiarity with the philosophical genre of the thought-experiment, whose deployment is a central technique in any analytical philosopher's tool-kit and may even be the way in which some achieve a kind of immortality (insofar as their imaginary case, like Nagel's, engenders a productive secondary literature of interpretation and argument). For a philosopher such as Norma, if Costello really did understand the nature of such thought-experiments, she would realize that her avowed literal-mindedness about Nagel's bat was essentially misplaced;

for thought-experiments are not in any way intended to provide an accurate representation of some stretch of reality. They are explicitly constructed so as to strip away the complexity and detail of real-life situations, in order to isolate a specific conceptual or theoretical issue in as stark and plain a manner as possible, thereby allowing us to exercise our judgement about it free of any distortions that might result from the actual entanglement of this particular issue with a range of others in everyday experience.

The aim of these imaginative exercises is thus importantly different from those undertaken by writers such as Elizabeth Costello, and they will be fundamentally misunderstood if they are measured against the kind of standards appropriate to literary criticism. Thought-experiments are devised rather than created, modified rather than rewritten, analysed rather than entered into; when successful, they invite praise in terms of their novelty or ingenuity, as opposed to their wisdom or insight. A thought-experiment is not a very short story; consequently (so one might think) the actual reality of bat-life is of precisely no relevance to Nagel's bat.

Both of the points I am speculatively attributing to Norma here are, however, no more beyond philosophical question than are Amy Gutmann's, and hence no more to be taken for granted as starting points for understanding Costello's mode of engagement with philosophy. To see why, it is worth examining another example of the use of this philosophical genre, this time explicitly in the domain of ethics. In a recent, much-praised, and influential book entitled *The Ethics of Killing*, which puts the technique of thought-experimentation to highly systematic and imaginative use, Jeff McMahan presents his readers with the following imaginary situation.[4] Suppose that a woman, without family or friends, dies giving birth to a healthy infant. At the same hospital there are three other five-year-old children, who will die if they do not receive organ transplants, and the newborn has exactly the right tissue type. If McMahan's moral theory is right, it is morally permissible to "sacrifice" the orphaned infant in order to save the other three children.

The most obvious worry about this moment is that, although McMahan recognizes that he seems to be confronting a *reductio ad absurdum* of his position and confesses that "I cannot embrace [this implication] without significant misgivings and considerable unease" (EK, 360), embrace it nonetheless does. For he continues his examination of abortion and euthanasia for a further 150 pages, still drawing on the theory that led us to the apparent *reductio* in the first place—quite as if simply acknowledging its existence constituted a sufficient settling of accounts with it.

---

[4] (Oxford: Oxford University Press, 2002), hereafter EK.

Reduction to absurdity is a fate that any philosophical theory might meet—although it is relatively rare for a theorist simultaneously to underline and ignore such a flaw. But such split-mindedness is peculiarly disturbing when the theory concerns itself with morality, since in such a context a *reductio* argument confronts us with moral absurdity—or, to put it more bluntly, with the morally intolerable, the morally unthinkable. The philosopher Elizabeth Anscombe once remarked that anyone who thought in advance that it is open to question whether an action such as procuring the judicial execution of the innocent should be quite excluded from consideration showed a corrupt mind.[5] She thereby expressed a (highly controversial but hardly unintelligible) fear not only of evil actions, but of thinking evil thoughts—a fear (familiar to Plato) of the dulling and degrading of moral sensibility that such acts of contemplation can encourage and express. The analogy with McMahan's moral absurdity is not exact, of course. A morally innocent victim is certainly central to his cautionary tale; but while (to his credit) he cannot bear explicitly to accept this evil consequence of his theory, neither can he bear to reject the theory on its account. On the contrary, he acts as if his claim to be a serious moral thinker would be rather more severely damaged if he took such evil consequences as a sufficient reason to abandon his theoretical endeavours. Being a fearless thinker matters more, it seems, than avoiding morally fearful thoughts.

Although there is a connection to be made between this worry and Costello's treatment of Nagel's treatment of bats (a connection one might articulate by asking whether merely contemplating another being in a manner untrue to its real nature is itself a way in which the moral imagination is degraded), this is not the aspect of McMahan's work that I want to focus on here. What matters more in this context is that his tale of the 'Sacrificial Newborn' is a paradigm case of the work done by thought-experiments in moral philosophy. For its sole rationale is to present us with a lightly clothed (in this particular instance, consequentialist) calculation, designed to bring out an implication of adopting a particular moral principle or value. The constructive process seems to have gone something like this: first eliminate anyone with whom the newborn might have a human relationship (since their distress might complicate the sums), then stipulate enough older children to outnumber our orphan (thereby reminding us that three is at least three times greater than one). It's a deliberately arithmetical tale, morality by numbers—and the simpler the texture, the clearer the point.

[5] "Modern Moral Philosophy," in *Collected Philosophical Papers*, vol. 3 (Oxford: Blackwell, 1981).

But what if our concern were not clarity but understanding, or an engagement of our moral imagination with something resembling the texture and complexity of human reality? Not only is medical unlikelihood bypassed for McMahan's purposes (no tissue-typing problems); we hear nothing of the family and friends of the three five-year-olds. This is presumably because their obvious joy at the redemption of their children would simply shift the balance of calculation even further in the same direction. But what if the mother of one of these children discovers the source of her daughter's new organs? Would her joy be untainted by this knowledge? Is it obvious that she, or any of the parents involved, would regard it as legitimate for this healthy orphan to be thus abused? Is it obvious that any of them, or indeed any of the hospital staff, would not feel an obligation to the memory of the newborn's dead mother that might make them hesitate over its "sacrifice"?

From Norma's point of view, such questions might seem as unfair to McMahan as Costello's questions are to Nagel; McMahan's purpose is not to produce a gripping and gritty exercise in literary realism, but rather to make a theoretical point—indeed, to acknowledge a point against his own theory that my carping questions simply underline. Certain possible complications in the telling of the tale are excised simply because they are irrelevant to the issue at hand, which is the relative strength of the moral claims made on us by human infants and young children. It is to this matter alone that McMahan wants us to direct our moral intuitions; hence, his case is constructed so as to clear the scene of any other, potentially polluting concerns to which our intuitions might be responsive.

This kind of disagreement about the value of thought-experiments in ethics was once raised from a different perspective by Carol Gilligan.[6] She recounts what transpired when a boy and a girl (both eleven years old) were presented by researchers with a problem case: would it be morally permissible for a poor man to steal medicine from a chemist in order to save the life of his sick wife? The boy understood the case to embody a conflict between the immorality of theft and the sanctity of human life, and he opted for the latter value; the girl wondered why the chemist wouldn't simply give the man the medicine he needed once the situation was explained to him. Some will take it that the girl had simply misunderstood the point of the problem case, and of problem cases in general; for to include such a dialogue between chemist and husband is to change the case, and thus to avoid responding to the particular issue of principle it was intended to abstract from the complexity of reality. Others will take it that the boy had been distracted by matters of principle from attending

---

[6] Cf. her *In a Different Voice* (Cambridge: Harvard University Press, 1982), chap. 2.

properly to the concrete reality of moral experience and the possibilities of human fellowship.

The difficulties I raised in the case of the "Sacrificial Newborn" are, I would suggest, analogous. First, its extreme condensation forces its deviser to take certain moral valuations for granted; hence McMahan treats it as obvious that the relatives of the sick five-year-olds will rejoice in their salvation, and that the death of the newborn's mother removes her wishes and concerns entirely from the equation—hardly self-evident assumptions from many moral perspectives. And this raises the general difficulty of separating the value-neutral facts of a case from the moral intuitions we are supposed to bring to bear on it. For if our differing intuitions will in fact lead us to contest more or less every step in the construction of the case, the idea that any value-neutral account of any such case is available even in principle will seem deeply questionable.

Second, thought-experiments in ethics presuppose that we can get clearer about what we think concerning a single, specific moral issue by abstracting it from the complex web of interrelated matters of fact and of valuation within which we usually encounter and respond to it. But what if the issue means what it does to us, has the moral significance it has for us, precisely because of its place in that complex web? If so, to abstract it from that context is to ask us to think about something else altogether—something other than the issue that interested us in the first place; it is, in effect, to change the subject.

Even if one were prepared to take these difficulties seriously, however, how smoothly do they transfer to the case of Nagel and his bats? Is not his concern with the nature of nonhuman and human consciousness essentially unrelated to ethical matters, and so must not his use of thought-experiments in the philosophy of mind be immune to the kinds of anxieties I have expressed about their use in moral philosophy? As it happens, the broader structure of McMahan's book suggests that this aspect of Norma's putative defence of Nagel is far from decisive. For McMahan's treatment of the specific issues of abortion, infanticide, euthanasia, and suicide (in parts 4 and 5 of his book) applies conclusions reached by his prior discussion of the nature of death and killing (in parts 2 and 3), which are in turn guided by conclusions reached in his opening account of the nature of persons. This approach appears so obviously right to McMahan that he barely pauses to explain it; but presumably the line of thought goes like this. Only if we understand the nature of persons can we understand what it is (and why it is bad) for them to die, and only then can we understand what is bad about causing them to die by killing them, and only then can we understand what, if anything, is bad about the specific forms of killing known as abortion and euthanasia.

This pattern of reasoning should sound familiar: it is precisely the model of grounding ethics on metaphysics that we earlier saw O'Neill invoke in her dispute with Diamond. For McMahan, as for O'Neill, these rational foundations are not themselves moral; clarifying the nature of persons is treated in the first part of his book as a metaphysical rather than an ethical issue. He aims, before doing anything else, to establish the essential nature of a certain kind of entity; doing so will have consequences for our moral thinking, which may be why we engage in it, but that metaphysical issue is ethically neutral in itself.

However, if we accept McMahan's view of rational grounding, we would undermine the assumption about content that I attributed to Norma earlier in this chapter, and so have grounds for criticizing any exasperation she directs on that basis towards her mother-in-law; for views about consciousness that are ethically neutral in themselves may well have significant ethical implications, for our treatment of both human and nonhuman animals. And of course, McMahan's model certainly does appear to be sensible; it seems to amount to the truism that we should settle the more general issue before moving to the more particular, or rather, get the rational foundations of our moral thinking in place before we engage in specific moral disputes. What I want to suggest, however, is (first) that this model is in fact untenable and hence cannot itself provide a reason to reject Norma's stance; but (second) that the nature of the flaws in McMahan's model themselves provide a different and better reason to question her stance.

McMahan's account of personhood builds upon one of the most influential contemporary pieces of metaphysical analysis in this area—that of Derek Parfit.[7] Parfit clams that, in normal circumstances, personal identity (what makes me one and the same person across time) is a matter of the holding of certain relations of psychological continuity and connectedness—relations of memory, desire, intentions and their fulfilment, and so on. McMahan revises this account so that psychological continuity is treated more broadly, and as a matter of degree; but most fundamentally, he argues (against Parfit, but with reference to Parfit's most famous thought-experiment, that of a Star Trek–style teletransporter) that identity is preserved only if the relevant psychological continuity is grounded in the physical and functional continuity of enough of those areas of the person's brain in which consciousness is realized. Hence, according to this "Embodied Mind" account, a person in the early stages of Alzheimer's has reason to be egoistically concerned about what may happen to his body even in the final phases in which the mental life associated

---

[7] Cf. *Reasons and Persons* (Oxford: Oxford University Press: 1984).

with his body will no longer be even weakly psychologically connected from day to day.

Whether this account really treats the mind as embodied is in fact dubious. McMahan seems rather closer to presenting us with a kind of brain-body dualism in place of the religious/Cartesian mind-body dualism he so detests (transplant the right part of a person's brain into a new body, and you preserve his identity). Certainly, when the embodiedness of his favoured brain-parts is really thrust upon his attention, he misses its true significance. This becomes most obvious in another of his "cases," that of Dicephalus. This is his version of a rare but real medical condition, which occurs when a human zygote divides incompletely, and results in twins conjoined below the neck. Referring to the specific, real-life case of Abigail and Brittany Hensel, McMahan flatly asserts that "no one doubts that they are separate and distinct little girls" (EK, 35). Each, he tells us, would have her own private mental life and her own character; there are "of course" two personal or biographical lives, although their shared set of organs sustains a single biological life.

But McMahan makes no effort to imagine the meaning of his claims to the girls themselves. Will Abigail feel that she has an utterly distinct personal or biographical life from her sister, or her sister from her? Neither can ever play on her own with other children, have a joyful or furious private conversation with her mother, retreat to her room to rage or sulk or think in solitude, or go out alone with a boyfriend. Suppose they were to have a child; as McMahan notes in passing (but only to confirm that their two minds share a single body), it would be the child of both, a child with three parents. What significance might their motherhood have for each of them ("biographically"), given its rootedness in their common flesh? Would it confirm, modify, or undermine their sense of separateness and union? And what significance will their private mental life have to them when it exists only in the context of such enforced, embodied intimacy with one another?

McMahan's treatment of this "case" utterly fails to acknowledge that the nature of their embodied lives simply cannot be broken down and distributed between biological union and psychological distinctness in any straightforward way. If a sense of the separateness of persons is part of our concept of personhood, and that sense would be radically disrupted in the case of dicephalic twins, then so would our concept of personhood. Our ordinary concept of a person has the sense and the significance it has because it is embedded in the normal circumstances of our ordinary embodied lives with others; alter those circumstances, and our ordinary concept will not simply carry over, hence its structure cannot be straightforwardly illuminated by their study.

It is quite as if McMahan thinks that we first develop a concept of a person (say, as a psychologically continuous entity) and then relate to those we identify as persons in ways we judge appropriate to their metaphysical genus, so that those relations might be evaluated for their consistency with our independently given nature. But in truth, our concept of a person is constituted by, finds its life and sense in the context of, the normal forms of our lives with other persons—with embodied, flesh-and-blood creatures inhabiting structures of language and culture. And since those lives have a moral dimension, since their commonality and variety cannot adequately be characterized except in terms that invite ethical questions (as Abigail's relations to her sister, her parents, and her children plainly do), the same is true of our concept of a person. Personhood is not the metaphysical foundation of an interpersonal ethics; it is itself an ethical notion. To attempt to analyse it while remaining morally neutral is bound to produce exactly the air of mad conceptual science with which McMahan's description of his Dicephalus case is imbued.

Now we can see why rejecting McMahan's model of rational grounding for ethics does not rehabilitate Norma's objection to Costello. If personhood is itself an ethical notion, then Nagel's exploration of the concept of human (and so nonhuman) consciousness cannot coherently be regarded as a philosophical enterprise with no ethical implications. And this is not simply because it will inevitably give expression to an ethically charged attitude towards human consciousness; for any such ways of viewing human animals will inevitably hang together with certain ways of viewing nonhuman animals. As it happens, this is another respect in which McMahan's book is symptomatic of broader philosophical patterns of thought whose identification at the outset of this study might help us better to appreciate the particular philosophical coherence and interest of Costello's lecture.

The pattern of thinking we have just sketched directly informs McMahan's sense of the relative moral status of human and nonhuman animals, in the following way. Recognizing that human interpersonal relations typically exhibit a requirement of mutual respect, McMahan looks for its rational and metaphysical basis. He finds it in the mature human being's possession of certain psychological capacities—a rationally guided will, or sophisticated forms of self-consciousness. He then points out that some human beings lack these capacities, and he concludes that they must fall below the threshold of respect. Their moral claims on us should be assessed not in terms of inviolable rights but in terms of their interest in continuing to live, and this interest can be compared with, and sometimes traded off against, competing such interests (hence the Sacrificial Newborn "case"). More specifically, certain higher nonhuman mammals, being possessed of at least analogous versions of the psychological continuity that grounds the human interest in continuing to live, should be seen as having analogous second-tier moral status to that of human foetuses, infants, and the severely disabled.

For McMahan, then, the moral status of human beings is not univocal, and moral status of the second-tier variety at least is not restricted to members of the human species. To deny this second claim is to exhibit speciesism; it is to load moral significance onto a purely biological category. Suppose, he asks us once again to imagine, we administer genetic therapy to a canine foetus that confers human levels of self-consciousness, rationality, and autonomy upon it as it develops; it would then have become a person in the morally relevant sense of that term. Why, then, do we have any more reason to administer the therapy to a severely retarded human adult than to a normal, healthy dog?

McMahan claims that this is a serious problem. Trying to convince us of this, he says, "Let us assume, for the sake of the argument, that a dog with human intelligence could have a life that would be well worth living even in a society in which it would be a freak, would have no acceptable mate, and so on. In short, let us put those contingent problems aside" (EK, 319). Easy for us to do, one might think; not so easy for the dog. Would a human being, deprived of any acceptable mate and regarded as a freak by his fellows, be faced with merely contingent problems that would leave his capacity to conceive of him/herself as a person essentially unaffected? What interpersonal relations (of friendship, family, gossip, common hobbies, and interests) would be conceivable for our Superdog; and in their absence, what would the sense be of calling it a person nonetheless? I don't say—one can't say—that there could be no sense in doing so. I say only that the sense it would have is not the sense it has when human beings acknowledge one another as persons. The forms of embodied common life open to distinctively human creatures provide the context within which our notion of personhood has the sense it has. These forms are not the practical enactment of a logically prior or analytically separable intellectual hypothesis about capacity possession that might turn out to be metaphysically ungrounded.

In other words, our concept of a person is an outgrowth or aspect of our concept of a human being; and that concept is not merely biological but rather a crystallization of everything we have made of our distinctive species nature. To see another as a human being is to see her as a fellow creature—another being whose embodiment embeds her in a distinctive form of common life with language and culture, and whose existence constitutes a particular kind of claim upon us. We do not strive (when we do strive) to treat human infants and children, the senile and the severely disabled as fully human because we mistakenly attribute capacities to them that they lack, or because we are blind to the merely biological significance of a species boundary. We do it (when we do) because they are fellow human beings, embodied creatures who will come to share, or have already shared, in our common life, or whose inability to do so is a result of the kinds of shocks and ills to which all human flesh and blood is heir—because there but for the grace of God go I.

This supposedly speciesist conception of humans as fellow creatures in fact provides a far more satisfying and powerful way of reconceiving our relations with nonhuman animals than anything McMahan's argument provides. For nonhuman animals, too, can be seen as our fellow creatures in a different but related sense of that term. Their embodied existence, and hence their form of life, is different; but in certain cases, the human and the nonhuman forms of creaturely existence can overlap, interact, even offer companionship to one another, and in many ways, some nonhuman animals can be seen as sharing a common fate with us. They too are needy, dependent, subject to birth, sexuality, and death, vulnerable to pain and fear—in short, they are fellow sons and daughters of life (to adapt a phrase from Walter de la Mare). Seen in this light, the excesses of modern factory farming stand out clearly enough without further metaphysical analysis.

This conception of nonhuman animals as our fellow creatures, as well as the conception of human beings as fellow creatures of which it constitutes an extension, plainly stand in need of far more elaboration than I have so far provided. I mention it now, however, because it will emerge that Costello's counterconception of animal life can plausibly be related to such thinking. To find such a conception more clearly and sustainedly articulated in literary works of outstanding quality is itself unsurprising; for the ethical significance of mortality is a literary as well as a philosophical perennial. Strikingly, however, McMahan shows himself to be incapable of attending to such sources of understanding—shows, in fact, that he has a tin ear for such things, and for reasons that may once again be regarded as exemplary of a certain kind of philosophical blindness to literature.

His discussion of the treatment of mortality by the greatest writers of Western culture is in fact the one point in his enormous book where McMahan's scrupulous equanimity deserts him, to inadvertently comic effect. For what he finds in this tradition is "a dreary record of evasion and sophistry" (EK, 95–98). Socrates "prates" about obtaining a great good in the other world while drinking his hemlock (no chance of irony here, just hypocrisy); Schopenhauer's attempt to reconcile us to our place in the unending cycle of life is "wringing a meagre drop of consolation from the rags of bad argument"; and Tolstoy's "The Death of Ivan Ilych," despite being "of course" a masterpiece, is also a "conspicuous piece of evasion." Ivan's deathbed vision is a deus ex machina that irritatingly leaves us to guess at what his reassuring illumination actually is. Even when one of Tolstoy's biographers tells McMahan that it is the acceptance of his own mortality that brings Ivan peace, he is profoundly unsatisfied. "Not only is there no textual support for this conjecture, but insofar as Ivan Ilych accepts mortality, this is not an explanation of his finding peace but is itself precisely what requires explanation."

Perhaps this degree of incomprehension is not surprising, since Tolstoy's story articulates its vision of the acknowledgement of our mortality through Ivan's gradual acceptance of himself as an utterly unexceptional human being, as confronting a fate common to all human creatures. That acceptance begins when he is himself accepted as a fellow creature by his servant, Gerasim ("we shall all of us die, so why should I grudge a little trouble?" Gerasim remarks, as he massages his master's aching legs), and so begins to accept Gerasim as his fellow. And it is furthered when his young son, his eyelids bruised by self-doubt and self-hatred, creeps in tears to his sickbed to gaze in pity on his sufferings.

McMahan certainly won't find a sentence in the story in which Ivan says "I must accept my mortality!"; nevertheless, every word in Tolstoy's text works to articulate just such a vision. But because that text contains no premises, independently established, allowing us to advance further hypotheses, perhaps even to draw novel and ingenious conclusions in the fulness of time, McMahan can identify no power of rational conviction in it. In this respect, he shares Gutmann's orienting assumptions about embedded argumentation as the only possible way in which fiction might be relevant to philosophy, even if Gutmann finds in Coetzee what McMahan cannot find in Tolstoy. If, however, we stop laying down such requirements in advance, then we have some hope of seeing that, in nothing less than the text taken as a whole, Tolstoy is inviting us to appreciate a particular way of seeing human life—a way of seeing ourselves as mortal creatures subject to a common and uncanny fate, but capable nevertheless of living well, of doing the right thing. In other words, there really is genuine sustenance for our moral imaginations, our ethical reflections, to be found in such contexts. Is it simply accidental that a gifted philosopher so much at home in the genre of the thought-experiment should be incapable of recognizing the rather different way in which that of the short story might provide it?

Returning from Tolstoy to Coetzee, in the light of McMahan's example, we might ask why Norma feels so strongly that Nagel has no responsibility to be true to the actual nature of bats when he invokes them in his philosophical reflections on consciousness. Is this because she thinks that when philosophers use any kind of creature as part of a thought-experiment, they can stipulate whatever they please about the nature of that creature and our capacities for understanding it, as long as it serves to further their philosophical purposes? This assumption of the philosophical author as the God of his thought-experimental world, as having merely to assert or stipulate that things are thus-and-so in order for things to be thus-and-so within the world of his fiction, might hold with respect to Nagel's use of Martians in that same article, since their existence is purely imaginary. But how can a philosophical claim about the human capacity to understand real (however putatively alien) forms of conscious life be worth making if it entirely fails to make contact with their true nature?

It might help here to recall that, as part of his argument, Nagel places other human minds more nearly within the grasp of his own mind than he does bats. Would Norma be equally exasperated if Costello had taken it that, in doing so, Nagel was in the first place making a claim about other human minds? Is Norma's exasperation, then, an indication of her idiosyncratic, indefensibly puritan notion of philosophy, or perhaps a function of her more general exasperation at her mother-in-law—or simply an expression of Coetzee's indefensibly narrow conception of philosophy's willingness to be held to account for the uses it makes of real beings, and of reality more generally, in its experiments? I propose to begin this study on the assumption that these requirements on what philosophy is, and so on what is to count as a genuine engagement with it, are being laid down by Norma, not by Coetzee and certainly not by Costello.

Accordingly, I want to take seriously the fact that Costello explicitly links her intention to take Nagel as writing in the first place about a bat with her status as a writer: "Like most writers, I have a literal cast of mind, so I would like to stop with the bat" (LA, 32). Even if we persist in thinking that such a cast of mind is actually inappropriate to the evaluation of Nagel's bat, we must recognize that Costello's lecture as a whole will manifest just this cast of mind, and so acknowledge that when she claims that she is engaging with particular philosophers and their particular arguments, we should attempt to understand her as, in the first place, doing just that. What she is doing in the second, third, and later places will emerge later and may well deepen our understanding of what she is doing in the first place; but we cannot reach those later places without a secure initial sense of the first.

This means that we would do well to dwell a little longer on what exactly Costello means by her "literal cast of mind." In effect, Norma takes this phrase literally: she assumes that Costello is indicating an intention to read Nagel in a literal-minded way, one that focuses on the fact that he employs the word "bat," which in its primary, literal sense self-evidently refers to real, live bats—a way of reading him that obliterates the central fact that his is an essentially imaginative exercise in the service of a philosophical rather than a zoological purpose. Hence, Norma takes the literal to be distinct from, even opposed to, flights of the imagination—whether philosophical or otherwise; she takes Nagel's imaginative flights to have only the most exiguous bearing upon reality, and she further takes it that it is up to Nagel just what kind of bearing upon reality his words can and should have. But why on earth should she, or we, imagine that a novelist of high repute should associate literature with the literal in this rather literal-minded way?

Costello's use of the phrase is in fact imaginative, even ironic: she takes it that anyone who takes up the word "bat" has a responsibility thereby, before any other responsibilities she might wish to take on, to use it in ways that really are responsive to the reality of the creature to which it refers, and hence she is obliged to exercise the imagination necessary to apprehend that reality. The imagination of the writer is primarily literal because it is primarily devoted to the attempt genuinely to capture reality, to make the real manifest in words. Such a genuinely literal use of words is not something to be taken for granted, as if amounting to no more than the most primitive aspect of linguistic competence, from which one might then go on to make more or less imaginative uses of words; it is rather a way of characterizing the deeply challenging goal towards which certain kinds of literature (certainly the kind Costello writes) endlessly aspire. Does this goal (call it a vision of words as an impression or cast of reality) imply a cast of mind essentially different from that of philosophy—one that philosophy can simply cast off? Or does it rather amount to challenging the philosopher's way of understanding what it is for reality to make an impression on us—challenging, for example, not the empiricist principle that genuine comprehension of reality is always grounded in impressions derived from it, but rather the empiricist's conception of what it is to derive a genuine impression from, to be genuinely impressed by, reality?

So when I say that I propose to take Costello's attempts to engage with philosophers and their arguments literally, I don't mean this in a literal-minded way. I mean that I am taking her to be attempting to engage with the reality of those arguments as she understands that task, which means acquiring and conveying an impression of the underlying reality of the ways these philosophers are using their words—the degree to which their uses of them allow the reality towards which those words are turned to impress itself upon them and us, the extent to which we can take what they say literally, that is, as seriously meant and so as imaginatively responsible to their subject matter.

Chapter Three

ELIZABETH COSTELLO'S LECTURE:
THREE PHILOSOPHERS AND A NUMBER OF APES

I N THIS CHAPTER I WILL attempt to take literally Elizabeth Costello's claim to be engaging with philosophers qua philosophers. That engagement will turn out to have three faces or aspects: an essentially internal critique of three exemplary instances of philosophical reflection on nonhuman animals; an attempt to contest a deeply held philosophical assumption about the essential comprehensibility of animate being and indeed being as such; and the deployment of a famous literary exemplar in such a way as to invite a radical reconception of the weight of every word in her lecture.

Stepping Three Times into the Great River:
Aquinas, Kohler, Nagel

In her first lecture, Costello claims to honour the philosophical ideal of genuinely clarificatory or edifying speech: "I want to find a way of speaking to fellow human beings that will be cool rather than heated, philosophical rather than polemical, that will bring enlightenment rather than seeking to divide us into the righteous and the sinners, the saved and the damned, the sheep and the goats" (LA, 22). But even before this claim acquires the strong patina of irony that acquaintance with the tone of her lecture as a whole might give it, and that is anyway implicit in her concluding citation of a divine, parabolic equation of nonhuman with human animals, she distinguishes acceptance of this ideal from a willingness simply to employ the language of the philosophers, even in the unoriginal, secondhand manner that she declares is the best she could manage.

> Although I see that the best way to win acceptance from this learned gathering would be for me to join myself, like a tributary stream running into a great river, to the great Western discourse of man versus beast, of reason versus unreason, something in me resists, foreseeing in that step the concession of the entire battle. (LA, 25)

Why so? It would not be hard, particularly for a reader trained in philosophy, to misunderstand the nature and motive of Costello's resistance. For she does not take very much care to distinguish her position from that of scepticism or relativism about the validity of human reason as such.

> Might it not be that the phenomenon we are examining here is, rather than the flowering of a faculty that allows access to the secrets of the universe, the specialism of a rather narrow, self-regenerating intellectual tradition whose forte is reasoning, in the same way that the forte of chess-players is playing chess, which for its own motives it tries to install at the centre of the universe? (LA, 25)

The analogy with chess suggests a conception of reasoning as a game, a self-sufficient cultural practice defined by an internally coherent system of rules, but without any genuine relation to reality—no more than an arbitrary way of legitimating the power of a particular social group, culture, or species in relation to its competitors, and identifying the satisfaction of its own goals with that of attaining truth.

The response to this is obvious, and indeed Norma forcefully articulates it later that day: "there is no position outside of reason where you can stand and lecture about reason and pass judgement on reason" (LA, 48). To lecture about or pass judgement on anything whatever (for example, by comparing reasoning with playing chess) is itself an exercise of reason, and hence subject to its requirements—that is, it stands in need of rational justification. Does this simply mean that, unlike chess, human reason is a game we are compelled to play, with which we simply cannot dispense, and so a form of power whose reach is total? In her lecture, Costello claims that

> seen from the outside, from a being who is alien to it, reason is simply a vast tautology. Of course reason will validate reason as the first principle of the universe—what else should it do? Dethrone itself? Reasoning systems, as systems of totality, do not have that power. If there were a position from which reason could attack and dethrone itself, reason would already have occupied that position; otherwise it would not be total. (LA, 25)

But this picture of the putatively totalitarian nature of reason is self-refuting. For if reason is total in this sense, not only is there no position outside reason from which it could be attacked, there could not possibly be any such position; but then our so-called subjection to reason is neither coercive nor limiting in any way, since there is no genuine position that it prevents us from inhabiting.

Must we think of this as Norma's retrospective deconstruction of Costello's stance? To do so would overlook the fact that Costello's own way of putting her point all-but-explicitly refutes itself—for she ends by appearing explicitly to demonstrate the necessary unavailability of the position that she begins by claiming to occupy, the fabled position outside the domain of reason. Why assume that she is not sufficiently aware of the logical relations within a continuous sequence of five of her own short sentences to grasp this fact—even to be in control of it, to be intending to show how an apparently inevitable intensification of this familiar vision of the coercive power of reason in fact renders it impotent? Is it that we take Costello in particular, or writers in general, to be essentially incapable of reasoning, as cultural representatives of that which is essentially opposed to the life of the mind? Costello invokes just such a picture of herself, in imagining her audience's initial response to her refusal to restrict herself to embroidering on the discourse of the old philosophers: "Do I in fact have a choice? If I do not subject my discourse to reason, whatever that is, what is left for me but to gibber and emote and knock over my water glass and generally make a monkey of myself?" (LA, 23). Literature is familiar with the idea of the fool who speaks more truly than the sane, as religion is familiar with the idea of a form of wisdom that is foolishness to the wise. Costello has her own way of embodying these ideas for the edification of the professional philosopher.

Let's go back to the final one of those five sentences on the totality of reason: "If there were a position from which reason could attack and dethrone itself, reason would already have occupied that position; otherwise it would not be total." This does not actually, literally say that there *is* no position from which reason could attack itself; it says that reason would already have occupied that position, otherwise it would not be what it is (that is, total). So another possibility the sentence leaves open is that reason, in accordance with its nature, not only is inherently capable of critically evaluating itself, but must already have done so insofar as it has genuinely or totally fulfilled its potential. This is hardly a position unfamiliar to philosophers: one might say that it is part of their definition of Western Enlightenment, and of philosophy's distinctive contribution to it—that of seeing the necessity for, and actually engaging in, a critique of reason by reason. And it is ultimately this task that Costello is taking on, and claiming to further, in her lecture.

> Both reason and seven decades of life experience tell me that reason is neither the being of the universe nor the Being of God. On the contrary, reason looks to me suspiciously like the being of human thought; worse than that, like the being of one tendency in human thought. Reason is the being of a certain spectrum of human thinking. (LA, 23)

A distinction is being drawn here between reason as such and particular modes or inflections of reason; more exactly, between human thinking, and one tendency within it that one might label reason or reasoning, and that philosophers in particular are prone to conflate with thinking as such. (It is not exactly the distinction later drawn by an academic from the Appleton College literature department, between "true reason and false reason" [LA, 55].) And drawing this distinction is itself presented as an exercise of reason, more precisely of human thinking, or that tendency of it that is conjoined with and informed by life experience—that is, by a lifetime of experience as writer and as human being, and by that writer's experience of life, animate being, animal existence in its human and non-human forms. This is how Costello characterizes literature's critique of reason by itself.

Let us look at three examples of this critique as they are threaded through the text of the lecture: they take the form of a literarily literal reading of Aquinas, Kohler, and Nagel (and so of theological, scientific, and philosophical modes of reason). Aquinas is represented as justifying his claim that our treatment of nonhuman animals has no moral significance (except insofar as cruelty to animals might encourage cruelty to humans) by identifying men as made in God's image and so as partaking in God's being, which he identifies with reason—a reason that must also pervade God's creation, constituting the rules by which the universe works, but which only God and humans can understand. In short, Costello's concern here is with the God of the philosophers, not only of "the philosopher" (as St. Thomas is known to Roman Catholics), since she holds that Plato and Descartes are equally committed to analogous views of human, worldly, and divine being as inherently rational.

Costello's response to this kind of vision is to tell the story of Srinivasa Ramanujan, originally a clerk for the Madras Port Authority but later brought to Cambridge University, and "widely thought of as the greatest intuitive mathematician of our time, that is to say, as a self-taught man who thought in mathematics, one to whom the laborious notion of mathematical proof or demonstration was foreign" (LA, 24). She asks first whether Ramanujan was "closer to God because his mind . . . was at one, or more at one than anyone else's we know of, with the being of reason? If the good folk of Cambridge . . . had not elicited from Ramanujan his speculations, and laboriously proved true those of them that they were capable of proving true, would Ramanujan still have been closer to God than they?" (LA, 24). And second, further invoking a performing ape, well-known in Europe at roughly the time of Ramanujan's residence in Cambridge, she asks: "How are we to know that Red Peter, or Red Peter's little sister, shot in Africa by the hunters, was not thinking the same thoughts as Ramanujan was thinking in India, and saying equally little?" (LA, 24).

Once again, it would be easy for a philosophical reader to see two rather straightforward lines of argument implied by these questions, and two rather bad ones at that. The first seems to rest on the assumption that the capacity to make correct mathematical judgements divorced from the capacity to prove or otherwise demonstrate their validity would be more purely rational than the two capacities conjoined; and the second seems to presuppose that a creature lacking either capacity might be thinking in mathematics, or more exactly exercising mathematical judgement in thought, despite showing no signs of any such intellectual activity in what she says and does.

The first assumption fails to appreciate that intuitive mathematicians are the exception that proves the rule, or rather could only be exceptional; for in the absence of a general capacity to prove the truth of mathematical judgements, the idea that such judgements could be valid as opposed to invalid (that is, constitute a particular part of the domain of reason) would lack any content. If all mathematicians were like Ramanujan, then none would merit the appellation "mathematician." because there would be nothing that counted as a domain of specifically mathematical judgement and expertise.

The presupposition of the second question is equally dubious: for even Ramanujan can be characterized as an intuitive mathematician because he actually arrived at and expressed judgements that accorded with the standards of derivability constitutive of the field of mathematics, and more generally because he said and did the kinds of things that make manifest a broader capacity on his part to think (about Port Authority dockets, travel plans, the hostile climate of England, and so on). An ape in the African jungle, by contrast, may manifest certain kinds of behaviour characteristic of simple thought processes, but she certainly manifests nothing recognizable as indicating that she is thinking sophisticated mathematical thoughts to herself. As Norma Bernard puts it later, with respect to squirrels, and the possibility of their thinking about anything other than acorns, trees, weather, and other animals: "hundreds of years of observing squirrels has not led us to conclude otherwise. If there is anything else in the squirrel mind, it does not issue in observable behaviour. For all practical purposes, the mind of the squirrel is a very simple mechanism" (LA, 48).

But are these assumptions ones that Costello is endorsing, or ones she sees at work in the views of her opponents and to which she is critically responding? Take the first worry, about the intelligibility of divorcing correct mathematical judgement from the capacity to prove those judgements. We need to recall that the Thomist position to which Costello is responding (and with which she associates Plato and Descartes) is one that invokes a conception of the divine as more intimately at one with reason than mere human beings. Does Aquinas think that God needs to construct proofs of mathematical hypotheses before he can endorse them as valid? The familiar picture here is rather the reverse: familiarity with what Costello calls "the protocols of academic mathematics" is required for humans, but that is because they lack divinity; for God, what Kant would call purely intellectual intuition is not only possible, but definitive of his divine status. God does not have reason, he is reason: he does not require any means towards the apprehension of truth, he embodies truth.

So Costello's point about Ramanujan might be that, if her philosophers really do regard God as being more at one with reason than the average human being, why do they not regard those untypical human beings who (it seems) can immediately intuit a certain range of the deliverances of reason as more at one with it, and so with God, than their fellows? It is not that she takes Ramanujan to be closer to the essence of reason, and so of reality and the divine, than her philosophers are willing to acknowledge; after all, she wishes to argue that the spectrum of human thinking, and so of reality, stretches far more widely than that of logic and mathematics. Her claim is rather that if we believe that our reliance upon the methodologies of reason is part of what distances us from God, if we really meant what those invocations of the divine appear to say, then those who have no need of such protocols to apprehend the essence of things ought to seem closer to the divine, on our understanding of that desirable status, than we are.

What, however, of the fact that, whilst the Ramanujans of this world have at least actually articulated the results of their intuitions, the Red Sallys of the African forests have remained utterly silent? What of Norma's point that hundreds of years of observations have given us no reason to believe that nonhuman animals possess anything other than highly rudimentary mental mechanisms? Here, we need to examine the second of Costello's three confrontations with thinkers about nonhuman animal; for if the basis of our rejection of the idea that nonhuman animals reason in sophisticated ways is our scientific observations of them, then much will hang on the reliability of those observations.

Wolfgang Kohler was an experimental psychologist who took apes from the African mainland to Tenerife, where he subjected them to a range of experiments designed to elicit their underlying capacities for rational thought. The structure of these experiments is familiar: food is left for them, but out of their immediate reach, and the apes are given objects such as sticks and crates that they might use to reach it; when they succeed in one such task, it is further complicated (for example, by filling the crates with stones, which have to be removed before the crates can be used to construct a tower to reach a bunch of bananas hanging out of reach).

Costello attempts to imagine one ape's experience of these experiments—the one Kohler names Sultan.

Sultan knows: now one is supposed to think. That is what the bananas up there
are about. The bananas are there to make one think, to spur one to the limits
of one's thinking. But what must one think? One thinks: Why is he starving
me? One thinks: What have I done? Why has he stopped liking me? One thinks:
Why does he not want these crates any more? But none of these is the right
thought. Even a more complicated thought—for instance: What is wrong with
him, what misconception does he have of me, that leads him to believe it is
easier for me to reach a banana hanging from a wire than to pick up a banana
from the floor?—is wrong. The right thought to think is: How does one use the
crates to reach the bananas? . . .

At every turn, Sultan is driven to think the less interesting thought. From the
purity of speculation (Why do men behave like this?) he is relentlessly propelled
towards lower, practical, instrumental reason (How does one use this to get
that?) and thus towards acceptance of himself as primarily an organism with
an appetite that needs to be satisfied. Although his entire history, from the time
that his mother was shot and he was captured, through his voyage in a cage to
imprisonment on this island prison camp and the sadistic games that are played
around food here, leads him to ask questions about the justice of the universe
and the place of this penal colony in it, a carefully plotted psychological regimen
conducts him *away* from ethics and metaphysics toward the humbler reaches
of practical reason. And somehow, as he inches through this labyrinth of con-
straint, manipulation, and duplicity, he must realise that on no account dare he
give up, for on his shoulders rests the responsibility of representing apedom.
The fate of his brothers and sisters may be determined by how well he performs.
(LA, 28, 29)

Norma Bernard is likely to see here the spectacle of a question begged:
Costello is simply attributing to Sultan from the outset the very conception of godlike human reason—capable of moral and speculative purity—
for which truly objective experimentation is supposed to provide independent evidence. But this is surely a rather literal-minded response to
Costello's literary exercise. Her point, in inviting us to imagine inhabiting Sultan's situation, is not to propose that, for all we know, Sultan's
way of inhabiting his situation was exactly the same as ours would be; it
is to encourage us to appreciate how little of our undoubted life of reason
would find expression if we were to inhabit Sultan's situation, and thereby
to encourage us to see that Kohler's modes of experimentation are no
more free of conceptual question-begging than her own literary thought-
experiment.[1] For such experiments cannot be designed so as to reveal
indications of reasoning without presupposing a particular conception of

[1] Eileen Crist's book *Images of Animals: Anthropomorphism and Animal Mind* (Philadelphia: Temple University Press, 1999) analyses the ways in which the very different vocabulary and concepts employed by biologists, sociobiologists, and behavioural scientists rein-

what it is to reason, and which range on the spectrum of thought might be expected to manifest itself in the life of the experimental subject. Kohler designs his experiments so as to find indications of instrumental reasoning; they offer no incentive for the apes to manifest signs of any other kind of mental activity, and a variety of incentives (including that of individual well-being and species survival) for them to suppress it. In other words, human observation of nonhuman animal life runs a very grave risk of producing only the results that those observers can imagine getting.

In the end, then, observation cannot discriminate neutrally between valid and invalid exercises of the imagination; it always presupposes a certain exercise of the imagination, or rather a certain lack of it, and so ought to acknowledge the possibility of imagining things otherwise. Costello will later call the imaginative substructure of these experiments imbecilic—an insult to human reason, let alone to Sultan (LA, 62). But the deep error here is not to employ the wrong imaginative and conceptual presuppositions; it is to fail to acknowledge that one is doing so, and hence to acknowledge that other presuppositions are at least possible.

Costello does not, however, regard Kohler as negatively as she regards Aquinas, Plato, and Descartes, in part because his observational results were not restricted to those concerning his experiments. She reports him also reporting a moment when the captive chimpanzees lope around the compound in a circle, some naked, some dressed in cords or old strips of cloth, some carrying pieces of rubbish. Kohler is perceptive enough to note that "the ribbons and the junk are there not for the visual effect, because they look smart, but for the kinetic effect, because they make you *feel* different—anything to relieve the boredom. This is as far as Kohler, for all his sympathy and insight, is able to go; this is where a poet might have commenced, with a feel for the ape's experience" (LA, 30). In part, this digression prepares the ground for Costello's seminar in the literature department, to which we shall soon turn; but it is also a preparation for her third encounter with the philosophers—the one involving Nagel's bat.

What interests Costello about Nagel's position is contained in her sole citation from his essay: "[W]hat it would be like for *me* to behave as a bat behaves . . . is not the question. I want to know what it is like for a *bat* to be a bat. Yet if I try to imagine this, I am restricted by the resources of my own mind, and those resources are inadequate to the task" (WLB, 169). Costello's question is whether the felt restriction here is a reflection of the resources of the human mind as such, or of the mind of Thomas Nagel. Are humans as such unable to think themselves into the mind, or

---

force their presuppositions about nonhuman animals and close off the availability of alternative approaches.

the perspective, or at least the position, of a bat, or are they (or at least some or most of them) unwilling? Is the nonhuman animal refusing our best imaginative efforts, or are we refusing to make our best efforts, or at least refusing to acknowledge the results of our best efforts—the efforts of the poets, for example?

As Costello reminds us, Nagel constructs a continuum of imaginative or sympathetic accessibility—with Martians at the far end, then bats, dogs, and apes, and finally other human beings at the closest point to us; and he implies that the relevant degree of accessibility depends upon whether or not we share something (what Nagel calls resources of the mind, or more specifically a mode of consciousness) with the object of our putative understanding. For when modes of consciousness differ, then mine gets in the way of the others', mediating its distinctive mode through my own, and generating at best an imaginative inhabitation of my being a Martian or a bat, not of a Martian's being a Martian, or a bat's being a bat.

There is a clear echo in Nagel's approach of that taken by McMahan and O'Neill in ethics; for all three, a creature's credentials for claiming a status undeniably attributable to human beings must be grounded on their possession of a certain metaphysical property or capacity. To be sure, Costello also sees an important difference here between Nagel and philosophers such as Descartes; for she notes that Nagel not only recognizes the reality of nonhuman modes of consciousness, he also ties each such mode very tightly to specific sensory modalities and modes of life, and hence is not committed to a picture of human beings as ghosts in a bodily machine, their thinking processes essentially unrelated to the biological machinery they inhabit rather like "a pea rattling around in a shell" (LA, 33). Even so, Nagel assumes that the distinctive modes of consciousness that different modes of life engender present an insuperable barrier to understanding, and in particular to the sympathetic imagination; and that is why Costello takes him to be wrong, or rather to be "sending us down a false trail."

> To be a living bat is to be full of being; being fully a bat is like being fully human, which is also to be full of being. Bat-being in the first case, human-being in the second, maybe; but those are secondary considerations. To be full of being is to live as a body-soul. One name for the experience of full being is *joy.*
>
> To be alive is to be a living soul. An animal—and we are all animals—is an embodied soul. . . . To thinking, cogitation, I oppose fullness, embodiedness, the sensation of being—not a consciousness of yourself as a kind of ghostly reasoning machine thinking thoughts, but on the contrary the sensation—a heavily affective sensation—of being a body with limbs that have extension in space, of being alive to the world. . . . I can think my way into the existence of a bat or a chimpanzee or an oyster, any being with whom I share the substrate of life. (LA, 33, 35)

Costello's reference to "joy" here is mysterious—except insofar as "full-ness of being" pictures every animal as brimming not only with life but with its own specific life, as if fully inhabiting its own skin, and so per-fectly fulfilling its allotted place in creation. Beyond this, however, she is contesting Nagel's assumption that differences in modalities of life are more important than the commonality of living, of aliveness, of embodied existence. Where he sees qualitative discontinuities between Martian, bat, ape, and human modes of conscious awareness, Costello sees a fundamen-tal continuity of animate being—a fellowship between different kinds of mortal creature, each in its own way participating in or enacting the possi-bilities and necessities (call it the finitude) of life: birth, reproduction and death, food and drink, confinement and freedom, being at-home or not-at-home in the world. How does Nagel know that the admitted differ-ences between bat-being and human-being make any understanding of what it is like to be a bat impossible? How hard has he, or anyone, tried to think their way into the existence of a bat or a chimpanzee? Where should we look for such essays or experiments, and how should we assess the degree of their success?

Elizabeth Costello thinks that she knows where to look; this will be the subject of her seminar on the poets and the animals. It is also not hard to imagine how little she will think of Nagel's claims about the limits of his imagination, given the things he says in passing about what the imagina-tion is and how it is exercised. For despite admitting that "the imagination is remarkably flexible" (WLB, 172 fn), all that he can imagine might be involved in trying to imagine another creature's experience is "imagining additions to my present experience, or . . . segments gradually subtracted from it, or . . . some combination of additions, subtractions and modifi-cations" (WLB, 169)—a crudely mathematico-physical model, to say the least. And he yearns in conclusion for a nonimaginative way of thinking about the subjective character of experience, "an objective phenomenol-ogy not dependent on empathy or the imagination" (WLB, 179). This desire to transcend the imagination reflects his essentially unimaginative conception of what the human imagination might be.

COMPREHENDING THE INCOMPREHENSIBLE:
DEATH, ANIMATE LIFE, LITERATURE

But Costello thinks that she can amass some provisional reasons for con-testing Nagel's rather more a priori, or say conceptual, doubts about this possibility of one form of life understanding another before she brings the poets explicitly into play. In effect, she helps herself to Nagel's model of a discontinuous continuum of understanding and tries to unsettle his (and our) confidence in our capacity to understand the mode of animal life closest to us, according to that model—human life. It is as if she is saying to him: if your confidence that we understand one another is misplaced, so too may your confidence that we cannot understand what it is like to be a bat. And unsurprisingly, her attempts to press this charge all circle around the human body—the challenges to and opportunities for understanding presented by its reality, the reality of its existence and of its absence.

Costello begins, in effect, by asking us whether we understand ourselves:

> For instants at a time . . . I know what it is like to be a corpse. The knowledge repels me. It fills me with terror; I shy away from it, refuse to entertain it.
>
> All of us have such moments, particularly as we grow older. The knowledge we have is not abstract—"All human beings are mortal, I am a human being, therefore I am mortal"—but embodied. For a moment we *are* that knowledge. We live the impossible: we live beyond our death, look back on it, yet look back as only a dead self can.
>
> When I know, with this knowledge, that I am going to die, what is it, in Nagel's terms, that I know? Do I know what it is like for me to be a corpse or do I know what it is like for a corpse to be a corpse? The distinction seems to me trivial. What I know is what a corpse cannot know: that it is extinct, that it knows nothing and will never know anything any more. For an instant, before my whole structure of knowledge collapses in panic, I am alive inside that contradiction, dead and alive at the same time. . . .
>
> That is the kind of thought we are capable of, we human beings, that and even more, if we press ourselves or are pressed. But we resist being pressed, and rarely press ourselves; we think our way into death only when we are rammed into the face of it. Now I ask: if we are capable of thinking our own death, why on earth should we not be capable of thinking our way into the life of a bat? (LA, 32–33)

Costello's point here is not just that it is part of understanding what it is like to be human that we understand what it is like to be mortal, that being alive as a human being is a matter of essentially finite existence, one that will inevitably end in death. Her point is even more specific: that part of understanding what it is like to be me is understanding that I am going to die. Costello patently thinks we can grasp this—that we can, each of us, think or know or understand that "I am going to die"; but she is also well aware that it is a highly peculiar kind of thought—not at all natural or easy to think, as if an achievement automatically conferred by the immediacy of our self-awareness (something simply given to any individual human consciousness). For, as she puts it, to think this thought is to be alive inside a contradiction, to be dead and alive at the same time, to live the impossible. Her point is that we must embody or be that knowledge (as opposed simply to having it, being able to recognize the application of the famous syllogism to our own case), and that to do so we must embody a contradiction or impossibility—we must think something that is essentially resistant to thought, something that when properly thought will engender the collapse of our whole structure of knowledge, and something that we, with all our being, resist thinking.

So when she concludes by bringing the thought of our own death, and so the thought of what it is like to be me, into alignment with the thought of what it is like to be a bat, it is not to suggest that understanding bat-being is as easy as Nagel thinks it is to understand human-being; it is to affirm that nonhuman animal life is no less (but not necessarily any more) resistant to human understanding than is human animal life. Her point is that the shared substratum of life, the fellowship of mortal creatures that provides our means of access to nonhuman animal being is a matter of resistance, contradiction, impossibility—that understanding any manifestation of animal life, of finite embodied existence, is a matter of deploying our imaginative capacity to be dead and alive at the same time, and risking the panic-stricken collapse of our whole edifice of knowledge.

If human self-understanding is such a fraught affair, what of understanding other human beings? Here, Costello invokes (and not for the first time) the horrors of the Holocaust:

> The particular horror of the camps, the horror that convinces us that what went on there was a crime against humanity, is not that despite a humanity shared with their victims, the killers treated them like lice. That is too abstract. The horror is that the killers refused to think themselves into the place of their victims, as did everyone else. They said, "It is *they* in those cattle-cars rattling past." They did not say, "It is I who am in that cattle-car." They said, "It must be the dead who are being burnt today, making the air stink and falling in ash on my cabbages." They did not say, "I am burning, I am falling in ash." (LA, 34)

Costello is exactly not denying that we can understand these killers—as if simply reformulating the perhaps too-familiar thought that we cannot grasp the evil of the Holocaust. On the contrary, this passage precisely records her attempt to understand its agents by attempting to do what she claims they refused to do with respect to their victims—namely, to think herself into their place.

But what is involved in so doing, and can it really be done? On the one hand, Costello tells us how things were from the killers' point of view—one articulated by a refusal to think of the victims as anything other than "they." On the other, that is exactly the pronoun Costello employs to articulate the killers' point of view: "They said . . . they did not say . . . ." So is her attempt to understand them a success or a failure? What does she suggest would constitute success? Apparently, thinking of them not as "they" but as "I": putting oneself in another human being's place is not simply a matter of being able to address them, to think of them, as "you"—the second-person pronoun usually in place in such relationships—but as "I," as if becoming them, seeing no real distinction between them and me.

Is that genuine understanding, or a factitious, sentimental caricature of it—a way of misunderstanding what it is really to understand another as an other, which surely involves acknowledging precisely their separateness from me, the essential fact that they are not me? Is it even possible to understand another that way? Is it really possible to think, to fully mean a statement such as "I am falling in ash"? When, in "Death Fugue," Paul Celan says "your ashen hair Shulamith . . . then as smoke you will rise into air . . . he grants us a grave in the air," does he mean it (does he mean "you" or "us," or both)?[2] If we think it is impossible, then how can we criticise these murderous others for failing to achieve it? Then Costello's stance must seem comprehensibly incomprehensible. But if we think it is possible—if we think that Celan can really mean what he says— then we seem committed once again to the idea that to understand another one must be prepared imaginatively to inhabit impossibilities and contradictions, to overcome resistances and refusals from those others, and within ourselves.

Costello has already signalled the complexities in this kind of supposedly automatic capacity to grasp another human being in their being, when discussing the relation of the Poles and Germans and Ukrainians who lived in the vicinity of the camps to what was going on within them.

> The people who lived in the countryside around Treblinka . . . said that they did not know what was going on in the camp; said that, while in a general way they might have guessed what was going on, they did not know for sure; said that, while in a sense they might have known, in another sense they did not know, could not afford to know, for their own sake. . . . [W]e said, a sickness of the soul . . . marked those citizens of the Reich who had committed evil actions, but also those who, for whatever reason, were in ignorance of those actions. . . . We look (or used to look) askance at Germans of a certain generation because they are, in a sense, polluted; in the very signs of their normality (their healthy appetites, their hearty laughter) we see proof of how deeply seated pollution is in them.
>
> It was and is inconceivable that people who *did not know* (in that special sense) about the camps can be fully human. (LA, 19–21)

---

[2] I quote from Michael Hamburger's translation, collected in his *Poems of Paul Celan* (London: Anvil Press, 1988).

The point here is not just that those people who failed to know what was going on in the camps found themselves living out a contradiction in their relation to the camps, and so to themselves; for one might say that this contradiction—of knowing and not knowing, of refusing to know what one nevertheless knows all too well—is an indication of a failure of understanding. But in understanding these people in these terms, are we actually understanding them, or failing to? Is talk of sin and pollution—particularly a kind of pollution whose special signs are those of unpolluted normality—a way of articulating an understanding, or the expression of a sense that we have come up against the limits of human understanding? And if the latter, is that because these people resist any form of human understanding, or because we refuse to accept them as humanly comprehensible? If we find it inconceivable that people who did not know, in that special sense, about the camps can be fully human, then are we saying that to understand them is to understand that these human beings are not human beings; or are we rather saying that these are human beings we simply cannot understand—and that anyone who thinks otherwise is not properly understanding what they did?

No matter which interpretation we prefer, we seem destined to treat a contradiction in the content of our putative knowing as the sign of its genuineness. And once again, Costello's point seems to be that, if contradiction, impossibility, and resistance or refusal are marks of genuine understanding of the human animal, then their presence in our attempts to understand nonhuman modes of animate life may indicate their success rather than their failure, and so indicate something about the reality of embodied existence as such.

The third of Costello's budget of counterexamples to Nagel's continuum of cognitive access concerns an aspect of her own mode of human being, in more than one sense:

> [T[here is no limit to the extent to which we can think ourselves into the being of another. There are no bounds to the sympathetic imagination. If you want proof, consider the following. Some years ago I wrote a book called *The House on Eccles Street*. To write that book I had to think my way into the existence of Marion Bloom. Either I succeeded or I did not. If I did not, I cannot imagine why you invited me here today. In any event, the point is, *Marion Bloom never existed*. Marion Bloom was a figment of James Joyce's imagination. If I can think my way into the existence of a being who has never existed, then I can think my way into the existence of a bat or a chimpanzee or an oyster, any being with whom I share the substrate of life. (LA, 35)

What should the philosopher say in response to this "proof"? Does the fact that Marion Bloom is a fictional human being mean that we should place her (qua human being) pretty much on the same part of Nagel's continuum as any other human being we encounter in real life; or does it mean that, qua fictional, she should be placed at least as far away from other humans as are Nagel's Martians, whose existence (as far as we know) is similarly imaginary? Costello's concluding comparison appears to suggest that she is inclined to find our capacity to make sense of Marion Bloom's individual being far more puzzling than our ability to know what it is like to be a bat, but primarily because we do not, in any straightforward sense, share the substrate of life with her. But once again, we should be careful: for Costello is not denying that her capacity to think her way into Marion Bloom's existence is puzzling—indeed, deeply enigmatic, given her prior association of such exercises of imaginative sympathy with the commonality of genuinely animate existence. It is not as if she shows any sign of thinking that the human capacity to become completely absorbed in the vicissitudes of merely fictional beings is either morally pure (George Steiner is not the only thinker to express bewilderment at the conjunction of aesthetic sensitivity and evil to be found in the prime movers of the Holocaust) or metaphysically transparent (since there is, in reality, nothing there to understand). In this respect, she is reminding us that a fundamental dimension of the human form of life is inherently paradoxical or mysterious—as much to the philosopher as to any other inhabitant of culture; and as a consequence, so is a fundamental aspect of certain human beings—not only the creators of these fictional beings, but those who encounter them in their reading or viewing.

And to which category should we assign Elizabeth Costello, whose most famous novel involves re-creating another author's creation? Is contesting the truth about a fictional character with his creator more or less easy to comprehend than creating a fictional character ex nihilo? Is the latter possibility ever really possible? However we adjudicate these matters, the fundamental implication of her comparison of literary understanding with the understanding of nonhuman animals is once again to suggest that in the latter case, as with the former, we should expect to find genuine understanding, but of a kind that is marked with contradiction, impossibility, and a potent mixture of resistance and refusal.

KAFKA'S APE: OPACITY, PROGENY, MADNESS

This concluding "proof" of the enigmatic nature of distinctively human modes of being certainly encourages us to consider again the fact that we are attempting to understand the lecture of a very particular fictional character—one who is herself a creator of fictions, and whose most characteristic literary achievement was a text that contested the nature and reality of another writer's most famous fictional characters. For that reminder invites us to return to the beginning of Costello's lecture, where she explicitly identifies the canonical literary text upon which her present text is essentially parasitic.

> Ladies and gentlemen . . . it is two years since I last spoke in the United States. In the lecture I then gave, I had reason to refer to the great fabulist Franz Kafka, and in particular to his story "Report to An Academy," about an educated ape, Red Peter, who stands before the members of a learned society telling the story of his life—of his ascent from beast to something approaching man. On that occasion I felt a little like Red Peter myself and said so. Today that feeling is even stronger, for reasons that I hope will become clearer to you.
>
> Lectures often begin with lighthearted remarks whose purpose is to set the audience at ease. The comparison I have just drawn between myself and Kafka's ape might be taken as such a lighthearted remark, meant to set you at ease, meant to say I am just an ordinary person, neither a god nor a beast. Even those among you who read Kafka's story as an allegory of Kafka the Jew performing for Gentiles may nevertheless—in view of the fact that I am not a Jew—have done me the kindness of taking the comparison at face value, that is to say, ironically.
>
> I want to say at the outset that that was not how my remark—the remark that I feel like Red Peter—was intended. I did not intend it ironically. It means what it says. I say what I mean. I am an old woman. I do not have time any longer to say things I do not mean. (LA, 18)

Kafka's ape is the lens through which Costello views all of the material she discusses in her lecture: various putative originals, relatives, and doppelgangers of that literary creature are invoked at critical junctures, and their conjunctions or disjunctions (I imagine them threading through the text rather as that text reports Kohler's band of chimpanzees loping in a ragged circle around their compound) are what provide the lecture with such overarching coherence as it possesses. Kafka's Red Peter first recalls its historical original—an ape named Peter briefly famous on the variety circuits of middle Europe; then his briefly mentioned, half-mad female companion prompts Costello to imagine the real Peter as having a silent sister, presented as akin to Ramanujan; a melodramatic and mocking pretence of scholarship (amounting to an employment of coincidence in exactly the way she condemns in her opponents) next allows her to claim Kohler's Sultan as another historical source for Kafka's invention; then Red Peter's condemnation to sterility and hybridity generates a startling vision of the human animal as suffering its interpretation of itself as "monstrous thinking devices mounted inexplicably on suffering animal bodies" (LA, 30); and finally Red Peter's tortured confinement to a cage as he is shipped back to Europe gives Costello a complex image for the freedom that fullness of being requires and confers, for the ways in which

philosophers confine reason within the human body, and for the con-
finements (to cattle-trucks, to camps) emblematic of the Holocaust. Is this
a way of presenting ideas, proposals, assertions, and sheer speculations
that philosophy can recognize as a way of thinking without reconfiguring
it into a parade of arguments—thinking devices mounted inexplicably on
suffering animal bodies?

But the primary point of Costello's initial reference to Red Peter is to
articulate her sense of identity, or at least uncanny intimacy, with him:
before he comes to present us with an image of masochistic humanity, he
is introduced as a way of introducing Costello herself to her audience.
She says that she feels like him, and that she is not being lighthearted or
ironic, but simply saying what she means; so what does Red Peter feel
like, according to Kafka's account—more precisely, what does it feel like
to be Red Peter?

He is an African ape who reports that, after five years of intensive training, he has managed to attain the cultural level of an average European;
he performs in variety shows, attends social gatherings and scientific semi-
nars, and has now received the ultimate accolade—an invitation to give
an academy an account of the life he led as an ape. He begins by declaring
that he cannot comply with the specific terms of the invitation, since his
transformation depended upon letting go of his ape origins, and his memory no longer gives him access to the form of his experience and existence
before his capture. More precisely, the strong wind that blew after him
from his past has diminished to a gentle puff of air playing around his
heels; and the opening through which it and he came

> has grown so small that, even if my strength and my willpower sufficed to get
> me back to it, I should have to scrape the very skin from my body to crawl
> through. To put it plainly, gentlemen, as much as I like expressing myself in
> images, to put it plainly: your life as apes, gentlemen, insofar as something of
> that kind lies behind you, cannot be further removed from you than mine is
> from me. Yet everyone on earth feels a tickling at the heels; the small chimpan-
> zee and the great Achilles alike.[3]

Accordingly, his report begins after his capture, the shots that brought
him down having resulted in a large red facial scar that misleadingly leads
people to associate him with another performing ape named Peter, and a
severe wound below his hip (caused by what he calls a "wanton" shot),
the scar from which he hides beneath his human clothing, but which
makes him limp even now. He came to himself on a boat, in a cage whose
dimensions forced him to squat with knees bent and trembling, arms

---

[3] "A Report to an Academy" (hereafter RA), trans. W. and E. Muir, in *The Complete
Short Stories of Franz Kafka*, ed. N. N. Glatzer (London: Vintage, 1983), 250.

raised, face turned towards the solid planks of a locker, and the cage bars elsewhere cutting into his flesh. He could see no way out, where before he had had so many ways out of everything; thinking with his belly, he realised that his only means of escape was to stop being an ape, and to become instead like the men on ship who moved around unimpeded. So after careful observation and much trial and error, Red Peter masters the business of smoking a pipe and drinking schnapps from the bottle, until this fight against his ape nature resulted in "a brief and unmistakeable 'Hallo!' breaking into human speech, and . . . into the human community, and [I] felt its echo: 'Listen, he's talking!', like a caress over the whole of my sweat-drenched body" (RA, 257).

Once in Europe, faced with a choice between the zoo and the stage, he chose the latter and fought his way through the thick of things, working and socializing by day, and by night taking comfort from a half-trained little chimpanzee. He cannot bear to look at her by day, "for she has the insane look of the bewildered, half-broken animal in her eye" (RA, 259). Such is Red Peter's report.

In part, then, Kafka's ape manifests Elizabeth Costello's sense of being a performing animal in and for the academy. As a practising writer of fiction, she experiences the invitation to deliver a lecture and seminar to academics, but particularly to literary critics and (above all) to philosophers, as fundamentally incoherent in its demands; for it asks her to articulate the distinctive nature, ideas, and insights of the writers in what amounts to the manners and modes of expression of an entirely different species of human discourse, or at least one that regards itself as evolutionarily superior—as having transcended the more primitive modes of human thought and speech, those associated with the body (the belly) and the image (understood as opposed to the concept, or to reason).

Red Peter finds himself unable to regain access to his life as an ape prior to his capture and so cannot do what his audience explicitly invited him to do; but then again, if he could—if he retained immediate access to his ape-being—he would not be in a position to respond to that or any other invitation in the first place. In other words, his declaration of the opacity of his apehood to himself is his declaration that he has effected an ascension to humanity; what the tale more quietly evaluates "through [its] ironies and silences" (LA, 27) (which crystallize in its implication that his animal origin is his Achilles heel) is the cost of that achievement.

So is Costello saying that the thoughts of a writer, authentically expressed, would be as intelligible (that is, as unintelligible) as those of another animal species? Should we conclude from the relative articulacy and coherence that we have discovered in her engagements with an array of academic authorities that her thoughts can no longer be grounded in or authorised by her capacities as a creator of fictions—the very basis for her invitation in the first place? Or is it rather that she considers the lecture she is about to give as essentially hybrid, monstrous, a sterile crossing of two otherwise healthy and fruitful ways of being human? Can her academic audience engage with what she is saying in a way that acknowledges both the mode of expression it has attained and the mode of expression it has had to relinquish?

But Costello's sense of intimacy with Kafka's ape runs more deeply than this.

> Red Peter was not an investigator of primate behaviour but a branded, marked, wounded animal presenting himself as speaking testimony to a gathering of scholars. I am not a philosopher of mind but an animal exhibiting, yet not exhibiting, to a gathering of scholars a wound, which I cover up under my clothes but touch on in every word I speak.
>
> If Red Peter took it upon himself to make the arduous descent from the silence of the beasts to the gabble of reason in the spirit of the scapegoat, the chosen one, then his amanuensis was a scapegoat from birth, with a presentiment, a *Vorgefuhl*, for the massacre of the chosen people that was to take place so soon after his death. . . .
>
> In return for the prodigious overdevelopment of the intellect he has achieved, in return for his command of lecture-hall etiquette and academic rhetoric, what has he had to give up? The answer is: much, including progeny, succession. If Red Peter had any sense, he would not have any children. For upon the desperate, half-mad female ape with whom his captors, in Kafka's story, try to mate him, he would father only a monster. It is as hard to imagine the child of Red Peter as to imagine the child of Franz Kafka himself. Hybrids are, or ought to be, sterile; and Kafka saw both himself and Red Peter as hybrids. (LA, 26, 30)

I take it that Costello's claims about Kafka are also claims about herself—in other words, that she (like Kafka and Red Peter) sees herself as a hybrid, as a scapegoat, and above all as a wounded animal who touches on that wound in every word she speaks. Red Peter's wound results from a wanton shot; it is the mark of his capture, and it marks his gait in the world with a limp; and his sense of outrage at the outrage some people feel when he exhibits it itself exhibits a failure fully to have absorbed the cultural level of the average European as he claims—both their prudish sense of modesty about their bodies, and their inhibition or displacement of their violent impulses ("the hand which wrote that [my ape nature is not yet quite under control] should have its fingers shot away one by one" [RA, 251]).

The taint of madness in that wanton imprecation, despite its responsiveness to the suffering that words can inflict as easily as fists, as well as the way it seems to embody a more general abhorrence of the distinctively human transformation of paw into hand, hence into a means of linguistic expression, connects directly to Red Peter's inability to look his chimpanzee mate in the eye. For he refuses thereby to confront the wound touched on in every word he speaks—the possibility that the fully broken-in ape of this story is in fact fully broken, that in the process of acquiring human speech and reason he has driven himself mad.

What would Costello's son, John Bernard, make of his mother's willingness to identify with a creature that, she declares, would not have children if it had any sense? Costello has patently not chosen sterility—she has two children and (in the vicinity of Appleton College) two grandchildren; but her lack of any apparent concern for or genuine attentiveness to her family, not to mention her son's and daughter-in-law's various discomforts with her presence, strongly suggest that she is not exactly at home amidst such relations of blood and law. And the idea of herself as scapegoat—a creature familiar to Jewish and Christian thought as the beast who bears the burden of our sins, and bears away our pollutedness by accepting that pollution itself—invokes (in all seriousness, as well as in the accents of irony and self-pity) a theological perspective that recurs throughout her visit.

But the open wound that most thoroughly pervades her lecture, and that threatens to poison the hospitality of college and family alike, is her sense of the continuing human treatment of animals in farms, trawlers, abattoirs, and laboratories throughout the world—the sadistic games we play around the production of meat for food—as comparable to the Holocaust:

> Let me state it openly: we are surrounded by an enterprise of degradation, cruelty, and killing which rivals anything that the Third Reich was capable of, indeed dwarfs it, in that ours is an enterprise without end, self-regenerating, bringing rabbits, rats, poultry, livestock ceaselessly into the world for the purpose of killing them.
>
> And to split hairs, to claim that there is no comparison, that Treblinka was so to speak a metaphysical enterprise dedicated to nothing but death and annihilation while the meat industry is ultimately devoted to life (once its victims are dead, after all, it does not burn them to ash or bury them but on the contrary cuts them up and refrigerates and packs them so that they can be consumed in the comfort of our homes) is as little consolation to those victims as it would have been—pardon the tastelessness of the following—to ask the dead of Treblinka to excuse their killers because their body fat was needed to make soap and their hair to stuff mattresses with. (LA, 21–22)

Costello understands herself as being branded or marked, wounded by this knowledge; and in giving expression to it as she does, in the form of a comparison that identifies her audience, and her fellow human beings more generally, as being in the sinful, polluted state of those Germans, Poles, and Ukrainians who knew but did not allow themselves to know what was going on in the death camps, she at once understands those she addresses as psychically wounded by their knowledge precisely because of their denial of it, and aims to wound them further by articulating that understanding to their face—more precisely, by pressing or ramming their (and our) faces into it.

She is hardly unaware of the offensiveness of her comparison, or of the charge it allows and requires her to make; indeed, part of what marks or brands her is the further awareness that what she sees as a murderous enterprise of degradation and cruelty is simply not so regarded by most of her fellow citizens—and not because they are unaware of the facts of industrial meat production processes (a recital of which she consequently skips at the beginning of the lecture). A further part is her knowledge that she will be expected to give expression to her views in the manner of the academy—part of the great stream of Western discourse on human versus beast, and reason versus unreason, the very discourse that she takes to underpin the possibility of the murderous enterprise she wishes to protest against. But what wounds her most deeply is not the likelihood that her comparison and charge will be thought morally incompetent and intellectually disreputable to the point of insanity; it is the fact that the position into which she places herself by making both is one that makes *her* seriously contemplate the possibility that she is going mad—a fact that emerges later, during the culminating exchange of Coetzee's pair of lectures.

> It's that I no longer know where I am. I seem to move around perfectly easily among people, to have perfectly normal relations with them. Is it possible, I ask myself, that all of them are participants in a crime of stupefying proportions? Am I fantasizing it all? I must be mad! Yet every day I see the evidence. The very people I suspect produce the evidence, exhibit it, offer it to me. Corpses. Fragments of corpses that they have bought for money.
>
> It is as if I were to visit friends, and to make some polite remark about the lamp in their living room, and they were to say, "Yes, it's nice, isn't it? Polish-Jewish skin it's made of, we find that's best, the skins of young Polish-Jewish virgins." And then I go to the bathroom and the soap-wrapper says, "Treblinka—100% human stearate." Am I dreaming, I say to myself? What kind of house is this?
>
> Yet I'm not dreaming. I look into your eyes, into Norma's, into the children's, and I see only kindness, human-kindness. Calm down, I tell myself, you are making a mountain out of a molehill. This is life. Everyone else comes to terms with it, why can't you? *Why can't you?* (LA, 69)

If Costello is right, most of the people she encounters in the world are morally insane, or psychically wounded, with polluted souls; if she is wrong, then she is morally insane—living in a fantasy, dreaming, utterly disoriented. When she really looks at her fellow human beings, when she attends to her kin and her kind, the thought of utterly degraded animals retreats to the realm of fantasy; but when she really attends to her fellow-animals and their fate, the thought of human beings as fundamentally normal or well-balanced loses its grip. But these are not simply two exhaustive and mutually exclusive interpretative possibilities between which she must choose, or endlessly oscillate. They are both equally well-grounded in her experience, in the kindness that is all she can see in the eyes of those who nevertheless present her with fragments of corpses that they bought for money; so she cannot choose between them, she must endorse both—must see the very normality of her fellows as proof of the depth of their pollution. Her experience of the human world is thus itself scarred or seamed, internally contradictory; it resists her understanding, and hence so too does the world it is an experience of and the subject whose experience it is.

What does it say about the human animal, that ape swathed in clothing more complex than rags and cords, that its experience of its fellows and its world, and in particular its experience of the other animals with whom it shares the substrate of life, should ram its face into the possibility of its own insanity? Is that simply the fate of all apes who make the transition to humanity, incapable either of entirely losing touch with their animality or of wholly acknowledging it (as if that transformation were always incomplete, as Achilles' early-acquired invulnerability fatefully omitted his heel), so that we drug ourselves to repress our disgust at what we have become, while knowing that we would have to scrape the very skin from our bodies to recover our original nature? Is the naked ape simply the insane animal, or is that understanding of humanity itself insane? Can philosophy understand it as a vision of reality that is responsive in any way to the claims of reason?

Chapter Four

FOOD FOR THOUGHT: TWO SYMPOSIA

L IKE RED PETER'S REPORT to the academy, which is at once a con-
summate demonstration of his human acculturation and yet every-
where touched by the threat of insanity, Costello's lecture is both
a complete and subtle exercise of imaginatively grounded thought and an
extended cry of pain. How, therefore, should one respond to her words?
  This is a question that arises within and without Coetzee's fiction. It
confronts Costello's academic hosts, who have arranged a dinner in her
honour at the Faculty Club, where it will be the topics of conversation at
least as much as the construction of the menu that raise issues of tact,
civility, and civilization. But it is also an issue for the organizers of the
Tanner Lectures, one of whose obligations is to arrange for a number of
academics to respond immediately to Coetzee's address in brief but ideally
question-provoking ways (no doubt a dinner was in the offing here, too).
In both contexts, then, one might detect in the background the Platonic
ideal of the symposium, with its famous synthesis of physical and intellectual sustenance, hence its celebratory affirmation of such mutual acknowledgment of the life of the mind and the life of the body as a pinnacle
of human culture. In this chapter, I propose to examine the dynamics of
both symposia more closely; in the following two chapters I will organize
a third symposium of my own, the guest list for which contains a number
of philosophers whose thinking and writing can be seen as directly and
indirectly in dialogue with that of Costello and Coetzee.

The Appleton College Symposium

The Appleton College symposium is concisely rendered by Coetzee, but in
such a way as to relocate its aspirations within three rather less grandiose
conditions or constraints. First, there is the simple value of politeness:
despite Elizabeth Costello's unusually blunt and uncompromising refusal
to meet the expectations of her hosts in her lecture, they do their best to
treat her with respect. It soon becomes clear, however, that Costello is not
entirely willing to reciprocate. Take the following exchange between the
college president and his guest (narrated by that guest's son):

"But your own vegetarianism, Mrs. Costello," says President Garrard, pouring oil on troubled waters: "it comes out of moral conviction, does it not?"

"No, I don't think so," says his mother. "It comes out of a desire to save my soul."

Now there truly is a silence, broken only by the clink of plates as the waitresses set baked Alaskas before them.

"Well, I have a great respect for it," says Garrard. "As a way of life."

"I'm wearing leather shoes," says his mother. "I'm carrying a leather purse. I wouldn't have overmuch respect if I were you."

"Consistency," murmurs Garrard. "Consistency is the hobgoblin of small minds. Surely one can draw a distinction between eating meat and wearing leather."

"Degrees of obscenity," she replies. (LA, 43–44)

The reader is torn between amusement at Costello's obdurate refusal to smooth away social difficulties, satisfaction at her literal-minded responses to remarks that give priority to civility over truth, and sympathy with those forced to confront ideas of salvation and obscenity over a baked Alaska (the ice cream stubbornly retaining its frozen solidity beneath that sweet, whipped covering).

Part of academic civility on such occasions finds expression in the ability and willingness of people in disciplines other than the guest's own to find ways of responding to her ideas from their own perspective on the world; this is the second of the three constraints I mentioned earlier. Once again, a certain ideal of human civilization is registered here; for it is precisely the capacity of any given academic discipline to find intelligible ways of engaging with other such disciplines, and so of revealing the essentially dialogical unity of human forms of understanding and inquiring into the world, that is meant to be recognized and embodied in the institution of a university. And once again, the value of that aspiration has to be measured against the forms of failure and degradation to which it is necessarily open—as, for example, in a given discipline's refusal to give any weight to the perspective of another, or its willingness to trade intellectual seriousness in its contributions to this cultural conversation for some other value (say, institutional power, or etiquette, or personal point-scoring).[1]

Unfortunately, but perhaps unsurprisingly, it is one of the two philosophical members of the Appleton symposium whose main contribution exhibits a form of such failures, and in so doing she points us towards the third of the constraints I mentioned earlier. Responding to Costello's

[1] For a much more detailed elaboration of this theme, see my *The Conversation of Humanity* (Charlottesville: University of Virginia Press, 2007), esp. chap. 1.

association of human disgust at eating certain sorts of animal with religious horror, Norma objects that

> "Disgust is not universal . . . [s]o perhaps it's just a matter of what you learned at home, of what your mother told you was OK to eat and what was not."
> "What was clean to eat and what was not," his mother murmurs.
> "And maybe"—now Norma is going too far, he thinks, now she is beginning to dominate the conversation to an extent that it totally inappropriate—"the whole notion of cleanness versus uncleanness has a completely different function, namely to self-define ourselves, negatively, as elite, as elected. We are the people who abstain from *a* or *b* or *c*, and by that power of abstinence we mark ourselves off as superior: as a superior caste within society, for instance. Like the Brahmins."
> There is a silence.
> "The ban on meat that you get in vegetarianism is only an extreme form of dietary ban," Norma presses on; "and a dietary ban is a quick, simple way for an elite group to define itself. Other people's table habits are unclean, we can't eat or drink with them."
> Now she is getting really close to the bone. (LA, 42)

On the one hand, genuine contributions to a conversation should be something that the individual speaker can stand behind, own or disown, as an individual as well as merely a representative of their discipline; genuine speech should be the expression of the individuality of the speaker. On the other hand, even if we regard John's anxiety about Norma's contribution as itself unreliable because we know of his broader anxieties about the hostility between Norma and his mother, what Norma actually says gives us reason to think that this hostility really is getting the better of her. For we know that a key point of domestic dispute between Costello and her daughter-in-law is the former's refusal to eat dinner with the Bernard family because of Norma's refusal to remove meat from the children's menu simply to please her mother-in-law. Here, then, seeking truth and saying what one thinks are on the verge of subversion from within, by virtue of the very condition (the investment of the individual in the thoughts to which they give conversational expression) that is supposed to make progress in genuine understanding possible.

To say that pure intellectual inquiry in the form of a dialogue is necessarily conditioned in this way, and hence sometimes flawed and always questionable in these terms, is not of course to say that it is always reducible to or exhausted by such flaws. But it is to say that it can never float free of such complexities, which are as much a part of any realistic picture of human intercourse as is the aspiration it embodies. Indeed, to repress or deny this embeddedness would amount to a failure to live up to that aspiration towards genuine understanding of reality.

The Princeton Symposium

It is not hard to sympathize with the position of Coetzee's four respondents—the literary theorist Marjorie Garber, the philosopher Peter Singer, the scholar of religion Wendy Doniger, and the primatologist Barbara Smuts. For they were asked to comment on a text that already incorporates (within its own symposium and elsewhere) most modes and directions of academic commentary upon it that might easily be imagined. No wonder that one of them (Garber) identifies Coetzee's strategy here as a technique of control (although not only that); but in so doing, she doesn't seem willing to consider the possibility that it is also a technique of emancipation. For Coetzee's fictional anticipation of his respondents might also be intended to give them the opportunity to free themselves from their normal modes of response (from control or dictation by the perceived or imposed duties of their office and discipline) in order to take up the simpler, and more difficult, challenge of responding as individual readers—hence as individuals.

How should we think of Peter Singer's response in relation to that opportunity? In many ways, the position in which he is placed by Coetzee's text is the most difficult of the four. Singer is one of the most famous, influential, and uncompromising contemporary philosophical defenders of the rights of nonhuman animals; but the conclusions Costello reaches on the topic appear to propose a far more radical egalitarianism between humans and other animals than he has ever endorsed; and the means by which he has argued in defence of nonhuman animals would appear to embody exactly the conception of reason, and so of philosophy, that Costello's lecture attacks. In short, not only would Costello reject Singer's views as insufficiently radical; she would regard the form in which he advocates them as subverting even that insufficiently radical content. Moreover, since Costello is a fictional character, Singer is forced to recognize a distinction between her views and those of her author, and indeed to recognize that there is a fundamental difficulty involved in assuming that any opinion or argument advanced in this text is attributable to its author. And yet Singer's invitation is to respond qua philosopher to Coetzee's Tanner Lectures, not to Costello's Gates Lecture.

Singer's solution to these multiple difficulties is commendably radical, even if inherently risky. He chooses to respond to Coetzee's lectures by writing a very short story—a fictional piece in which a philosopher of animal rights named Peter, who has been asked to reply to J. M. Coetzee's Tanner Lectures, discusses his difficulties with respect to the form and what he takes to be the content of those lectures with his daughter Naomi, in the company of their dog Max, over the family breakfast table (yet another variant of the symposium model). Since this choice leaves Singer completely vulnerable to assessments of relative literary quality that are hardly likely to redound to his credit, his readers will be tempted to assume that there must be some very important reason why he sees no possible alternative to adopting this form of address—even that something about Coetzee's own choice of this form for his lectures mandates Singer's choice of responsorial form.

What, then, might it be? Since Singer's fiction is presented with no introductory or explanatory frame, his readers have nowhere to look for guidance on this matter but to the fiction itself, in which—as it happens—Peter expresses a very clear view about the key philosophical point (or consequence) of Coetzee's choice of form. After he has identified and discussed what he takes to be Costello's arguments in her lecture, Naomi suggests that none of them would supply Coetzee with acceptable grounds for a radical egalitarianism with respect to animals; and Peter responds as follows:

> "But *are* they Coetzee's arguments? That's just the point—that's why I don't know how to go about responding to this so-called lecture. They are *Costello*'s arguments. Coetzee's fictional device enables him to distance himself from them. And he has this character, Norma, Costello's daughter-in-law, who makes all the obvious objections to what Costello is saying. It's a marvellous device, really. Costello can blithely criticize the use of reason, or the need to have any clear principles or proscriptions, without Coetzee really committing himself to these claims. Maybe he really shares Norma's very proper doubts about them. Coetzee doesn't even have to worry too much about getting the structure of the lecture right. When he notices that it is starting to ramble, he just has Norma say that Costello is rambling!"
>
> "Pretty tricky. Not an easy thing to reply to. But why don't you try the same trick in response?"
>
> "*Me*? When have I ever written fiction?" (LA, 91)

Where Garber sees a technique of control, then, Peter more specifically sees a means of advancing arguments without commitment, and otherwise avoiding intellectual responsibility—for example, when the lecture Coetzee gives Costello to deliver begins to lose rigour, he has a marvellous means of avoiding the hard work that might be needed to restore its coherence and structure. Patently, then, Peter shares the view of the other philosopher obliquely involved in the Princeton symposium (Amy Gutmann) viz that Coetzee's fiction is a frame or container for arguments of various kinds. But he adds to this the thought that the space a fictional frame creates between what it contains and its creator thereby enables its creator to pull off a number of intellectually disreputable tricks (not to mention making it extremely difficult for any respondent to such a text to take up his distinctive responsibilities).

What, then, are we to make of the last exchange in the above passage, which makes up the final words of Singer's response? Naomi seems to be urging her father to try the same trick as Coetzee; and although his reply expresses an initial demurral, it is based solely on pointing out that writing fiction would be a new departure for him, and the existence of the response as a whole in fictional form further suggests that he manages to overcome it. But for him to follow Naomi's advice would surely amount to his deciding to indulge in what he has just characterized as an intellectually disreputable practice: more particularly, it would imply that his response contains arguments to which he does not commit himself, and exhibits an insufficiently rigorous rational structure. Does the author of this response really mean to take responsibility for these specific consequences of adopting such a literary form?

Perhaps, however, its author could respond by pointing out that I am not taking sufficiently seriously the central feature of Coetzee's fictional technique that the central character of Singer's fictional tale underlines—namely, the distinction it allows and requires readers to draw between main character and author. For all the views about fiction and philosophy that I have thus far drawn on are those of Peter the character and not, or at least not necessarily, Singer the author. Could one therefore argue that, strictly speaking, I am no more in a position to establish Singer's relation to any of the views advanced by his namesake in the text than either Peter or Singer is with respect to Coetzee and his character Costello? Could one even go further and argue that it is precisely Singer's intention to exploit this gap between author and character in his response, in such a way as to establish an ironic distance between Peter's old-fashioned beliefs in the distinction between truth and fiction, the value of thinking about feeling rather than just feeling, and the disreputability of fiction? For all I know, perhaps Singer finds these views as questionable as I do. Who can say, when faced with a piece of fiction about philosophical issues?

Certain aspects of the fictional tale might be taken to support this suggestion of willed or intended distance. After all, Peter does not exactly come across as an attractive character in his brief exchanges with his daughter—certainly not as someone for whom anyone, including his creator, might wish to be mistaken. By this I don't simply mean that his basic philosophical stance on animals rights is intellectually unattractive. To be sure, precisely because his approach exemplifies the "metaphysics as a ground for ethics" model assumed by O'Neill, and in doing so draws upon a conception of the morally relevant capacities and interests of human and nonhuman animals that resembles the one advanced by McMahan, many of the flaws I tried to identify in earlier chapters of this study are also manifest in Peter's thinking.[2] But the unattractiveness I am referring to now is as much a matter of character as intellect, or more precisely a matter of intellectual flaws that shade into flaws of character.

Take one central example, where Peter is arguing that painless, unanticipated killing may not be wrong in itself. Naomi disagrees:

> "What are you saying—that we could painlessly kill Max, get another puppy to replace him, and everything would be fine? Really, Dad, sometimes you let philosophy carry you away. Too much reasoning, not enough feeling. That's a *horrible* thought."
>
> Naomi is so distressed that Max, who has been listening attentively to the conversation, gets stiffly up from his rug, goes over to her, and starts consolingly licking her bare feet.
>
> "You know very well that I care about Max, so lay off with the 'You reason, so you don't feel' stuff, please. I feel, but I also think about what I feel. When people say we should *only* feel—and at times Costello comes close to that in her lecture—I'm reminded of Goering, who said 'I think with my blood.' See where it led him. We can't take our feelings as moral data, immune from rational criticism. But to get back to the point, I don't mean that *everything* would be fine if Max were killed and replaced by a puppy. We love Max, and *for us* no puppy would replace him. But I asked you why painlessly killing is wrong *in itself*. Our distress is a *side effect* of the killing, not something that makes it wrong in itself. Let's leave Max out of it, since mentioning his name seems to excite him and distress you." (LA, 88–89)

To begin with, taken as a rational response to Naomi's objection, this is surprisingly poor stuff. First, when Naomi suggests that her father is reasoning too much, and not feeling enough, Peter reflects her claim back to her as the charge that he is all reason and no feeling: since Naomi claims neither that we should feel rather than think, nor that our feelings should be immune to rational criticism, this is a blatant misrepresentation of her position (as well as that of Costello), which also happens to make it far easier to criticize. Even so, however, Peter's chosen criticism—to cite Goering—fails to work. For to point out that some thinking guided by feeling leads to horrific conclusions no more discredits all feeling-guided thinking than pointing out that some feeling-free thinking leads to horrific conclusions can discredit all such thinking.

Second, Peter's suggestion that his and Naomi's distress at Max's painless, unanticipated destruction would simply be one (morally undesirable,

---

[2] The resemblance to McMahan's work is unsurprising, since both are utilitarian consequentialists, and McMahan's work draws explicitly on that of Peter Singer. For a more detailed critical evaluation of Singer's views about the moral status of nonhuman animals, see C. Diamond, "Eating Meat and Eating People," in *The Realistic Spirit*.

because unhappiness-embodying) side-effect of a deed that is not in itself wrong is incoherent. For if it really were the case that Max's killing were not wrong in itself, there could be no rational basis for anyone, including Max's owners, to feel distressed about it; if they reflected with the appropriate degree of rigour upon their feelings, they would realize that they had nothing to be distressed about. And what this shows is that such feelings are not causally determined side-effects of an event or occurrence, but rather modes of response to it, and ones that are inherently open to rational evaluation (hence instances not of feeling as opposed to thinking, but rather of feeling informed by thought).

Third, when Peter makes his final rhetorical move of suggesting that they stop thinking about Max, and start thinking instead of a different species of animal with whom neither Naomi nor he has any direct relations in their everyday lives, he does more than reinforce his disreputable attempt to cast his daughter as someone who not only prefers feeling to thinking, but is herself incapable of preventing her rational faculties from being disrupted by emotional partiality. He also exemplifies one of Costello's key criticisms of philosophers. For he presents it as a requirement of reason that one insulate oneself from specific, individual existing animals, and our concrete experience of them, in favour of the intellectual contemplation of the concept of an animal species or of animality in general. (This is an issue that recurs in Costello's seminar, to which we shall soon turn.)

Small wonder, then, that we wince when a little later he "smiles triumphantly" at his daughter and declares. "Ah, but now you are conceding my point" (LA, 89); for these are ill-gotten argumentative gains. One would, accordingly, certainly like to think that a philosophically trained author would wish to establish as much distance as possible between himself and this particular creation. And that hypothesis would also allow us to account for certain other features of both main character and text that might otherwise create problems for its author, since they would otherwise seem to suggest a tendency on his part to identify with his fictional protagonist. Take the following exchange between father and daughter, over Costello's talk of the being of animate existence:

> "She talks about bat-being and human-being both being full of being, and seems to say that their fullness of being is more important than whether it is bat-being or human-being."
>
> "I can see what she's getting at. When you kill a bat, you take away everything that the bat has, its entire existence. Killing a human being can't do more than that."
>
> "Yes, it can. If I pour the rest of this soymilk down the sink, I've emptied the container; and if I do the same to that bottle of Kahlua you and your friends

are fond of drinking when we are out, I'd empty it too. But you'd care more about the loss of the Kahlua. The value that is lost when something is emptied depends on what was there when it was full, and there is more to human existence there is to bat existence."

Naomi says quietly: "Oh. I didn't think you'd noticed the Kahlua." (LA, 90)

Peter's representation of Costello's position is literal-minded in the worst sense. The only sense he can attach to the idea of "fullness of being" is a breathtakingly literal one; his assumption seems to be that Costello imagines the relation of an animal's being to the animal itself on analogy with the relation between the contents of a bottle and the bottle itself. Without this assumption, his argument by analogy cannot work; but to take it seriously is to attribute to Costello a picture of the relation between life and body of exactly the dualist, Cartesian kind against which her whole lecture is directed.

But those bottles are more than just the vehicle for a crude simplification of an opponent's position; they are also positioned by their author in such a way as to confirm Peter's sense of his own relation to Naomi. They immediately declare that, even with respect to her attempts at a private life, he knows everything: nothing is hidden from him; he is in effect omniscient. They thereby reinforce the fact that she is a mere child, and a female child at that; he is the all-knowing father, the paradigm of male authority—an embodiment of the Law of the Father. But if he is omniscient, then of course he knows the truth about animals and she must not. Why else, after all, does she lose every argument into which she enters in this little narrative?

In other words, the Kahlua bottle exemplifies the extent to which the author of this tale systematically stacks the deck against one of his characters, in favour of the other; it also exemplifies the ways in which the tale itself is structured in such a way as to align Peter's (in fact illusory) demonstration of his intellectual superiority with his gender and his parental role in a thoroughly unattractive way. It would therefore be a relief to be able to hold that these, too, are best understood not as ways in which the author's straightforward identification with his main character has got altogether out of hand, to his intellectual and ethical detriment, but rather as delicate authorial hints to the reader that we should distance ourselves from his main character's unquestioning sense of himself as the intellectual alpha male of his world.

Even given these substantial points in its favour, however, serious grounds for doubt about the plausibility of such an approach to this text must in all honesty be acknowledged. After all, in the Coetzee text, the possibility of straightforwardly identifying author and character is discouraged by a variety of strategies, prominent among them the fact that the character concerned is an older female whose personal circumstances and literary track record offer at most very general points of resemblance with those of her author. In the Singer text, matters are very different; for his main character not only possesses the same first name, gender, occupation, and immediate task as his creator, but has also written a book with an opening chapter whose title matches that of one of his creator's books, holds views about animals that are indistinguishable from those expressed in other contexts by his creator *in propria persona*, and bases them on exactly the same arguments that his creator has also advanced in his own name.

Furthermore, if Singer did hold the views about literature advanced by his character and thought of fictional frames as essentially optional containers for self-evidently philosophical arguments (like bottles into and from which the intellectual Kahlua could be poured, without affecting it in the slightest), then it could do no harm to the rational force of those arguments if they were, on this particular occasion, presented by a fictional character of the same name. For that would amount to closing the space within which Coetzee gets up to his intellectually irresponsible tricks, in the name of philosophical integrity and the old-fashioned distinction between truth and fiction. Then, even while ensuring that everyone grasped that he stood behind every word Peter says, Singer could nevertheless use his fictional frame to make a few jokes, and also to make an apparently gracious gesture to the author of the lectures to which he is responding, without in any way threatening his sense of philosophy's superiority to the childish, feminine, and essentially emotional domain of the literary. On this reading, one might say that casting Costello and Coetzee as Naomi to his Peter is Singer's way of trumping what he thinks of as Coetzee's attempt to cast Singer and philosophy as Norma to his Costello.

There is, however, a way of avoiding the attribution of such thoughts and intentions to Singer—namely, by hypothesizing that he intends us to regard Peter as the author as well as the protagonist of this fictional exercise. This would, after all, be one way of understanding its ending, in which Naomi precisely encourages her father to take up Coetzee's fictional challenge. Then the apparent sense of identification between author and character that we have repeatedly run up against could be interpreted as part of Singer's authorial strategy, but in a way that doesn't implicate him in Peter's rational, ethical, and fictional misdeeds. For it could be viewed as part of Singer's plan to utilize a further literary-theoretical distinction (between fictional author and real author) in order to buttress the case against Peter, now understood as a character who also writes the story in which he stars, as the creator of the fictional universe which centres upon him—the divinity of the fiction as well as the divinity incarnate within it. Then Singer's creation of Peter could be seen as his silent dis-avowal of everything that his earlier philosophical work stood for, and hence as a genuinely graceful acknowledgment of the superiority of Coet-zee's distinctive marriage of thought and feeling in fiction. The charitable reader is therefore able to avoid the more unpalatable implications of Singer's literary experiment, should she wish to exercise that virtue.

Chapter Five

FOOD FOR THOUGHT: A THIRD SYMPOSIUM

T HREE YEARS AFTER THE Tanner Lectures and responses first appeared in print, Cora Diamond gave a paper at a different kind of symposium—a conference at the New School for Social Research in New York, in honour of Stanley Cavell.[1] The paper was entitled "The Difficulty of Reality and the Difficulty of Philosophy" and has now itself appeared in print, in a much-expanded version of the New School conference proceedings.[2] In it, Coetzee's Tanner Lectures provide one among a range of examples of what Diamond wants to call (using a phrase from John Updike) "the difficulty of reality," and of philosophy's capacity to be deflected from those difficulties precisely because of its characteristic ways of attempting to respond to the claims of reason. Stanley Cavell appears in the paper as one philosopher who is sensitive to philosophy's tendency so to be deflected, practised at diagnosing its various occurrences (as opposed to being further deflected from their true nature), and so able to avoid succumbing to that tendency. Cavell himself was also at the New School conference, and he took (he actually says that he felt compelled to take) Diamond's paper as the subject of his contribution to a collection of essays about—call it a disembodied or virtual symposium on—Diamond's work. His paper, entitled "Companionable Thinking," accordingly responds both to Diamond's response to Coetzee and to Coetzee (among other things); and it is in turn the subject of a brief response by John McDowell in the same volume.[3]

At one point in an earlier draft of his essay, Cavell characterized Diamond as one of the original respondents to Coetzee's Tanner Lectures—as if giving expression not only to his sense of Diamond's inwardness with Coetzee, but also to the depth of his wish that Coetzee might have been shown that philosophy's capacity to respond to his writing was not really

---

[1] I attended this conference, and it was hearing Diamond's paper that confirmed me in my desire to embark on this project.

[2] A. Crary and S. Shieh, eds., *Reading Cavell* (London: Routledge, 2006).

[3] A. Crary, ed., *Wittgenstein and the Moral Life: Essays in Honour of Cora Diamond* (Boston: MIT Press, 2007). Diamond's, Cavell's, and McDowell's papers have now been republished in one volume—Cavell et al., *Philosophy and Animal Life* (New York: Columbia University Press, 2008), hereafter PAL. All page references to these essays are keyed to this volume.

as restricted as Gutmann's and Singer's actual responses must have suggested. Since I share that wish, in this section of the chapter I propose to
imagine its fulfilment, to inhabit and extend Cavell's hallucination, by
treating Diamond, Cavell, and McDowell as if they had taken on that
responsibility—hence, as contributors to an alternative, and in my view
far superior, Tanner symposium.

What, then, does Diamond mean by the difficulty of reality?

> [T]he phenomena with which I'm concerned [are] experiences in which we take
> something in reality to be resistant to our thinking it, or possibly to be painful
> in its inexplicability, difficult in that way, or perhaps awesome and astonishing
> in its inexplicability. *We take things so.* And the things we take so may simply
> not, to others, present that kind of difficulty, of being hard or impossible or
> agonizing to get one's mind around. (PAL, 45–46)

Coetzee's lectures exemplify this phenomenon primarily because, in Diamond's view, they present a woman who is wounded, haunted in her
mind, first by what we do to animals, and second by the fact that this
horror, which reduces her to a terrible rawness of nerves, is treated as if
it were nothing, as simply part of the accepted background of ordinary
life, by most other people. Diamond sees clearly that Costello's sense of
having her sanity under threat is as much a matter of the second horror
as of the first—that an essential part of what is driving her mad is that
what she experiences as an inexplicable horror is not so experienced by
others, and that this divergence between herself and her fellow human
beings is itself painfully inexplicable.

Costello's repeated resort to Holocaust imagery is, therefore, in the
first instance Coetzee's way of conveying a sense of what it is like to
hang on the frightful, no-man-fathomed cliffs of Costello's mind, from
which only the reality of sleep and the thought of death offer her any
relief. At the same time, however, it gives us a way of seeing a difficulty
of reality to which Costello is blind: for her use of it, in all its offensiveness, suggests that her understanding of what we do to animals seems
to throw into shadow the full, painfully inexplicable horror of what we
do to each other, as if we could not simultaneously use the Holocaust as
an image for what we do to animals and retain a grip on the reality of the
Holocaust itself, on what it shows us about what we are (inexplicably,
agonizingly) capable of doing to other human beings. In other words,
insofar as we strive to keep one sort of difficulty of reality in view, we
seem blocked from seeing another; we simply cannot keep both inexplicable horrors in proper focus simultaneously. And this is as true of Costello
as it is of at least some of those who find her use of the Holocaust as a
figure of comparison utterly offensive.

The character in Coetzee's story who makes this point clear is the one whose contribution to the Appleton College symposium takes the form of his absence from it, and the message that absence is intended to convey—the well-respected poet Abraham Stern, a longtime resident on campus. The morning after the dinner, Costello receives a note from him:

> *Dear Mrs. Costello,*
>
> Excuse me for not attending last night's dinner. I have read your books and know you are a serious person, so I do you the credit of taking what you said in your lecture seriously.
>
> At the kernel of your lecture, it seemed to me, was the question of breaking bread. If we refuse to break bread with the executioners of Auschwitz, can we continue to break bread with the slaughterers of animals? You took over for your own purposes the familiar comparison between the murdered Jews of Europe and slaughtered cattle. The Jews died like cattle, therefore cattle die like Jews, you say. That is a trick with words which I will not accept. You misunderstand the nature of likenesses; I would even say you misunderstand wilfully, to the point of blasphemy. Man is made in the likeness of God but God does not have the likeness of man. If Jews were treated like cattle, it does not follow that cattle are treated like Jews. The inversion insults the memory of the dead. It also trades on the horrors of the camps in a cheap way.
>
> Forgive me if I am forthright. You said that you were old enough not to have time to waste on niceties, and I am an old man too.
>
> *Yours sincerely,*
> *Abraham Stern* (LA, 49–50)

It is Cavell who points out an implication of this letter that might otherwise have escaped our attention: the connection between one of its motivating images and the behaviour of its author. For whether we take the breaking of bread in secular or religious terms (as exemplifying the subsumption of nature into culture, or as commemorating an exodus from slavery, or as ingesting the body and blood of divinity), the human communion it embodies, and from which Stern agrees we must banish the Nazis, is one in which he refuses to participate with Costello.

> [A]re we to take it that Stern finds Costello's offensive fault of assimilation to warrant assimilating her (receiving a treatment of shunning precisely marking the treatment warranted by) the executioners of Auschwitz, beyond the pale of shared bread? This reaction would seem to make his perception of Costello's fault quite as inordinate as he takes her perception of the slaughterers of animals to be. And/or should this count as Stern's doing what he promised at the outset of his letter to do, namely doing Elizabeth Costello the credit of taking what she said in her lecture seriously? (PAL, 100–101)

From the perspective of Diamond's reading of Coetzee, of course, these perceptions of Stern are not alternatives (as Cavell's "and/or" implicitly acknowledges). For Stern's sense of Costello's analogical use of the Holocaust as painfully, inexplicably horrible is such that he blinds himself to the inordinately monstrous analogy that his own stance towards Costello embodies. Once again, using the Holocaust as a way of bringing one kind of painful difficulty into focus throws into shadow an equally agonizing moral problem.

For both Cavell and Diamond, then, to take Coetzee's lectures seriously as literature (whatever that difficult project might turn out to involve) in the first instance means taking them seriously as a presentation of specific, individual characters; they certainly have opinions and engage in and with arguments of various kinds, but the full significance of the opinions and arguments to which they relate cannot be grasped unless they are grasped in relation to the people who hold, advance, and contest them. On Diamond's view, for example, Stern's characterization of the kernel of Costello's lecture would amount to a failure to appreciate the specific way in which she aims to engage with the canonical patterns of philosophical argument. For he summarizes her use of the Holocaust as follows: "The Jews died like cattle, therefore cattle die like Jews, you say." But this transforms Costello's traumatizing perception into an inference; it makes her expressions of horror pivot upon a "therefore," when in Diamond's view Costello's stance towards philosophy centrally involves a "rejection of the '*therefore*'—[of] arguments that go from characteristics of animals to its therefore being permissible to treat them this or that way" (PAL, 83).

In effect, then, Stern's inordinate indignation at Costello's perceptions leads him to misperceive Costello's real, particular relation to the canonical techniques of reason; it allows him to deflect himself (and us) from any proper appreciation of the force and the limits of her stance towards nonhuman and human animals. And in Diamond's view, Stern here offers us a poet's (and a religious believer's) version of the very phenomenon of which Gutmann and Singer offer us a philosophical inflection. Indeed, for Diamond, such deflections are a besetting, even a defining, temptation of philosophy in its relation to literature—part of what makes acknowledging the reality of that relation so difficult for both parties.

She castigates both Gutmann and Singer for regarding Costello as one particular, dispensable vehicle or container for the presentation of a position on the issue of how we should treat animals—that is, for treating Costello herself, in all her psychological and moral particularity, as of vanishing significance in comparison with the opinions and the fragments of argument that are undeniably embedded in her lecture and her conversation. By putting Coetzee's lectures in the context of argumentative discourse on moral issues, these philosophers move themselves and us away from the various interrelated difficulties of reality that Coetzee's writing attempts to present, and hence from the specific conception of the human animal (as capable of being wounded and haunted by the real, of suffering a painful inability to comprehend what is nevertheless undeniably there) that emerges from it, in favour of a very different conception (of humans as essentially rational animals, of nonhuman animals as essentially distinct from humanity, and of reality as essentially graspable in its entirety by a specific dimension or aspect of distinctively human rationality) that it cannot even register as one conception to which there might be intelligible and powerful alternatives.

To be sure, there is a hardness or difficulty in the familiar modes of philosophical argumentation, and so the effect of this kind of deflection is not necessarily to relieve us of difficulty. But it is not the kind of difficulty we face when trying to appreciate what Diamond calls the difficulty of reality. In philosophy, the difficulties are real but not hard to understand: they are the difficulties of confronting hard problems, ensuring that arguments are valid or sound, watching out for distortions caused by inappropriate emotional responses, unquestioned assumptions, or assertions ungrounded in reasoning. A difficulty of reality is, on Diamond's view, an apparent resistance by reality to one's ordinary modes of life, which include one's ordinary modes of thinking; to appreciate that kind of difficulty "is to appreciate oneself being shouldered out of how one thinks, how one is apparently supposed to think" (PAL, 58). Costello's immense isolation is in large part a function of how her experience of how we treat animals is such as to compel her to resist any invitation or compulsion to articulate her experience in terms of the resources available in a certain, massively familiar way of thinking, the great river of Reason in Western culture; she aims to rely instead, and to invite her audience to rely, upon our capacity to inhabit in imagination nonhuman animal bodies. And just as we may reject that invitation by requiring whatever results from it to be reformulated in the terms of philosophical argumentation, so we may (in reading his lectures) reject Coetzee's invitation to exercise our capacity to imagine the bodily existence of Elizabeth Costello as she tries to confront the difficulty of what we do to animals, and do so by deflecting the whole business of reading him into the familiar terms of a discussion of difficult moral issues.

As the perspective I adopted in chapter 3 should already have made clear, I do not entirely share Diamond's apparent sense that Costello's relation to philosophical argumentation is absolutely negative. Diamond's way of putting the point is as follows:

> She does not engage with others in argument, in the sense in which philosophers do. . . . She comments on the arguments put to her, but goes on from them in directions that suggest her own very different mode of approach. She does not take seriously the conventions of argumentation of a philosophy text, as comes

out in her image of the dead hen speaking in the writings of Camus on the guillotine. (This is clearly, from the point of view of conventions of argumentation, no way to respond to the argumentative point that animals cannot speak for themselves and claim rights for themselves as we can. The image itself is reminiscent of Wittgenstein's image of the rose having teeth in the mouth of the cow that chews up its food and dungs the rose.) (PAL, 52)

I would prefer to say that Costello's lecture does indeed go on from the philosophical arguments made in the canonical texts she confronts, but only after a moment or phase in which she really does take their conventions seriously—specifically by following out their own preferred terms of articulation in such a way as to reveal their internal fissures. And even in those phases of her engagement with philosophers in which she seems most flatly to refuse their preferred terms of articulation, something other than a mere assertion of absolute difference in approach, something more like a kind of response to the argumentative points that so provoke her, seems to me to be under way.

Let us recall in more detail the invocation of Camus to which Diamond refers. Costello makes this move in her final session at Appleton College, which takes the form of a debate with a professor of philosophy named Thomas O'Hearne, who puts forward three positions or theses, to which Costello is invited to reply. The second involves the claim that since animals cannot speak or think in any full-blooded sense of those terms, the panoply of rights concepts simply cannot have any intelligible application to them. Costello's reply culminates in the following suggestion.

> As for animals being too dumb and stupid to speak for themselves, consider the following sequence of events. When Albert Camus was a young boy in Algeria, his grandmother told him to bring her one of the hens from the cage in their backyard. He obeyed, then watched her cut off its head with a kitchen knife, catching its blood in a bowl so that the floor would not be dirtied.
>
> The death cry of that hen imprinted itself on the boy's memory so hauntingly that in 1958 he wrote an impassioned attack on the guillotine. As a result, in part, of that polemic, capital punishment was abolished in France. Who is to say, then, that the hen did not speak? (LA, 62)

There is no denying that there is a strong element of flat denial here—an attempt to refuse the terms for thinking with which O'Hearne presents her. But it is worth bearing in mind that this is the penultimate exchange in the final formal encounter of a long sequence of such encounters that have not gone well, and have patently begun to exhaust the rather limited reserves of Costello's patience. So we need not think of her undeniable peremptoriness here as exemplifying her default attitude to philosophy and its claims throughout her visit, let alone in her lecture. And there is anyway much more to be registered in the content of her response.

To begin with, the Camus story offers the reader a further instance of someone being haunted or wounded by a difficulty of reality. That difficulty may in part be a matter of being struck by a certain conflict in the condition of animals reared in farms and homesteads for human use, in the utterly familiar tension between their being cared for in life and destined for the pot. But it is more immediately a matter of being struck by the simultaneous practicality and odiousness of the grandmother's desire to catch the hen's blood in a bowl; for that entirely understandable concern to avoid besmirching a floor somehow accentuates the brutality of the beheading, crystallizing the hen's status as flesh-for-food that happens to contain large and potentially messy amounts of blood.

The grotesque delicacy of that carefully angled bowl exemplifies the ways in which human civilization can sometimes be seen as dressing up the horrifying realities of its practices in ways that are so blatantly concerned with the appearance of cleanliness that they betray a lingering sense of the underlying uncleanness of what is actually being done. And it is this sense of the perverse human tendency to attempt to deaden self-disgust in ways that actually intensify it that Camus finds himself confronting in a new field—that of human judicial execution. There is here, in other words, the discovery or revelation of an analogy, of the kind Costello so offensively draws between factory farming and the extermination camps of the Holocaust; and it actually helps to bring about revolutionary change.

In short, Camus may not have deployed an argument, in any conventional philosophical sense, but he does present a way of seeing certain connections between the past and the present, the private and the public, and between the nonhuman and the human, with passionate conviction of a kind that elicits a deep and transformative imaginative response in other human beings. But it is not just that this way of seeing the world embodies a perception of fellowship between human and nonhuman animals; Costello's attribution of speech to the hen depends upon the idea that the hen speaks not only in or through the mouth of a human being, but also about and on behalf of human beings rather than her nonhuman fellows. In this sense, the hen speaks through Camus on behalf of mortal creatures in general, the fellowship of animate, embodied existence.

What, however, is happening to the idea of animals as speaking, and so to the idea of speech, in Costello's hands (and mouth)? Diamond usefully compares it to the following example from Wittgenstein:[4]

---

[4] *Philosophical Investigations* (Oxford: Blackwell, 1958), hereafter PI.

"A new-born child has no teeth."—"A goose has no teeth."—"A rose has no teeth."—This last at any rate—one would like to say—is obviously true! It is even surer than that a goose has none. And yet it is none so clear. For where should a rose's teeth have been? The goose has none in its jaw. And neither, of course, has it any in its wings; but no one means that when he says it has no teeth.—Why, suppose one were to say: the cow chews its food and then dungs the rose with it, so the rose has teeth in the mouth of a beast. This would not be absurd, because one has no notion in advance where to look for teeth in a rose. (Connexion with "pain in someone else's body.") (PI, 221–22)

On one vision of words and their ordering, the idea of "teeth" has no application to roses: it violates the grammar of our language games with the word. A mode of application to roses can be invented for it, of course; but that amounts to sheer invention, to the construction from scratch of a new and utterly different language game for it. According to another vision of language, closer to Diamond's and Costello's hearts, words are inherently capable of projection beyond their familiar contexts, as if there is always already more to their meaning than is captureable in the grammatical rules for particular language games with them. Such projectiveness is guided or governed by the existing ways in which that word relates to a range of other words, insofar as each concrete, realized case of projection is an expression of our willingness to find a point of purchase for some proportion of that range of interrelated expressions, some specific way in which the relevant word can be seen as bringing some inflection of that field of terms into the new context.

The sense in which a rose might be said to have teeth is neither an entirely familiar nor an entirely new application of those words; it is an extension or projection of them that is neither determined by the rules for their use nor forbidden by them. Rather, we are invited to make sense of that expression in the light of our everyday understanding of the relation between teeth and eating, and eating and feeding, in the lives of human and nonhuman animals, crops and flowers, and of the ways in which animals of either kind can help or be utilized by their fellows to eat and to feed. We make an intelligible context for their use, but in a way that feels like a discovery or revelation of a possibility (at once in and of the words, and in and of reality) rather than its essentially arbitrary construction.

What then, of Costello's concluding question: "Who is to say, then, that the hen did not speak?," and even more specifically, that it spoke of pain in another's body (in the beheaded bodies of human beings, but also in the hearts of those contemplating the practice that demands this beheading, and what that practice reveals of the human heart and its perversities)? We might say that her way of presenting this aspect of Camus' life in its relation to his writing is an invitation to see that, by seeing how, the idea of speech might find application in such a context—in important part by inviting us to recall our everyday understanding of ways in which the world of our experience can be said to speak to us, to intimate modes of understanding and ways of seeing the world, to indicate possibilities that are at once original and yet utterly natural, even compelling, once delineated. This is an essentially imaginative exercise of speech, which is not to say that it is essentially irrational. For who is to say what counts as "saying" if not those animals whose form of life is complex enough to burden them with speech? And what authority might any of them claim to determine what counts as a legitimate use of this or any other word, that is not equally claimable by any other speaker, simply by virtue of the fact that they are speakers? It is not, then, for philosophy to say that the hen did speak, or that she did not, or that she could not. It is for any and every one of us to judge, by judging whether or not we can accept any specific invitation to find a particular projection of those words worth going along with, something that we can follow.

I have no reason to think that Diamond would disagree with any of the morals I have been drawing from Costello's invocation of Camus and the hen. But it does seem at least misleading to describe them as not taking seriously the conventions of argumentation; they seem to me to be better characterized as reminders of other familiar, everyday ways of attempting to convince others of one's way of seeing the world, of the kind that Diamond specifies in her other work (for example, that cited in chapter 1). They would therefore seem to be forms of discourse that philosophy need have no qualms about admitting as modes of thought or ways of reflecting about the world, hence as possible ways of meeting its own distinctive burden—that of acknowledging the claims of reason.

That qualification aside, however, Diamond's paper goes on to link Costello's idea of our capacity to inhabit bodily existence in imagination, and of philosophy's reluctance to acknowledge it, to Stanley Cavell's lifelong engagement with scepticism. For she sees in his work a related case of someone recognizing and resisting philosophy's tendency to deflect a difficulty of reality into a difficulty of argumentation, and (even more importantly) of recognizing and resisting forms of resistance to that tendency that are in fact further expressions of it. She cites in particular his treatment of expressions of scepticism about other minds, and certain familiar Wittgensteinian attempts to dismantle or dissolve such forms of scepticism.[5]

---

[5] The Cavell paper to which she particularly refers is "Knowing and Acknowledging," in his *Must We Mean What We Say?* (Cambridge: Cambridge University Press, 1976).

It is common for sceptics about other minds to claim that we cannot ever know or be certain of what another is feeling, because we cannot ever feel what the other person is feeling. And it is common for Wittgensteinians to respond to such claims by asking whether it makes sense to think of our inability to feel another's feelings as a limitation upon us. It appears to reflect a picture of our relation to another's inner life as analogous to our relation to a flower in a garden on the far side of a wall over which we cannot see or climb; but what the sceptic takes to be an inability is in fact a misperception of the difference between two language games. In the language game with "flower," even if we cannot in fact penetrate beyond the wall, it makes perfect sense to imagine us doing so, and so it makes perfect sense to think of ourselves as at present excluded from that garden; but in the language game with "pain," there is no such thing as occupying the position of another with respect to what that other is feeling, and in fact no such thing as a position that the other has with respect to his pain (he simply has his pain, is in pain). In short, the form of words "I am feeling your pain" simply has no use in the game. We are not unable to be there if there is no "there" where we are unable to be.

Now those Wittgensteinians who respond in this way to the sceptic might well summarize their position by saying that, according to their diagnosis, the sceptic is inherently confused—misusing the words he needs in order to articulate his scepticism. And Cavell would not exactly deny this; rather—and this is what Diamond describes as astonishing—he claims that the truth of this diagnosis about the way the sceptic tends to express himself does not show that the sceptic's experience of powerlessness has been shown to boil down to a simple grammatical error. For since he, as well as any other speaker, already knows and so can be brought to acknowledge the grammatical points of which the Wittgensteinian philosopher has reminded him, why did he call on those particular words in the first place? More particularly, why does a traumatic perception of one's inability to have what another has find expression in the claim that one cannot know what that other has?

In Cavell's view, what is happening is that the sceptic is giving expression to an inordinate experience of metaphysical finitude (our separateness from the other, the "fact" that I am not him or her, and hence that I may—for all that either of us can do—miss his or her suffering, or have my own suffering missed by others) in terms suggestive of an intellectual lack (a picture of myself as locked out from what they are thinking or feeling, so that what is at issue are the limitations of human cognition, not the limits of human acknowledgment). But if an experience of powerlessness is deflected into an expression of ignorance, then simply to point out that the concept of ignorance is here misplaced, and to regard the matter as thereby settled, is precisely to accept the deflected terms in which the sceptic has given expression to her experience. It therefore amounts to a continuation of that deflection, a way of continuing to miss the difficulty to which that initial deflection is a defensive response.

Diamond thereby presents Cavell as having shown her that what the sceptic sees of the human condition is such that it threatens to unseat his reason; it shoulders him out from our ordinary ways of talking about pain, although it does not render him wordless. But the traditional Wittgensteinian response treats it as a difficulty caused solely by the sceptic's (presumably thoughtless or careless) failure to recall or respect those ordinary ways; and such a response deflects us from considering the possibility that certain aspects of our everyday experience of reality might compel us to repudiate our ordinary language games (without thereby rendering us mute or our experiences empty). By contrast, Cavell takes his way of thinking to be heading towards the conclusion that "scepticism about other minds is not scepticism but tragedy"; otherwise put, it opens up the thought that what philosophy knows as scepticism is presented in literature as tragedy, and hence that philosophy might in this respect find literature indispensable to its own distinctive business.

The particular aspect of Cavell's treatment of scepticism upon which Diamond focuses patently foregrounds the issue of human embodiment (one might less misleadingly say human ensoulment), and so of the human body, since it is this aspect of our metaphysical finitude—the distinctness of our bodies confirming our separateness—to which the sceptic is responsive. At one point, Diamond in fact describes herself as "inviting you to think of what it would be not to be 'deflected' as an inhabiting of a body (one's own, or an imagined other's) in the appreciating of a philosophical difficulty" (PAL, 59). And in his response to Diamond, Cavell picks up on this far from clear line of thought by suggesting a further way of understanding Costello's wound.

> That she conceals it under her clothes immediately alerts us to the most obvious, or banal, unlikeness, between her condition and that of other animals, namely just that her species wears clothes. And since what is concealed, and not concealed, under her clothes, we are allowed to assume, is an ageing but otherwise unharmed woman's body, the torment she expresses is somehow to be identified with the very possession of a human body, which is to say, with being human. (PAL, 110)

Cavell draws out two key implications from this reading of Costello's wound. One is that, since Costello claims that her wound is touched on in every word she speaks, and yet every word she speaks are the words of others, common bread, then "to speak, the signature expression of the human life form, is to be victimized by what there is to say, or to fail to say" (PAL, 115). Not to speak of our treatment of animals is to subject oneself to anguish; but the only words with which one finds that one can speak about that treatment are such as to impute moral insanity. And for Costello, what is at stake in this topic of our treatment of other animals, and so what is at stake in our obligation to talk about it, is the moral status of humanity as such.

This is the second implication that Cavell draws from his interpretation of Costello's wound.

> [S]ince the stigmata of [Costello's] suffering are coincident with the possession of the human body, the right to enter such a claim universally to other such possessors, has roughly the logic of a voice in the wilderness, crying out news that may be known to virtually none, but to all virtually. It is a voice invoking a religious, not alone a philosophical, register: it is uninvited, it goes beyond an appeal to experiences we must assume all humans share, or recognize, and it is meant to instil belief and a commentary and community based on belief, yielding a very particular form of passionate utterance, call it prophecy. . . . The right to voice it is not alone an arrogation of a claim every human being should be in a position to make, which philosophy requires of itself, in speaking for all; it is rather a judgement that distances itself from the human as it stands, that finds human company itself touched with noxiousness. (PAL, 111–12)

This returns us to the religious themes first broached by Cavell's interest in Abraham Stern's refusal to break bread with Costello, and it expresses a legitimate anxiety about philosophy's capacity to acknowledge Costello's (and so Coetzee's) ways with words. But it is important to see that Costello's inherently offensive utterance does not absolve her from implication in the crime she perceives, hence in the noxiousness of the human condition as it stands. As Cavell points out, she phrases her indictment in the first-person plural: "Ours is an enterprise without end" (LA, 21); and when she deflects the college president's admiration of her moral purity, she does so by pointing to her leather shoes and handbag. We saw earlier that, on Cavell's reading, Costello's concealment of her wound under her clothes is a pointer to the fact that it is only the human species of animal that wears clothes; so covering one's body with animal skin while abstaining from ingesting animal flesh cannot be defended as a merely superficial form of moral aberration, but rather suggests an internal contradiction of such depth that it pollutes one's humanity. When Costello talks of "degrees of obscenity," it is her reference to "degrees" that fails to convince, not her invocation of that which depraves and corrupts. This is what Diamond refers to as her, and our, sense of human beings as inherently vulnerable to experiences of bitter compromise.

By following out his interest in registering and developing these aspects of Costello's prophetic stance, issues of what he calls "inordinate knowledge." Cavell's discussion tends to remain focused directly on difficulties of reality that concern our relation to nonhuman animals, and indirectly on the ways in which this relation informs our understanding of ourselves and other human beings. In Diamond's paper, by contrast, while that knot of difficulties is also central, the full range of her examples takes us far beyond this ground of bitter philosophical, moral, and religious compromise with the body and its wounds. John McDowell begins his "Comment on Stanley Cavell's 'Companionable Thinking'" by emphasising this difference; and he goes on to argue that it amounts to a serious limitation in Cavell's response—one that risks obscuring Diamond's broader aims, and thereby risks obscuring the light she aims to cast on Cavell's own work on scepticism. But I find that I do not share McDowell's perception of risk here, because I do not entirely share either his sense of the risks run by Cavell's narrowness of focus, or his conception of Diamond's larger purpose.

In fact, McDowell is not entirely consistent in specifying exactly what Diamond's purpose is. He concludes his short paper as follows:

> The role of Coetzee's Costello in Diamond's paper is not to raise the question whether Costello's unhinging perception is a perception of how things indeed are—that is, whether meat eating is what she thinks she sees it to be, which would certainly have implications about whether we meat eaters should continue with the practice. The role of Coetzee's Costello for Diamond is rather to provide an analogue for the unhinging perceptions of separation and finitude that according to Cavell himself constitute the real point of philosophical scepticism. (PAL, 137–38)

The suggestion here seems to be that Cavell perversely fails to appreciate that his own work is the true subject of Diamond's paper. But this is hardly plausible. Since her paper was first delivered in Cavell's presence at a conference honouring his work, and has since appeared in a collection of essays on that work, it would be hard for him not to know that illuminating his own thought was at least one important part of Diamond's purposes. The question this knowledge posed for Cavell was rather how to acknowledge it—how to respond to that fact about it with due tact, in a way that made manifest the new possibilities opened up for his thinking by her recontextualization of it, and in the particular context of a collection of papers intended to honour Diamond's own lifetime of philosophical work. Evidently enough, his answer was to focus on an example (chosen from the many under discussion in Diamond's paper) that permitted him to engage seriously with a central theme in her wider philosophical writing—that of the moral status of nonhuman animals.

Moreover, without denying Cavell's centrality in Diamond's paper, it seems strange to assume that casting new light on Cavell's work was Diamond's sole concern. For McDowell himself emphasizes that the range of examples she discusses extends far beyond that of Coetzee and Cavell: as we shall shortly see, it includes several other writers working in a variety of genres other than that of the novel (such as poetry or autobiography). And earlier in his paper, he seems to draw a rather different conclusion from this fact: "Costello figures, for Diamond, only as exemplifying, in a richly elaborated way, something that is also exemplified [in other texts], and the specifics of what obsesses Costello are in a way irrelevant" (PAL, 133).

Here, then, McDowell suggests that Cavell is mistaken not in taking Costello to be Diamond's real focus when it is in fact Cavell himself, but rather in taking any individual example she discusses to be her real concern, when it is in fact what these various examples are supposed to exemplify that matters most to her. And what, on McDowell's view, these various difficulties of reality exemplify is the way in which "the special kind of animal life we lead comes into question" (PAL, 134). For in defeating our ordinary capacity to get our minds around reality, difficulties of reality defeat our capacity to capture reality in language; and the capacity to speak (and so the capacity to make sense of things in the way that this capacity to speak enables) is a distinguishing mark of human animals in general. In other words, such difficulties "can dislodge one from living one's life as a speaking animal" (PAL, 135)—from comfortably inhabiting that special kind of animal existence. It is, McDowell says, as if a beaver found dam building to be beyond its powers; and we can (he thinks) appreciate the particular significance of such difficulties of and for the human condition without sharing Costello's or Diamond's sense that eating meat constitutes one of them.

This is a powerful and penetrating perception of one way in which Diamond's various difficulties of reality might be seen as hanging together, or forming a family. It redefines the nature and depth of our woundedness, by presenting our nature as what makes us so deeply vulnerable to such damage; it explains why Costello—whose vocation makes words a particularly central element of her individual inflection of the human form of life—should be particularly sensitive to such difficulties; and it directs our attention once more to the continuities and discontinuities of human and nonhuman forms of animality. But McDowell's way of articulating his perception leaves him open to some deep, and potentially damaging, questions.

To begin with, his formulation implies that we can properly appreciate the general nature of our woundedness only if we regard the specific qualities of any particular example of it as irrelevant; and this makes sense only on the assumption that attention to the particularity of an example inherently tends to occlude attention to that which it exemplifies—quite as if generality and particularity must war with one another, in rather the way Plato assumed when presenting the specificity and concreteness of literary creations as tempting us away from the domain of genuine knowledge (that of the universal, the abstract).

But why assume that one cannot attend to the specificity of an example in a way that permits a proper appreciation of its resemblances and links to other specific examples, and so of what holds them together? There is no reason to assume in advance that Cavell's specific attentiveness to the case of Elizabeth Costello's woundedness must block a perception of how that woundedness relates to our nature as speaking animals; and in fact (as we have seen) he is specifically attentive to Costello as exemplifying our victimization by the human capacity for linguistic expression—a concern that (as McDowell, like anyone familiar with Cavell's work more generally, surely knows) reflects Cavell's wider interest in the ways human beings are marked or branded by speech.

Furthermore, McDowell's own way of characterizing the general nature of our woundedness strongly suggests that the specific case of our relations with nonhuman animals should have a particular significance for anyone interested in that woundedness. For he emphasizes that difficulties of reality can be seen as casting a particularly illuminating light on what he takes to be distinctively human about our form of animality—our relation to language. And Elizabeth Costello's engagement with various philosophical discourses suggesting an abyssal distinction between human and nonhuman animals, not to mention her characterization of Camus' hen as speaking, explicitly isolates for sustained critical questioning the idea of language as a distinguishing mark of the human. If McDowell were not so eager to redirect our attention towards human woundedness in general and away from one particular, and particularly wounding, manifestation of it, he might be forced to attend more closely to Costello's suggestion that we are prone to utilize our inwardness with words to deflect attention from the difficult reality—the uncanny intimacy—of our fellowship with nonhuman animals.

More unease about McDowell's approach is generated when, before attempting to deflect Cavell's, and so our, supposedly inordinate interest in the issue of nonhuman animals and our willingness to eat them, he offers "a brief, and necessarily oversimplified" (PAL, 129) sketch of Diamond's attitude towards eating what she calls our fellow creatures. According to McDowell, just as anyone who thought it might be all right to eat other human beings merely shows that her use of the phrase "human being" does not express everything many of us mean by it, so "for Diamond it is not a matter for debate whether it might be all right to eat our fellow creatures. . . . Those who make meat eating into a philosophical topic of the usual kind just reveal that they do not mean what Diamond means by 'fellow creature' " (PAL, 129). In particular, it is part of what

Diamond means by that term that no form of rearing nonhuman animals for human consumption could possibly be right.

> It should not seem to change the situation if we imagine animal husbandry being as it is depicted in a certain genre of children's stories, in which the relations between farmers and their animals are like the relations between people and domestic pets. Such stories necessarily leave unmentioned how the animals' lives end, and if one views animals as Diamond does, one would have to see sending them to be turned into food, however friendly one's previous relations with them were, as a betrayal. Factory farming . . . amplifies the evil of meat eating, but it is not the essential thing. (PAL, 130–31)

But this account of Diamond's views is, it seems to me, so brief and oversimplified that it risks encouraging serious misunderstandings of her position.

First, not all forms of vegetarianism are as radical as Costello's. There is no necessary connection between being a vegetarian and believing that all ways of rearing nonhuman animals for food are impermissible; some vegetarians may abstain from eating meat precisely because of the particular farming methods currently used to produce it, and would rescind that abstention should those methods change. Diamond's various discussions of the ethics of eating meat may suggest, but they do not declare, which version of vegetarianism she personally endorses (and deliberately so, in my view, since it is not clear what philosophical relevance that biographical fact should have); they rather strive to make clear which philosophical approaches to this ethical matter may clarify, and which risk obscuring, the real sources of conflict that it provokes. Certainly, the fact that Diamond finds philosophical illumination in Coetzee's presentation of Costello's radical hostility to eating meat provides no evidence either way. But suppose that McDowell is right in assuming that there are no circumstances in which Diamond would think it permissible to eat meat. Must she therefore (as McDowell appears to suggest) believe that anyone who thinks that there might be such circumstances, and wishes to discuss what they may be, either cannot regard animals as her fellow creatures, or cannot mean what Diamond herself means by that phrase?

Much in Diamond's own writing suggests that this is something like the reverse of her own view. To begin with, she illustrates what she means by regarding nonhuman animals as fellow creatures by quoting a poem by Walter de la Mare about a titmouse (which talks of "this tiny son of life" flitting off "into Time's enormous Nought"), without giving any indication of thinking that the meaning of the vision embodied in the poem is determinable only by establishing its author's views on eating meat. And another of her frequent literary reference points—Laura Ingalls Wilder's "Little House on the Prairie" books—offer a powerful vision of a rural American world in which human beings treat the nonhuman animals surrounding them (both domesticated and wild) with compassion, dignity, respect, and even awe, in ways that naturally suggest a perception of them as "fellow creatures." But these people would be utterly bewildered at the suggestion that eating some of these animals would essentially betray that perception. The question of how the animals they rear for food should be treated is not only intelligible to them, but morally central to their relationship with those animals—as we see when they condemn those among them who treat their livestock with neglect or cruelty, or despise those who hunt for wild game in certain ways. In such a context, the difference between farming and factory farming would be essential, not amplificatory. And they certainly regard some animals as vermin, and so as treatable in ways that cows and sheep, or wolves and cougars, are not. In fact, it is precisely insofar as they relate to their animals in ways that embody such distinctions that they manifest their conception of them as fellow creatures—as each living out different forms of mortal existence, and so as each relating differently to one another and to their human fellows.

To be sure, other human communities might embody different understandings of how to treat nonhuman creatures as our fellows; and those of our contemporaries (such as Elizabeth Costello or Albert Camus, or perhaps even Cora Diamond herself) who are profoundly impressed by the moral claims nonhuman animals make upon us might find this older, rural American vision of that fellowship to be flawed or internally contradictory in certain ways. But that is precisely my, and I think Diamond's, point. The notion of nonhuman animals as our "fellow creatures" is neither the repository of a single, unified sense to which anyone who grasps the notion must conform, nor a fundamentally multivocal concept that must mean something essentially different to everyone who applies it at all differently; it is rather a relatively stable locus of historically extended, thoughtful contestation.

The idea of animals as our fellow creatures is certainly shared by or at least familiar to many and has been long embedded in our thinking; but its precise range of application and its particular inflections of moral significance have been and are the subject of historical and cultural variation, and of reasonable but real disagreement. For the idea can be employed in various intelligible ways, and each such pattern of use can be comprehensibly extended (and each such extension comprehensibly contested) in various ways—extensions and contestations that differently exploit the way any such pattern of use, as embodied in a human form of life, ties together (or conflicts) with our existing and envisageable ways of employing a range of related ideas (such as "wild animals" or "vermin"). Since there is no reason to assume that any given human community's many and varied ways of thinking about and treating nonhuman animals across the full range of its encounters with them—even one for which the idea of "fellow creatures" has real purchase and resonance—will interweave so tightly and coherently as to form an impregnable, monolithic whole (and no reason to view the attainment of such an airless, self-confirming, and profoundly monotonous state of affairs, entirely immune to alteration or unexpected renewals of interest, as either desirable or even conceivable), then we should expect to discover a variety of gaps, points of friction, and even flat-out contradiction that might be utilized in order to reorient our moral imagination in a number of different ways.[6]

This is the vision of words as imaginatively projective that emerged a little earlier in my discussion of Costello's citation of the story of Camus and the hen. It is utterly central to Diamond's (and to Cavell's) conception of language; and yet McDowell's sketch of Diamond's stance seems to presuppose a contrary vision—when, for example, he claims that anyone who suggests that some nonhuman animals might be eaten, or that some ways of treating nonhuman animals are worse than others, is seen thereby to reveal that they do not mean what Diamond means by "fellow creature." For this implies that different ways of understanding what treating nonhuman animals as "fellow creatures" might or should amount to in a given context indicates that the phrase differs sharply and decisively in its meaning when employed by these two speakers—quite as if each is playing a different language game with the same term (so that "fellow creature" is ambiguous in the way "bank" is ambiguous between "money bank" and "riverbank").

McDowell thereby risks returning Diamond into the hands of Onora O'Neill, and her vision of Wittgensteinian moral philosophers as necessarily presupposing a shared linguistic and moral community, and as rendered utterly impotent by the possibility of linguistic and moral disagreement. For if McDowell's account were correct, invoking the notion of nonhuman animals as "fellow creatures" would not allow Diamond and her interlocutor even to clarify the nature and extent of their moral disagreement, let alone to find a way of alleviating or overcoming it. Unless they already agree on the meaning and the essential implications of the idea of nonhuman animals as fellow creatures, its invocation could only underline their disagreement, showing each to be armed with a way of meaning the idea that merely reflects her own initial judgement and insulates it and her from that of her interlocutor. (In a similar vein, McDowell tells us that it is only because most of us still use the phrase "human

---

[6] We will examine in chapter 7 one way in which such internal contestation might be conducted, as it is exemplified in one of Diamond's more extended discussions of eating meat.

being" in a certain way that the idea of cannibalism is not up for debate [PAL, 129]; so what happens if we stop using the phrase that way, or if some of us start using it differently?)

By contrast, Diamond thinks that, insofar as the idea of nonhuman animals as our fellow creatures makes sense to her and her interlocutor, pointing them both towards a multifarious but familiar (if often over-looked) range of thoughts, feelings, and ways of engaging with animals, it indicates a horizon within which each can make sense to the other, each can account for her own way of understanding that notion and of living out that understanding, and one might even succeed in bringing the other to see that her present way of regarding animals might bear refinement. Such an outcome is not guaranteed; but the traumatic reality of moral disagreement about such matters is difficult enough without characteriz-ing it in terms of a vision of language that appears to remove the very possibility of enhanced understanding of one's differences, let alone that of alleviating or overcoming the disagreement.

Of course, none of these concerns about McDowell's way of going on from his initital perception of the broad range of Diamond's examples of difficulties of reality invalidates that perception. We, too, need to attend to that fact about her discussion; and in particular, we must acknowledge that there is no necessary conjunction in Diamond's mind between the difficulty of reality and evil, anguish and suffering—say, disvaluation. For according to her account, certain instances of goodness or beauty can throw us, shoulder us out of our ordinary ways of talking and thinking, with equal force.

Diamond cites Czeslaw Milosz talking of beauty as something that should not exist, for which there are no reasons for and indeed reasons against, but which nevertheless undoubtedly exists—so that the architec-ture of a tree, the slimness of a column crowned with green, or the voices of birds greeting the dawn, which might strike some as the most quotidian of quotidian phenomena, strike Milosz as inexplicable in their reality. She quotes Ruth Kluger's Holocaust memoir, in which the author records the fact that a young woman's act of encouraging a terrified child seemed to her incomparable and inexplicable, as well as the fact that many people to whom she tells her tale wonder at her wonder, seeing nothing mysteri-ous in the fact that some people are altruistic. And she refers to the philos-opher Roy Holland's claim that one concept of the miraculous is that of the occurrence of something that is at one and the same time empirically certain and conceptually impossible.[7] The New Testament tale of Christ's public ministry being initiated at a wedding feast in Cana, where at his

---

[7] "The Miraculous," in his *Against Empiricism* (Totowa, NJ: Barnes and Noble, 1980).

mother's instigation he turns water into wine, is just such a story: it narrates an occurrence that is impossible for us to grasp in thought, which refuses to fit into our conceptual categories, and yet there it is, happening before our very eyes (and on our very tongue).

One might say with respect to this last case that there are hardly likely to be people who would take such occurrences in their stride. But of course, there will be many people (and not only philosophers) who would rule any such "concept" entirely out of order in advance, because it violates the very idea of a conceptual order in the absence of which the possibility of genuine thought will vanish; and there will be others who are willing to take seriously (or at least, are not willing to—can see no authoritative basis on which to—rule out in advance) the possibility that one's experience might force one to violate one's idea of what a well-ordered concept must be.[8]

There might also be those for whom the key point about our New Testament example is not its putative divine origin, nor its instantiation of a situation that one might meet in one's own experience, but rather the fact that it is a narration—that we relate to it in the first instance as readers or hearers of a story. Whether we think of that story as an accurate report on a real event or not would then be less significant than the fact that we can make sense of it as a story. For not all of us will respond to it as straightforwardly unintelligible qua tale, but rather we may see it as hanging together with literary devices and techniques of a more explicitly modernist nature; they might, in other words, see it as related to the many ways in which the teller of a tale can violate what appear to be the most basic conventions or conditions for narrative intelligibility, and find that readers are (or discover that they are not) willing to go on with him, to continue to find sense and interest in the world of that narrative.

We shall touch on these matters more systematically when we broaden our focus from *The Lives of Animals* to *Elizabeth Costello*, and indeed to the wider range of Coetzee's fiction taken as a whole. In the meantime, however, it is worth stressing that Diamond's primary reason for invoking Holland is to connect the awe that Kluger expresses at the reality of goodness and that Milosz expresses at the reality of beauty with the kind of astonishment and awe one would feel at a miracle. Some difficulties in reality, then, are not ones we would wish to wish away.

Nevertheless, her other major example of such a difficulty—the one that actually opens her essay and prepares the ground for her discussion

---

[8] For a representative sample of the full spectrum of such responses, cf. the first three essays in R. Gaita, ed., *Value and Understanding: Essays for Peter Winch* (London: Routledge, 1990).

of Costello and Coetzee—does concern pain rather than joy. It derives from a poem by Ted Hughes, entitled "Six Young Men."

The celluloid of a photograph holds them well—
Six young men, familiar to their friends.
Four decades that have faded and ochre-tinged
This photograph have not wrinkled the faces or the hands.
Though their cocked hats are not now fashionable,
Their shoes shine. One imparts an intimate smile,
One chews a grass, one lowers his eyes, bashful,
One is ridiculous with cocky pride—
Six months after this picture they were all dead.

All are trimmed for a Sunday jaunt. I know
That bilberried bank, that thick tree, that black wall,
Which are there yet and not changed. From where these sit
You hear the water of seven streams fall
To the roarer in the bottom, and through all
The leafy valley a rumouring of air go.
Pictured here, their expressions listen yet,
And still that valley has not changed its sound
Though their faces are four decades under the ground.

This one was shot in an attack and lay
Calling in the wire, then this one, his best friend,
Went out to bring him in and was shot too;
And this one, the very moment he was warned
From potting at tin-cans in no-man's land,
Fell back dead with his rifle-sights shot away.
The rest, nobody knows what they came to,
But come to the worst they must have done, and held it
Closer than their hope; all were killed.

Here see a man's photograph,
The locket of a smile, turned overnight
Into the hospital of his mangled last
Agony and hours; see bundled in it
His mightier-than-a-man dead bulk and weight:
And on this one place which keeps him alive
(In his Sunday best) see fall war's worst
Thinkable flash and rending, onto his smile
Forty years rotting into soil.

That man's not more alive whom you confront
And shake by the hand, see hale, hear speak loud,
Than any of these six celluloid smiles are,
Nor prehistoric or fabulous beast more dead;
No thought so vivid as their smoking blood:
To regard this photograph might well dement,
Such contradictory permanent horrors here
Smile from the single exposure and shoulder out
One's own body from its instant and heat.

A central link between this poem and Elizabeth Costello's lecture is of course the theme of death—more specifically, the "contradictory permanent horrors" of the imagination of death, and the way in which the photograph exposes the poet, as his poem in turn exposes us, to the impossibility of encompassing in thought the reality of mortality. Furthermore, as we shall see, Hughes's poetry forms a pivotal part of her later seminar, which reflects on the poets and their relation to the reality of nonhuman animals. But these links are complicated by elements in this particular poem that have no counterpart in either stretch of Coetzee's text.

One possibly relevant difference is the fact that the deaths of these six men are the result of war and so may also be thought of as encapsulating a sense of war as senseless, as a perfectly familiar and perennial aspect of human experience that is nevertheless capable of driving us to the point of madness in attempting to encompass its reality in thought. What, after all, is more obvious and entirely to be expected than that human beings should regularly fight with one another to the point of death? And yet what, in another mood, from another perspective, is more resistant to comprehension?

Beyond this, however, there is the central relevance of photography to the poet's sense of exposure. For what is threatening to drive him mad here is the simultaneous sense that no one could be more alive than these six men smiling in front of his eyes, and yet no one and nothing could be more dead; and his ability to see six dead men alive and smiling before his very eyes is possible only because he is looking at a photograph of them taken shortly before they went to war, and to their deaths. It is therefore perfectly possible to describe the situation in a way that makes it seem the very reverse of impossible or insane: what could be more familiar than the idea that the subjects of photographs might be dead? And so what could be more amenable to straightforward description and thought than the idea of dead men smiling in a photograph? As Diamond puts it, the terms of this language game could easily be explained to a young child; and at that stage the "point of view from which she sees a problem is not yet in the game; while that from which the horrible contradiction impresses itself on the poet-speaker is that of someone who can no longer speak from within the game. Language is shouldered out from the game, as the body from its instant and heat" (PAL, 45). The difficulty of reality that Diamond is trying to locate here is thus inseparable from the fact of photography: the instant and heat of the rending flash that shoulders out language and thought registers both the worst of war (the rifle-barrel and the bomb) and the camera's reliance upon the dazzling light of a flash-bulb to take its single exposure. Indeed, the difficulty can arise even when the subjects of a photograph are neither victims of war nor even dead. For what any photograph, by its very nature, can expose us to is the mysterious relation between a photograph and what it is a photograph of—between the real person, object, or environment in front of the camera when the photograph was taken and what the resulting photograph presents to its viewers.

As Diamond is well aware, this issue is central to Stanley Cavell's substantial body of work on film and philosophy. That project finds its initial orientation in a consideration of the material basis of film, and so in reflections on the relation between photographs and reality.[9] And Cavell begins those reflections by claiming that, whereas it makes perfect sense to say that a painting presents us with a likeness of something or someone, it would not be quite right to say that a photograph presents us with a likeness: what Cavell thinks we want to say is that it presents us with the thing itself. A photograph of an object is not, as a painting of it may be, a visual representation of that object (it does not stand for that object, nor form a likeness of it), but rather a visual transcription of it. However, it does not transcribe the sight or look or appearance of an object in the way in which a recording can be said to transcribe the sound of an object; for objects do not have or make sights in the way that objects have or make sounds. There is, one might say, no way of reproducing the "sights" they make without reproducing them; or better, there is nothing of the right sort for a photograph to be a photograph of short of the object itself.

When we look at a photograph of Tom Cruise, we see Tom Cruise—the man before the camera when the photograph was taken; we do not see a representation or reproduction or image or replica of him, we see the man himself. And yet we know that a photograph of Tom Cruise is not Tom Cruise. But saying that amounts only to saying that a photograph is not a human being; who would deny it? And this reminder of what no one could reasonably be expected to have forgotten does not address the real difficulty, which is precisely that of understanding what it is for something to be a *photograph* of Tom Cruise (as opposed to, say, a painting

---

[9] Cf. *The World Viewed* (Cambridge: Harvard University Press, 1971), esp. chaps. 2–4 (hereafter WV).

of him or a recording of his voice). The man himself is not there; but there he is, nevertheless, in the photograph; what seems for all the world to be happening, ontologically speaking, when we look at a photograph is that we see things that are not really there. Cavell finds that he wants to say: The reality in a photograph is present to me while I am not present to it. And so the motion-picture camera can make a world present to us from which we are absent, can cause live human beings and real objects in actual spaces to appear to us when they are in fact not there.

These matters would bear much more detailed discussion.[10] But for present purposes, my concern is not to persuade anyone that Cavell's formulations of the matter are correct, or even worthy of further investigation. What interests me is rather the fact that his analysis of photography in its relation to reality is designed from the outset not to dissipate or dissolve the aura of magic and mystery with which he takes it to be imbued, but rather to maintain itself within it. As he puts it: "It may be felt that I make too great a mystery of these objects. My feeling is rather that we have forgotten how mysterious these things are, and in general how *different* things are from one another, as though we had forgotten to value them" (WV, 19). Where his interlocutors elide important differences between aural, pictorial, and photographic representations in such a way as to occlude the specificity of the photographic, in all its mysteriousness, it is precisely Cavell's orienting assumption that obscurities are internal to our experience of photographs and so of film, rather than something blocking our way to a transparent understanding of those phenomena. Hence: "The commitments I set myself as I wrote were, first, to allow obscurities to express themselves as clearly and fervently as I could say, and, second, to be guided by the need to organize and clarify just these obscurities and just this fervour in the progression of my book as a whole" (WV, 162).

The point is not to avoid the achievement of clarity, but to recognize that such clarity that can be achieved must be clarity about just these obscurities, hence clarity that must be the result of working through those obscurities rather than banishing them, and so may result only in making it clearer to both author and reader that obscurity is internal to the phenomenon of photography and so of film. In other words, Cavell sees in the domain of photography as such exactly the kind of difficulty of reality, the possibility of experiencing something that is perfectly everyday as constitutively enigmatic, that Diamond sees as central not only to Coetzee's writing about Costello but to ordinary human experience more generally.

---

[10] I have developed some of these themes in chapter 9 of my *Stanley Cavell: Philosophy's Recounting of the Ordinary* (Oxford: Oxford University Press, 1994).

In this respect he registers a general willingness, as a philosopher, to avoid assuming that an appearance of paradox or contradiction or mystery is an infallible sign of a failure of understanding; he remains open to the possibility that appearances can, even in this respect, amount to revelations of reality. But Cavell's way of staying true to the initial obscurities of his experience of photography and film are also strikingly parallel to Coetzee's way of expressing his sense of the inherent paradoxicality of novel-writing. For in response to one sympathetic critic, he makes the following remark: "Stories are defined by their irresponsibility: they are, in the judgement of Swift's Houynhnhms, 'that which is not.' The *feel* of writing fiction is one of freedom, of irresponsibility, or better, of responsibility towards something that has not yet emerged, that lies somewhere at the end of the road."[11] Coetzee here uses one of his most significant novelistic predecessors to articulate a sense of the negative relation between fictional reality and reality, and of the novelist's paradoxically positive sense of responsibility to the nonexistent reality of his fictions, that is very close to Cavell's sense of film as presenting us with an absent or nonexistent reality. For one of Cavell's ways of making his point about the worlds of film is to declare: "That the projected world does not exist (now) is its only difference from reality. (There is no feature, or set of features, in which it differs. Existence is not a predicate.)" (WV, 24). This final parenthetical remark, recalling Kant's famous criticism of the ontological argument for God's existence, points out that any property possessible by a real object can be possessed by an object in a film, and hence that there is not and cannot be any specifiable respect in which the projected world and the real world differ. So, the reality of the real world is not a property of it any more than unreality is a property of the world of a film. And likewise, to say of a fictional tale that it is not, that neither it nor the people and objects it contains are real, is not to specify a property that those fictional beings lack, any more than to say that they are fictional is to specify a property that they possess but that real beings lack. What, then, are we saying when we say that these projected or narrated worlds do not exist? Can this obscurity be clarified without being dissipated?

For Cavell, it does not follow from his claim about the unreality of the world of film that seeing an object and seeing that object in a film are not distinguishable, any more than Elizabeth Costello is indistinguishable from a real person; what follows is that that undeniable distinction must be made out not in terms of perceptible differences between them, but rather in terms of the different relationships in which we stand to them

[11] *Doubling the Point*, ed. David Attwell (Cambridge: Harvard University Press, 1992), 246 (hereafter DP).

(for example, in the fact that we share neither a space nor a time with the beings of the film—we can neither enter their presence nor their present). It remains to be seen whether, and how far, Coetzee's understanding of narrative fiction can support a parallel elucidation of his claim that stories are that which is not—that the world of a story does not exist. Even at this point, however, it is clear that both Coetzee and Cavell are inclined to align themselves with those who would see the fictionality of fictional persons as making our capacity and willingness to respond to them as we do real people genuinely enigmatic. We shall return to this.

Chapter Six

FOOD FOR THOUGHT: AN UNINVITED GUEST?

BEFORE CONCLUDING THIS sequence of symposia, I cannot avoid confronting in more detail what will—from a philosophical perspective—appear to be at once an obvious and an utterly disabling objection to Diamond's idea of a "difficulty of reality." For if it really does depend upon taking seriously the possibility that phenomena, or at least our experience of them, might be constitutively resistant to our thinking, so that to understand them is to comprehend them as incomprehensible, and so to resort to forms of words that violate the limits of our language games and the order of our concepts, then we can rule out any such thing in advance; for it relies upon self-evidently incoherent talk of violating the limits of sense, of grasping that which is beyond our intellectual grasp. If that kind of talk does not simply boil down to the familiar possibility of having our intellectual and imaginative complacency challenged by the actual course of events, but really does mean to point us towards phenomena it is impossible to think, experiences that are contradictory, and concepts that are incoherent, then the very idea of a "difficulty in reality" is and must be empty. It amounts to a contradiction in terms; and to confront such a contradiction in one's thinking is an infallible sign that something has gone wrong with the thinking, not—not ever—an indication that whatever it is about which one is thinking might itself be contradictory.

Is Diamond's willingness to take seriously the very idea of a "difficulty of reality" simply an inexplicable mystery, although no more (or less) than one might expect of a certain kind of obscurantist Wittgensteinian influence on philosophical thinking? But we have already seen that the more familiar kinds of Wittgensteinian work in philosophy tend rather to exclude the possibility of sense and significance that Diamond is aiming to hold open for her readers. Other philosophers might talk of the rational order of our conceptual scheme, whereas these Wittgensteinians talk rather of the grammar of our language games; but this shift from "conceptual order" to "grammatical order" can result in the same laying down of requirements for sense to which Diamond is attempting to offer some resistance, on behalf of what she sees as the reality of everyday human experience of language and the world. For the simple fact is that we (some of us, sometimes) *take things so* (cf. PAL, 45), and philosophy has a duty to acknowledge that fact, to look and see what is there to be seen.

If, however, in this respect, Diamond's (and Cavell's) Wittgensteinian-ism is itself a form of resistance to our ways of thinking about Wittgen-steinians, and so in a sense not even authorised by what we think we know about Wittgenstein, there are other conceptions and traditions of philosophy within which the idea of a "difficulty of reality" would find ready acknowledgment. The work of the early Heidegger is the most obvious example of a mode of philosophical thinking that is open to the possibility of its own limits, more specifically to the idea that philosophy might have to overcome a fantasy of its own omnipotence if it is truly to articulate the nature of human reality and the broader reality of which it is a part.

Stanley Cavell's essay in fact touches on the possibility of such a link when he declares that he is assuming that "Coetzee leaves a sub-textual question to be directed to Heidegger" (CT, 15); but on his account, this concerns the relation between Elizabeth Costello's perception of the moral equivalence between factory farming and death camps and Heideg-ger's notorious linking of those same institutions (together with Stalin's forced starvation of the Ukranian kulaks), as part of his critique of West-ern culture in the age of technology. Here I want to explore a different, although not unrelated, connection; for viewed against the background of Coetzee's lectures, it is striking that the elements of human reality that bring out a certain humility in Heidegger's thinking about difficulties in reality are precisely those of death, the self's relation to itself and to other selves, and the human being's relation to nonhuman animals (and hence to its own animality). As a final contribution to this alternative sympo-sium, then, I want to suggest that we can appreciate Heidegger's sense of the agonizing, awe-inspiring inexplicability of these aspects of our exis-tence only if we learn to appreciate the mysterious resistance that the form of his writing (as evident in its vocabulary, syntax, and style) poses to those wishing to comprehend it, and further acknowledge the internal relation between these two difficulties—one having to do with reality, one with any adequate philosophical account of that reality.

Heidegger's analysis of the human way of being (what he calls "Da-sein"), as presented in his early masterpiece *Being and Time*, is presented to its readers in two halves or Divisions (more were planned, and some of the material allotted to them eventually appeared, although not in the form originally envisaged); but many Anglo-American commentators have tended to focus their exegetical efforts on Division 1.[1] Hubert Drey-fus's highly influential commentary on *Being and Time* embodies just such

---

[1] *Being and Time*, trans. J. Macquarrie and E. Robinson (Oxford: Blackwell, 1962).

a tendency.[2] It presents a reading of Heidegger's analysis of Dasein as a sophisticated and nuanced species of what many would call "pragmatism"—an account of human beings as inherently social and socialized creatures who are necessarily embedded in a world of entities, who are unique among them in being able to apprehend themselves and others as they really are, and whose primary mode of apprehension lies in the know-how embedded in their practical activities. In so doing, however, his commentary notoriously restricts itself to Division 1 of *Being and Time* (with the very limited exception of a long, co-authored appendix that devotes more time to Kierkegaard than it does to Heidegger)—quite as if the second Division of the book had no essential role to play in Heidegger's analysis, or at least led the analysis of Division 1 off into essentially optional depths of existential obscurity.

I don't wish to deny that Division 1 does invite such a conception of itself as free-standing or self-sufficient, as having brought what Heidegger calls his "existential analytic" to a satisfying initial conclusion; very much the contrary. True, his account of Dasein as a being who necessarily inhabits a world proceeds by isolating and clarifying specific elements of that totality (first the world, then Dasein's relations with others and itself, and the mode of its relation to that world). Hence it can give the impression of merely accumulating local insights into the human way of being without ever bringing them together, so that we might perspicuously survey the whole they constitute. But the final chapter of Division 1 is explicitly presented as aiming to overcome that lack and so might well seem to exemplify an imperial conception of Reason's reach of exactly the kind that would disgust Costello.

For in that chapter, Heidegger tells us that there is a specific state of mind through which Dasein reveals its nature to itself in a simplified way, and thereby gives access to itself as a structural totality. This is the phenomenon of anxiety (angst, dread), a state of mind that Heidegger distinguishes from cognate states such as fear by underlining its lack of a specific object. Whereas a fearful person is fearful of something in particular (a gun, a dog, a revelation), an anxious person experiences anxiety as a response to nothing in particular, or to something beyond the particular event that occasions it (as when a student is not simply fearful of, but anxious about, final exams). Genuine anxiety accordingly frees our attention from specific entities, people, or goals (from what Heidegger thinks of as our specific, ontic, or existentiell situation) so as to recall us to the fact that human existence as such (the ontology of the human) is always a matter of being situated—that is, of encountering some or other objects, people, and circumstances in the course of aiming to achieve some particu-

---

[2] H. Dreyfus, *Being-in-the-World* (Cambridge: MIT Press, 1991).

lar goal and to realize one among a range of possibilities made available to us in contexts that are never wholly of our own devising or entirely under our own control.

This vision of finite or conditioned freedom is what Heidegger invokes when he talks of Dasein as "thrown projection"; and he attempts to summarize it at the end of Division 1 by claiming that Dasein's way of being is care (that is, a matter of always projecting itself into the future, from a context in which it relates at present to other entities in some specific way, in part because of its previous projections and the history of that context). The necessarily temporal nature of this definition of human existence is evident.

It is, then, not at all surprising that even sophisticated commentators should feel that Division 1 of *Being and Time* constitutes a self-contained whole, the unity of which resides in a certain emphasis upon practical activity and the realm of the social. Such a commentator might well acknowledge that Heidegger's hermeneutic conception of any act of human understanding implies that all such analytical claims are provisional, and hence capable of being rearticulated and refined; he might even acknowledge that Division 2 aims at just such a rearticulation of the care-structure in terms of temporality. But this can be seen as deepening our grasp of the full implications of what Division 1 initially articulates, and hence as not posing any threat to the thought that the care-structure constitutes a complete, even if initial and hence relatively superficial, articulation of Dasein's being as a totality.

But to anyone who goes on from here into Division 2, it quickly becomes plain that Heidegger himself is not at all satisfied with this supposedly unifying invocation of care; he rather finds that the perspective it delivers contains the seeds of its own subversion. One might say: once introduced into his analysis, the concept of angst can no more be anchored to its specific initial role than its existential counterpart can be anchored to a specific object of concern. And as a result, Heidegger finds himself thrown into a state of anxiety about the whole of his analysis in Division 1. But why?

First, according to Heidegger, anxiety reveals that we are typically living inauthentic lives, relating to ourselves and others as what Heidegger calls "das man." He analyses this in Division 1 as a state in which we not only fail to take responsibility for our choices and projections as our own, but lose our grip on the very possibility that there might be an alternative to disowning our existence, to living as if what we do (the particular ways we spend our time, the specific direction we give to our lives) is simply what one does, what is done, a sheer, impersonal necessity. But if we typically live inauthentic lives, then it must at least make sense for us to live authentically; and yet that kind of ontic state seems entirely absent from the supposedly complete portrait of human existence presented in Division 1. And this in turn raises the worry that any reading of Heidegger's existential analytic that focuses exclusively on that portrait risks being guilty of repeating at a methodological level the inauthenticity on which it focuses.

Second, one aspect of the structure of care all but declares that there is an aspect of human existence that resists the very idea of completeness. For this structure includes what Heidegger calls Dasein's "Being-ahead-of-itself"—the fact that human existence is a matter of being endlessly delivered over to the task of actualising some specific existential possibility. But then, for as long as Dasein exists, it can never achieve wholeness; it will always already be ahead of itself, essentially related to an unrealized possibility, to something that it is not (yet). And yet, of course, human life does have an end. In Being-ahead-of-itself, Dasein also understands itself as relating to, standing out towards, its own future completion, towards a point at which there will be nothing of itself left outstanding. But the point at which the human individual's span of existence is complete is also the point of its own nonexistence: its death. Hence, any human life will embody, and so any full philosophical analysis of human existence must include an account of, this structural paradox—the fact that Dasein's conception of itself as necessarily ahead of itself and hence incomplete nevertheless incorporates a conception of itself as subject to death, and hence as necessarily completing its existence.

But Heidegger's philosophical approach is such that taking death as his topic engenders a reiteration of this structural difficulty at the level of method. For his existential analytic of Dasein is supposed to result from an application of the phenomenological method in philosophy, which involves analyzing our experience in such a way as to allow the phenomena we encounter to disclose themselves as they really are, and in a manner appropriate to their nature. In other words, his account of the human way of being draws upon the fundamental capacity that it attributes to human beings—the capacity to encounter phenomena comprehendingly. But if a complete account of Dasein's kind of existence must include an account of its end, then this aspect of human existence constitutively resists Heidegger's method. For when Dasein reaches its end, it is also not there.

Death is not something that any Dasein could directly experience; a human being's death is not an event in her life, not even the last. I can of course experience the death of another; but that gives me access to the significance of another's death to me, not its significance for her, and hence not the significance of my death to me. Neither route therefore seems to give us any grasp of the significance of death to the human being whose death it is (to death in its mineness, as Heidegger has it). How, then, can there be any genuinely phenomenological understanding of death? How can a philosophical method that draws exclusively on the human capacity to allow every phenomenon to appear to it as it really is provide any access to a phenomenon that is essentially incapable of appearing to, of being experienced or grasped by, any human being?

So, the opening pages of Division 2 identify a constitutive resistance on three levels to any sense of an ending with which the conclusion of Division 1 might have left us. Completeness or totality with respect to Dasein's existence appears out of reach for any individual Dasein, for the existential analytic of Dasein's way of being as such, and for the philosophical method that generated that analysis. One might, following Diamond, call this the critical conjunction of a difficulty in reality and a difficulty in philosophy. Hence, where Costello talks of the whole structure of our knowledge collapsing in panic, Heidegger confronts a mood of anxiety that compels him to begin his thinking again. For even in the face of this threefold resistance, he doesn't want to give up on his desire for a full or complete analysis, on his sense that such completeness is an undismissable criterion for the adequacy of any philosophical account of phenomena.

His resolution of this difficulty is exemplary in its elegance, and in the themes it introduces; for they reverberate throughout the rest of Division 2, and entirely recalibrate our sense of its tone, or mood—its mode of attunement to the human way of being. It begins from the suggestion that to grasp death, we must understand it as we understand the nature of the being whose end death is—in existential terms. We must, in other words, grasp death not as an actuality but as an existential possibility—a possibility that we relate to, or fail to, not in our death but in our life, which is the life of a thrown, projecting individual. And in these terms, he claims, death should be understood as our ownmost, nonrelational, and not-to-be-outstripped possibility. It is that possibility in which what is at stake is nothing less than the entirety of Dasein's worldly existence; it impends at every moment of our existence, so that each such moment might be our last; its realization at some point or other is certain, and hence inescapable; and in relating to it, all our relations to any other Dasein are undone—for no one can die my death for me.

On the face of it, however, this analytical shift from actuality to possibility cannot resolve the methodological resistance that death poses to Heidegger's phenomenology; for in fact, death cannot coherently be viewed as an existential possibility in Heidegger's sense of that term. Any genuine existential possibility is one that might be made actual by the Dasein whose possibility it is; we might eat the meal we're cooking, or play the game for which we're training, become a novelist or an academic. But we cannot actualise our own death in our own life; if it becomes actual, we are no longer there. Death, then, is not just the possibility of our own nonexistence, of our own absolute impossibility; it is an impossible possibility—an existential impossibility, a contradiction in existential terms. Hence death still cannot, it appears, be made accessible by existential analysis.

This is where the true elegance of Heidegger's treatment—the full extent of his unwillingness to be deflected from the reality of mortality, even by his own favoured conceptual resources—reveals itself. For if death cannot be viewed as a very unusual, even a unique, kind of existential possibility (since an impossibility is not an unusual kind of possibility), then we cannot understand our relation to our own death on the model of our relation to any genuine possibility of our existence. And this shows that death does not stand on the same level—the ontic or existentiell level—as any genuine existential possibility. Accordingly, Heidegger talks instead of our relation to our own death as "Being-towards-death"; and those hyphens indicate that he is presenting it as an essential, ontological structure of human existence, rather than as one particular existentiell state of the kind that structure makes possible.

He thereby presents our relation to death as manifest in the relation we establish to any and every genuine, concrete possibility of our lives, and hence to our existence as such. Precisely because death is an ungraspable but undeniable aspect of every moment of Dasein's existence, Dasein can only relate to it in and through its relation to what *is* graspable in our existence. Death thus appears as graspable only indirectly, as a condition of every moment of Dasein's directly graspable existence. It is that against which specific features of the existential terrain configure themselves, an omnipresent self-concealing condition for the human capacity to disclose things (including itself) as they really are, and so something that is in a sense revealed in anything and everything we can genuinely grasp. In Costello's and Coetzee's terms, one might say that death is the self-concealing and self-revealing wound of human life, a wound that is touched on in every aspect and element of any such mode of existence.

For Heidegger, then death is a phenomenon of life; it shows up only in and through life, in and through that which it threatens to render impossible. Phenomenologically speaking, life is death's representative, the proxy through which death's resistance to Dasein's grasp is at once acknowledged and overcome, or rather overcome only in and through its acknowledgment. Heidegger's point, then, is that *life* is our ownmost, nonrelational, not-to-be-outstripped possibility. For Dasein to acknowledge that is for it to acknowledge that there is no moment of its existence in which that existence is not at issue—that its existence matters to it, and that what matters is not just its individual moments but the totality of those moments: its life as a whole. Its life is its own to live, or to disown; existence makes a claim on each of us that cannot be sloughed off onto others. And insofar as every human life is fated to be utterly nullified by death, we human beings must acknowledge the utter nonnecessity of that life—the nonnecessity of our birth, of the actual course of our life, of its continuation from one moment to the next. Authentic Being-towards-death is thus a matter of living in a way that does not treat the merely possible or actual or conditionally necessary as a matter of fate or destiny beyond any question or alteration—the stance that "das man" exemplifies and inculcates. It means stripping out false necessities, becoming properly attuned to the real modalities of finite human existence.

This is why angst, in its objectlessness, hangs together with Being-towards-death. For no object-directed state-of-mind could correspond to an existential phenomenon that utterly repels any objective actualisation within Dasein's worldly existence; only a state-of-mind that discloses the sheer worldliness of Dasein's Being, beyond any specific world in which it finds itself, could also disclose the sheer mortality of that Being, its inherent nonnecessity beyond any specific array of contingent circumstances and possibilities that it finds itself confronting.

In the objectlessness of anxiety, particular objects and persons fade away and the worldliness of our Being announces itself as such, that is, as more or other than any particular worldly situation in which we find ourselves. Hence, anxiety discloses that in inauthenticity we identify ourselves with the particularity of our situation—treat it as if a necessity or fate, regarding what we do as simply what is done, beyond any question; and anxiety thereby discloses authenticity as a recognition of ourselves as not identical with any particular worldly situation, as essentially not coincident with what we presently are, as always transcending our present articulation and so as uncanny, our worldliness precluding our ever being fully at home in any particular world.

This non-self-coincidence (which Heidegger calls uncanniness) becomes the binding thread of the analyses of Division 2, as the following chapters on guilt and conscience make abundantly clear. When Heidegger claims that human existence is a matter of Being-guilty, he means that we are doubly related to nullity or negation. As projecting beings, every possibility we actualise we negate *qua* possibility, and in so doing we reject or negate other accessible possibilities; as thrown beings, we find that our projectiveness has its ground outside itself, in the situation from which any specific projection must emerge and which is accordingly beyond its specific determination, so that each such projection necessarily lacks power over itself from the ground up. Dasein thus appears as necessarily not self-grounding; but since it remains the being whose existence is always ultimately to be determined through its own actions, it is also necessarily not grounded by anything outside itself. Dasein is, then, essentially lacking in ground, it is groundless or ungrounded—another way in which it necessarily fails to coincide with itself.

When Heidegger then introduces the voice of conscience as the pivot between inauthenticity and authenticity, he is concerned not so much with the familiar phenomenon of an inner voice blaming or praising our specific deeds (Dasein's Jiminy Cricket) as with what must be the case about us for that phenomenon to be possible. In that (ontological) sense of the phrase, he presents the voice of conscience as Dasein discoursing to itself about itself in the mode of keeping silent, that is, as saying nothing. After all, a demand that activates objectless angst concerning an existential impossibility cannot specify any particular existentiell state or act as capable of satisfying it (as scaling a wall might address our fear of a rabid dog). It demands simply that Dasein regard its existence as making demands on it at any and every moment, as being inherently demanding beyond the satisfaction of any specific demands we choose to address in and through that existence.

Heidegger's idea is thus not that the voice of conscience speaks silently at specifiable moments; it is rather that any specific demands we interpret it as making on us always also make the further demand that we regard our subjection to demand as such as unredeemable through the satisfaction of those specific demands. What the voice of conscience speaks against, therefore, is our inveterate tendency to conflate our existential potential with our existentiell actuality; what it silently opens up is the human individual's internal otherness, its relation to itself as other, as not self-identical but rather transitional or self-transcending.

But if inauthenticity is characterized by Dasein's enacting an understanding of itself as essentially self-identical, as capable of coinciding with itself and fulfilling its nature, then interpretations of Heidegger's existential analytic of Dasein that present it as simply to be identified with the structure of care must themselves count as inauthentic philosophical exercises. Deceived by the apparent completeness and self-sufficiency of Division 1, they fail to see that these features of that part of Heidegger's book reflect an inauthentic absorption in specific work environments (the self's untroubled identification with its world), and the undifferentiatedness of "das man" (the self's untroubled coincidence with others and with itself insofar as it relates to what it does as what one does, what is done). They therefore fail to see that the internal differentiation within *Being and Time* between Division 1 and Division 2 is pivotal to its claim to be providing an authentic existential analytic of Dasein; for it enacts the way in which an authentic self-understanding is to be wrenched from the inauthentic grasp of ourselves with which the book itself tells us we will always already begin, both as individual Dasein and as philosophers. Hence, an authentic grasp of Heidegger's existential analytic depends upon grasping it as deliberately, unavoidably disrupting itself from within, and thereby achieving the non-self-coincidence that is the mark of anxious, anticipatory resoluteness.

In a sense, therefore, it is absolutely right to claim that there is no difference between the conclusions of Division 1 and those of Division 2; for there is no specific difference between them, since what the latter adds to the former is nothing in particular—that is, "nothing" is solely and specifically what it adds. In other words, what enacts Division 2's internal disruption of the analysis of Division 1 is Heidegger's acknowledgment of nothingness, nullity, negation. When I talked earlier of non-self-identity, we should read that phrase as telling us *both* that the self is not identical with itself *and* that the self is internally related to nullity, or negation. And of course, as Heidegger's analysis of death exemplifies, it is at this point that the existential analytic reaches the limits of its methodological capacity to represent its subject matter. For just as Being-towards-death succeeds in allowing death to appear to us as it is in itself only by conceding the impossibility of it ever so doing, and Being-guilty shows us the true nature of our thrownness only by conceding that something about the ground of our projections will always exceed our comprehending grasp (will always be a brute datum), so the voice of conscience can be attested to in this analysis only as being beyond any particular speech-act, and as originating neither entirely within us nor entirely without.

In short, from the point of view of phenomenology, nothingness does not appear as such and is not an object of a possible discursive act; it is not a phenomenon of experience, at all. It is not a representable something, but it is not an unrepresentable something either; hence it can be represented only as beyond representation, as the beyond of the horizon of the representable, its self-concealing and self-disrupting condition. And genuinely phenomenological philosophy can only acknowledge it by allowing "nothing" first to conceal itself and then to disrupt its concealment, to constitute itself as that upon which the existential analytic is shipwrecked. It is in this way alone that any analysis of human existence can achieve the only kind of completeness that its condition allows—by presenting itself as essentially incomplete, beyond completion, because completed and completeable only by that which is beyond it.

The same Costello-like pattern of thought about the inherent, ungraspable difficulty of human reality manifests itself in Heidegger's early work beyond the disrupted unity of *Being and Time*, in the extended discussion of nonhuman animal life that is to be found in his 1929–30 lecture course *The Fundamental Concepts of Metaphysics*.[3] These lectures summarize

---

[3] Trans. W. McNeill and N. Walker (Bloomington: Indiana University Press, 1995), hereafter FCM.

Dasein's kinship with the nonhuman animal realm in the form of three interlinked theses: "The stone is *worldless*; the animal is *poor in world*; man is *world-forming*" (FCM, 177). This notion of impoverished worldliness appears to imply that animals have at least a diminished capacity to grasp entities as they really are; but Heidegger appears to deny this, declaring, for example, that "[w]hen we say that the lizard is lying on the rock, we ought to cross out the word 'rock' in order to indicate that whatever the lizard is lying on is certainly given *in some way* for the lizard, and yet is not known to the lizard *as* a rock" (FCM, 198).

He further specifies this mode of givenness as "captivation" ("Benommenheit"), claiming that animals relate to themselves and their environments as if fascinated, dazzled, dazed, benumbed. The instincts that drive them also ring them or fence them in: objects forcibly impinge upon them solely as disinhibitors of drives (as food or mate, predator or prey), and so as not only withholding other objects (until circumstances allow those other objects to disinhibit other drives in the ring), but also as withholding themselves *qua* objects.

Little wonder, then, that Heidegger has been accused of anthropocentrism—of attempting to understand nonhuman animals as if they were failed or flawed variants upon the human way of being, while at the same time trying to introduce an abyss of essence between human animals and their nonhuman fellow creatures, an attempt that simultaneously involves a denial of the animality of the human animal and a failure to discriminate within the nonhuman animal realm between different species and their differing capabilities. It is not hard to imagine Costello finding that these Heideggerian theses place him squarely within the great river of Western discourse about man and beast.

But matters are perhaps more complex than they appear. To begin with, Heidegger explicitly recommends that we read the phrase "world-poverty" under erasure, quite as if he wants to place animals at once within and without the reach of the term "world," as if animals place the limits of its reach in question. Further, he questions his very right to form the theses I just quoted, arguing that, far from presupposing a human capacity for self-transposition into three different domains of otherness, they instead show that this capacity is in fact elicited only by the animal realm (since the otherness of stones neither invites nor resists the transpositions of a self, and the otherness of other human beings is always already internal to Dasein's essentially social nature). More precisely, Heidegger declares that animality is "essentially a potentiality for granting transposedness, connected in turn with the necessary refusal of any going along with" (FCM, 211). In other words, the singularity of nonhuman animals in our world of experience lies in their having a mode of access to the world from which we are excluded. Animal dealings with objects are accessible to human understanding, but only as resistant to human understanding; hence, to grasp animality is to grasp it as a mode of being from which human beings are fenced out, that they can grasp only as beyond them. In short, animality, like mortality, confronts us with a difficulty of reality, and so a difficulty for (phenomenological) philosophy.

Heidegger's real, if limited, attention to domesticated animals further enforces this perception of animality as internalizable within the human form of life, even if never exactly assimilable to it.

> We do not describe them as [domestic animals] because they turn up in the house but because they belong to the house . . . they "*live*" *with us*. But we do not live with them if living means: being in an animal kind of way. Yet we *are* *with* them nonetheless . . . through this being with animals we enable them to move within our world. . . . [The] dog eats with us—and yet, it does not really "eat." Nevertheless it is with us! (FCM, 210)

These oscillating notations of our kinship with pets might equally be described as notations of an oscillation in our sense of that kinship. They act as a reminder of the way in which the distinction between wild and domesticated or domesticatable animals profoundly pervades our relation to nonhuman animality, as if embodying our sense of them as simultaneously open and resistant to the human realm. Heidegger's oscillations also remind me of the passage in Rai Gaita's *The Philosopher's Dog* when he recalls the ways in which he is struck by the mysterious otherness of his dog Gypsy.[4]

> Sometimes when I see her on the bedroom or kitchen rug or note the ease with which she wanders through the house, I experience the kind of perceptual flux that occurs when I see now one side and then the other of an ambiguous drawing. In all sorts of ways, she is part of the family, participating intelligently and with complex feeling in our lives. But then she does something—chase a cat, for example, her killer instinct aroused—whose nature is so deeply instinctual that she appears wholly animal in a way that invites a capital "A." . . . It is the apparent absence of a psychological dimension in Gypsy's drive to kill that is so disturbing and makes her seem so *other* to us, so much a different kind of being. The occasions for such perceptual shifts . . . are not always dramatic. The sight of her sniffing another dog's urine could do it. Or the sight of her staring quite vacantly into space, clearly without a thought in her head. Or as [Gaita's wife] Yael once put it, "seeing this thing with a tail walking through the house." (PD, 63–64)

Heidegger's particular way of capturing this perceptual flux as internal to our sense of animal kinship as otherness invokes ways in which an

---

[4] (Melbourne: Text Publishing, 2002), hereafter PD.

animal's encircling ring can intersect with, or be encompassed by, the human world; and this opens up the possibility of disrupting and expanding both ring and world, a vision of animal being becoming more fully itself within a human world that is itself enriched thereby. Against this carefully constructed figurative background, the thesis that animals are world-poor might appear as a projection of our own rejected animality, a defence against the animal capacity to address and even to cohabit with the inhabitants of human worlds because of what that implies about the never entirely transcended animality of those who form them.

After all, if we are fully to understand Heidegger's theses, we must (according to his own account of human understanding as always situated or contextualized, more specifically as oriented by some or other particular mood or state-of-mind) ask ourselves what mode of attunement to reality they make manifest. Heidegger explicitly asserts in these lectures that contemporary human society discloses its world through the fundamental mood of boredom; and since he and his audience are situated in that world, "we constantly already question concerning the essence of world [and thus the essence of animality] from out of this attunement" (FCM, 272). In short, by Heidegger's own testimony, his theses are informed by boredom. And it just so happens that the first half of his lecture series, as if setting the scene for its later analysis of animality, is devoted to an analysis of boredom.

Without going into the terms of that analysis in undue detail, we need to note that for Heidegger, fundamental boredom is "Dasein's being delivered over to beings' telling refusal of themselves as a whole" (FCM, 139), a discovery of beings in general as indifferent to us and hence of us as indifferent to them. The world we encounter does not interest us—we are not gripped or drawn into active existence by the possibilities it holds out to us; and the affective or desiring aspect of our nature is thereby revealed as essentially lacking, as if our greatest present need is genuinely to experience need or lack, without which our capacity to project upon possibilities will remain inert.

Hence, when the second thesis claims that animals exhibit a responsive refusal to humanity, their seductive self-withdrawals exemplify the revealing refusal of the world as such to go along with the essentially situated and attuned comprehension of human beings. But in further claiming that animals suffer deprivation in that they are benumbed by the world, Heidegger in effect transposes to animality as such the predicates he has just assigned to human beings in the grip of boredom—covering over the oppressive absence of a world in which they can take a genuine interest by an endless round of bustling attempts to manufacture and satisfy specific needs. This may seem to imply that boredom tends to reduce the human to the merely animal; but if this transposition is a further expression of our boredom, then it rather indicates that we are refusing genuinely to interest ourselves in animals as they are in themselves, and that this refusal exemplifies a general suspension of interest that is somehow internally related to our own animality.

So when Heidegger later declares that overcoming boredom is a matter of liberating the humanity in man (FCM, 165–66), this need not mean that the essence of man must be liberated from his animality; it might rather envisage the realization of what is genuinely human in human beings as a disruption of their animality from within. Dasein's existence is always a transcendence of animality, a disruption of it—but a disruption from within, because the thrownness from which Dasein's projections always emerge is an inflection of desire or need, and hence of Dasein's embodiedness or animality. Realizing Dasein's mooded comprehension of its world thus neither negates nor reiterates animality; it is a demand made upon a particular species of it (the ensouled animal), a radicalization of animality as such. To let the Dasein in man *be* is to do the most intimate, uncanny violence to one's animality, but it is also to answer the most originary demand that our particular inflection of embodiedness (our form of subjection to desire) makes upon us.

For, Heidegger, then, the continuity between human and nonhuman animals takes the form of discontinuity; where his theses assert the discontinuity, their mode of presentation gives expression to the continuity. For if animals were essentially bored, then human states of boredom are both essentially different from animality (not being part of the human essence), and yet essentially expressions of it (being states which the human is essentially capable of taking on). Heidegger's theses thereby delineate a conception of animality (of nonhuman animality and of the animality of the human) as both within and without humanity's grasp, and hence as essentially enigmatic. And the form of these theses implies that the essential mysteriousness of animality, in ourselves and in other animal species, is an ineluctable consequence of the radicalization of animality within us, of the distinctively human burden of realizing ourselves in a questioning comprehension of the world that reveals it to be worthy of our interest.

Hence, to conceive of nonhuman animals as if always already bored or poor in world is to use them to distract ourselves from our distractions (from our present distraught condition). It expresses a loss of any interest in them as they are in themselves (i.e., as essentially, mysteriously resistant to our interest in them), thus giving expression to our boredom with the world; and it also expresses a refusal to interest ourselves in our own animality as it really is (i.e., as essentially, mysteriously resistant to our understanding), thus giving expression to our boredom with ourselves. This is how we deform our commonality as fellow creatures; this is how the nonhuman animal becomes an externalized figure of our inner perversity—our consignment to a mode of creatureliness that confronts its own animality as always already turned away from itself.

And this analysis returns us directly to the main theme of *Being and Time*, first sounded in its opening pages, when Heidegger declares that his account will "make manifest that in any way of comporting oneself towards entities as entities—even in any Being towards entities as entities—there lies *a priori* an enigma" (BT, 1: 23). Since the human way of being just *is* Being-towards-entities, this amounts to the claim that there is an enigma at the heart of Dasein's Being—or better, that the human way of being, in any and every mode of its comportment, is enigmatic, mysterious, riddling. Dasein is not unknown, or unknowable (as if further information were either guaranteed to solve the difficulty or utterly irrelevant to it); it does not present us with a puzzle (which might, in principle, have a solution). An enigma is an obscure or allusive sign; a riddle requires not just a solution but the imaginative construction of a space or horizon in which that solution can appear as such, as a solution to just this riddle; a mystery is to be acknowledged, not dissipated. A conception and mode of philosophy that is willing to take seriously such a sense of our incomprehensibility to ourselves is one that will find much food for thought in Elizabeth Costello's lecture, and in the lectures by J. M. Coetzee in which it appears.

Chapter Seven

ELIZABETH COSTELLO'S SEMINAR:
TWO POETS AND A NOVELIST

A LTHOUGH COSTELLO WAXES LYRICAL in her lecture about philosophy's apparently constitutional aversion to the imaginative inhabitation of the body, and all the contradictions it generates, she is far less forthcoming about her more favoured mode of access to the life of nonhuman animals—the poet's feel for the ape's experience. She fulfils this obligation more extensively, and so supplements and refines her conception of this mode of access, in her seminar on "The Poets and the Animals." the second academic set-piece of her visit, which forms the core of Coetzee's second Tanner Lecture.[1] In this chapter, I will focus on clarifying its major themes; in the following chapter, I will examine a range of material that either explicitly is, or might usefully be construed as, responsive to Costello's line of thought.

We are not present throughout the seminar, as we are with the lecture: instead, we arrive (with John Bernard) in the middle of Costello's account of the nature of and connections between three animal poems. The poems have been photocopied and distributed to the seminar; but John has time only to note their titles and authors. I reproduce here what Coetzee does not:

THE PANTHER
JARDIN DES PLANTES, PARIS

The bars which strike and pass across his gaze
　　have stunned his sight. The eyes have lost their hold.
To him it seems there are a thousand bars,
a thousand bars and nothing else. No world.

And pacing out that mean, constricted ground,
So quiet, supple, powerful, his stride

---

[1] As we saw in chapter 5, there is a third such set-piece, after the seminar, when Costello responds to three extended comments on her lecture offered by a philosophy professor, Thomas O'Hearne. I hope that my decision to incorporate those comments and responses at various points throughout this commentary, rather than treating them as a distinct, self-contained exchange, does not occlude anything of significance for Coetzee's purposes.

is like a ritual dance performed around
the centre, where his baffled will survives.

The silent shutter of his eye sometimes
slides open to admit some thing outside;
an image runs through each expectant limb
and penetrates his heart, and dies.
　—Rainer Maria Rilke

THE JAGUAR

The apes yawn and adore their fleas in the sun.
The parrots shriek as if they were on fire, or strut
Like cheap tarts to attract the stroller with the nut.
Fatigued with indolence, tiger and lion

Lie still as the sun. The boa-constrictor's coil
Is a fossil. Cage after cage seems empty, or
Stinks of sleepers from the breathing straw.
It might be painted on a nursery wall.

But who runs like the rest past these arrives
At a cage where the crowd stands, stares, mesmerized,
As a child at a dream, at a jaguar hurrying enraged
Through prison darkness after the drills of his eyes

On a short fierce fuse. Not in boredom—
The eye satisfied to be blind in fire,
By the bang of blood in the brain deaf the ear—
He spins from the bars, but there's no cage to him

More than to the visionary his cell:
His stride is wildernesses of freedom:
The world rolls under the long thrust of his heel.
Over the cage floor the horizons come.
　—Ted Hughes

SECOND GLANCE AT A JAGUAR

Skinful of bowls he bowls them,
The hip going in and out of joint, dropping the spine
With the urgency of his hurry
Like a cat going along under thrown stones, under cover,
Glancing sideways, running
Under his spine. A terrible, stump-legged waddle
Like a thick Aztec disemboweller,
Club-swinging, trying to grind some square

Socket between his hind legs round,
Carrying his head like a brazier of spilling embers,
And the black bit of his mouth, he takes it
Between his back teeth, he has to wear his skin out,
He swipes a lap at the water-trough as he turns,
Swivelling the ball of his heel on the polished spot,
Showing his belly like a butterfly.
At every stride he has to turn a corner
In himself and correct it. His head
Is like the worn down stump of another whole jaguar,
His body is just the engine shoving it forward,
Lifting the air up and shoving on under,
The weight of his fangs hanging the mouth open,
Bottom jaw combing the ground. A gorged look,
Gangster, club-tail lumped along behind gracelessly,
He's wearing himself to heavy ovals,
Muttering some mantra, some drum-song of murder
Intolerable, spurred by the rosettes, the Cain-brands,
Wearing the spots off from the inside,
Rounding some revenge. Going like a prayer-wheel,
The head dragging forward, the body keeping up,
The blackjack tail as if looking for a target,
Hurrying through the underworld, soundless.
  —Ted Hughes

Costello claims that, despite the shift in attention from panther to jaguar, Hughes is writing against Rilke. She associates Rilke's use of his panther with the kind of poetry in which animals are emblems—the lion of courage, the owl of wisdom: "the panther is there as a stand-in for something else. He dissolves into a dance of energy around a centre, an image that comes from physics, elementary particle physics" (LA, 50). Rilke sees his panther as having been deprived of the world by the bars of his cage; the world is thus the human world, and his eyes have lost their hold on it, as if he has been shut out from the world we occupy, and thus as if panther and human share a world—the pathos of loss is one that places the poet, and us, on the other side of the bars, and places the panther purely in relation to the world as we apprehend and construct it. (The resemblance to the apparent content of Heidegger's theses on the world poverty of nonhuman animals, fenced out of the human circle, is striking.) Hughes's jaguar occupies a cage in a zoo, just like Rilke's panther; but

the jaguar's vision, unlike the panther's, is not blunted. On the contrary, his eyes drill through the darkness of space. The cage has no reality to him, he is *elsewhere*. He is elsewhere because his consciousness is kinetic rather than abstract: the thrust of his muscles moves him through a space quite different in nature from the three-dimensional box of Newton—a circular space that returns upon itself. (LA, 51)

Costello sees Hughes as feeling his way towards a different kind of being-in-the-world, and asking us to imagine our way into the way the jaguar moves, or the way the currents of life move within the jaguar—to inhabit that body.

Although she does not spell this out in the exchanges we witness, the second Hughes poem if anything makes her point more forcefully than the first. It offers us a second glance—in other words, it is both a supplement and a correction to the first poem, its radically revised conception of appropriate form matching its claim to amount to a glance at the animal (that is, to embody a glimpse rather than a portrait or photograph, to which both Rilke's and Hughes's earlier poems seem formally to aspire), and in so doing it takes on the mode of vision of the jaguar itself (early said to be glancing sideways, in the manner of a cat at someone— the poet?—throwing stones in its direction). The poem runs along under its spine of long, sinuous sentences (only six in the whole poem), its stumpy clauses at once shoving their way forward and swivelling on their punctuation points, picking up and reformulating or recontextualizing ideas (club and blackjack, bowls and bowels, head and jaw, grinding and rounding, wearing out and wearing off, spots, rosettes, and brands) as they turn the corners of the irregularly paced lines, and yet always aware that each word it deploys is like a square being ground into a circular hole, the price of its confinement in even the loosest of poetic forms being an inevitable failure to find its target—a glance that glances off the reality of the animal itself. It is the sheer extravagance of Hughes's imagery, the blatant excess of his range of comparison (with Aztec, butterfly, gangster, prayer-wheel), and the tumbling, incantatory clumsiness of its swipes and laps that precisely secures our sense of the initial alienness of the form of bodily life he strives to inhabit, without ever repressing our sense that our striving can never be successful. It is in this way that Hughes's second poem fits Costello's characterization of a kind of poetry "that does not try to find an idea in the animal, that is not about the animal, but is instead the record of an engagement with him" (LA, 51).

Costello does not claim to understand the means by which Hughes achieves his success—"the process called poetic invention that mingles breath and sense in a way that no one has explained and no one ever will" (LA, 53), the process that Plato castigates as lacking *techne* (a body of intelligible principles). Costello certainly doesn't think that Hughes himself understands this mysterious interfusion of the body and soul of words; or rather, given that she responds so dismissively to a question that presupposes an unproblematic continuity between the author of these poems and the Devon sheep farmer of the same name, she sees a discontinuity between the insight embodied in the poem and the theories or manifestoes espoused by its author ("Writers teach us more than they are aware of" [LA, 53]).

For Costello, Hughes is a primitivist, mingling shamanism, spirit possession, and archetype psychology with an essentially ecological vision of individual animals as transitory occupants of the quasi-Platonic form of its species, of its niche in the interacting systems of Gaia.

> The irony is a terrible one. An ecological philosophy that tells us to live side by side with other creatures justifies itself by appealing to an idea, an idea of a higher order than any living creature. . . . Every living creature fights for its own, individual life, refuses, by fighting, to accede to the idea that the salmon or the gnat is of a lower order of importance than the idea of the salmon or the idea of the gnat. . . . Animals are not believers in ecology. (LA, 54)

This critique of Hughes (as ultimately just as guilty as Rilke of treating animals as emblematic of something other than themselves) looks rather like a version of a line of thought very familiar in modern philosophy; it is perhaps most often associated with existentialism, is often articulated in terms of the threat posed by the universal to the particular, and is very often looked on with great disfavour. It might therefore be worth exploring the trustworthiness of this impression of a family resemblance.

The proponent of this familiar argument first points out that to subsume any particular phenomenon under an idea or concept involves assigning it to a necessarily general or universal category; if that concept is rightly applied to this particular instance of the relevant type, then it is equally rightly applied to this other instance of that type ("this is a salmon, and that is a salmon"). But each of these particulars is, necessarily, distinct from the other; if the two did not differ, we would not have two particulars but only one. Hence, their subsumption under a single concept in effect obliterates that which distinguishes them from each other, which means that it fails to grasp that which individuates them— that which makes them this particular thing rather than that. And if we attempt to grasp in thought the relevant respect in which the one differs from the other, then we will necessarily do so by applying another, inherently universal concept to it, which is bound to subsume it within a group of other individuals who share the relevant feature and so to repress its difference from those others ("this is a young salmon, and this is an old salmon"). Hence, no matter how many such refinements of discrimination we employ ("this is a two-year-old salmon from the River Tay, with a damaged dorsal fin, caught on the morning of July 18"), we will never fully succeed in capturing this particular in all its particularity. In short, the inescapable generality of any category in terms of which we organize and grasp our experience, and so anything we can say or think about what makes the particular object of that experience the thing it is will, inevitably, fail to capture it in its individuality.

To this line of thought, there is a very swift response. If the business of grasping particularity is set up in such a way that it is inconceivable that any thought or assertion could succeed in doing so, then we should not represent the situation in terms of there being something we cannot do— some specifiable task that we are unfortunately but inherently unable to perform. For in such circumstances, we cannot in fact specify what would count as success in this task; so there isn't anything—any particular thing—that we are unable to do. (Compare the orthodox Wittgensteinian response to the sceptical claim that we cannot know another's pain because we cannot feel it, encountered in chapter 5.)

As in the earlier Wittgensteinian case, the logic of this response may leave some dissatisfaction; so it should be acknowledged that there is a more positive aspect to this argument, namely, that we *can* do anything we might conceivably want to do. Take any two salmon: if they are two, then they are distinct from each other, which means that they differ from each other in some respect(s), and it is perfectly possible for us to specify which respect(s)—age, location, fin damage, and so on. Of course, any such distinguishing property is one that our salmon might share with another salmon (a third one, not—*ex hypothesi*—the one with which we are now comparing it); but then, if this third salmon really is distinct from our salmon, then there must be some other, specifiable respect in which it differs from ours, and that in turn can be perfectly well captured in thought and speech.

Putting the counterargument in more general terms, we might say that we must distinguish between judging that one object falls within a general class into which other objects also fall, and judging that two apparently distinct objects are in fact one and the same object. The mere fact that to subsume an object under a concept is, necessarily, to subsume a particular under a universal is not to say that any attempt to grasp a particular object in thought is tantamount to obliterating or abstracting from its particularity. It is in fact a partial contribution to the task of grasping it in all its particularity.

This need not, however, amount to a decisive rebuttal of at least some versions of this anxiety about the particular in relation to the universal. Put aside for the moment the unworthy suspicion that philosophers are rather more likely to focus on the question of whether an accurate description of particular things is possible in principle than to attempt to provide one in practice, and thereby to give themselves a chance to appreciate the sheer, stubborn difficulty of portraying the simplest of things truthfully in words. Even then, one might (and in some cases undoubtedly should) interpret those who express the anxiety we have been evaluating as anxious not about the medium of human thought and speech as such, but rather about some particular human conception of this medium and of its relation to reality. It is not, after all, too difficult to imagine ways in which the picture of a concept as subsuming a particular, or of concepts as ways of grasping reality, might encode a kind of imperialism of reason with respect to the real. Heidegger, for example, noted the echo of "greifen" in the German term for concept (*Begriff*), and the possibility it opens up of picturing thinking as grasping or clutching at things, even pawing or clawing at them, rather than (say) allowing them to make an impression on us, or taking them to heart.[2] And the figure of subsumption might be developed in such a way as to suggest that our ways of thinking and speaking embody an a priori order (whether conceptual or grammatical) to which our experience of reality in all its vagaries must conform (on pain of failing to count or qualify as experience), without its ever being able to put that order in question, or in any way to suggest that making sense of some particular experience might require creative work on the part of the thinker rather than the mechanical application of a conceptual rulebook.

Philosophical readers of differing persuasions might wish to flesh out these possibilities in different ways—perhaps by reference to Kant's distinction between determinant and reflective judgement, perhaps by invoking the Aristotelian perception of the priority of the particular over principle (which is not equivalent to the elimination of principles in favour of sheer particularity) in moral judgement, perhaps by developing Adorno's suspicion of the internal relation between certain philosophical accounts of the concept and certain totalitarian formations of moral, political, and religious thought and practice. Costello's critique of Hughes might then be seen as forming another, more literary alternative to these argumentative strategies. For of course, her point is not that some poets foolishly try to articulate the reality of salmon in terms of ideas, whereas the true poetic task is to do without any such ideas. It is rather that the distinctively shamanistic version of ecological thinking to which Hughes appears to cleave both in his prose and in some of his poetry is in fact a literary way of avoiding or deflecting attention from the individual animals we confront in our experience.

For Hughes's way of thinking ecologically can and does encourage the thought that any specific fish and insect is a mere transient instantiation of the ecological genus or species, no more than a bearer of something

---

[2] Cf. *What Is Called Thinking?*, trans. J. Glenn Gray (New York: Harper and Row, 1968), 212–13.

greater than it, even something essentially beyond the realm of material particulars. But precisely because the salmon and the gnat have no access to ideas, and so to ideas of themselves as participating in a species and so in some greater ebb and flow of nature, the mode of their embodied being will exceed anything that might be articulated in the terms that track those larger movements. This excess is most evident in their wholehearted investment in the struggle against death; for this struggle is a struggle not for life or salmon-life but for the continuation of their individual existence, and so to this extent such ecological frameworks of understanding threaten to repress the full individuality of that existence.

Costello returns to this point about the animal relation to death, when giving her final response to Thomas O'Hearne's final comment on her lecture and seminar, just before she leaves for home; and she thereby indicates another way in which she sees even the poet's insight as limited—or rather, as capable of being supplemented, even superseded. O'Hearne suggests that dying is, for an animal, just something that happens, the breakdown of systems that keep the physical organism functioning, and nothing more—certainly not something about which they can feel horror, because they are incapable of understanding death as human beings do. Costello has this to say:

> Anyone who says that life matters less to animals than it does to us has not held in his hands an animal fighting for its life. The whole of the being of that animal is thrown into that fight, without reserve. When you say that the fight lacks a dimension of intellectual or imaginative horror, I agree. It is not the mode of being of animals to have an intellectual horror: their whole being is in the living flesh.
>
> If I do not convince you, that is because my words, here, lack the power to bring home to you the wholeness, the unabstracted unintellectual nature, of that animal being. That is why I urge you to read the poets who return the living, electric being to language; and if the poets do not move you, I urge you to walk, flank to flank, beside the beast that is prodded down the chute to his executioner. (LA, 65)

The contact of human flesh with animal flesh, the direct relationship between one creature and another, can do what even the poet's words may not do, or at least cannot as easily be gainsaid or neutralized or abstracted in ways that poems can. Costello later characterizes her reaction to this philosophical comment as Swiftian: "if this is the best that human philosophy can offer. . . . I would rather go and live among horses" (LA, 65). And here she returns to the other main theme or reference point of her seminar—*Gulliver's Travels* or, more precisely, one aspect of that tale.

Costello aims to read Swift as a dark ironist rather than as a facile pamphleteer; but she also aims to contest some of the terms and limits of his vision, as well as contesting the more general idea that his fables are easy to digest—or more exactly, the general tendency vehemently to stuff one particular way of reading him (and so presumably anyone) down the reader's throat. As a warm-up exercise, she makes the modest proposal that we reexamine the premises of the orthodox reading of "A Modest Proposal." The consensus begins from the assumption that Swift cannot mean what he says, in proposing that Irish families could make a living by raising babies for the table of their English masters, since that would amount to endorsing an atrocity; so he must mean us to recognize that the English are already, in one sense, killing human babies by letting them starve, and so are already mired in atrocity. Costello questions whether this is the right, or at least the only legitimate, moral orientation to be found in Swift's "Proposal"; why not contemplate the possibility that we are being invited to extend our settled conviction of the atrociousness of raising human babies for the table to the settled practice of raising piglets for the table? Swift's fable actually begins, beyond question, by drawing a parallel between farming nonhuman animals and farming animals; why repress that fact by interpreting its significance in terms of a putatively parallel parallel between practices lying entirely within the human world (linking the policy of starving people with cannibalism)?

For Costello, this reading effectively eliminates the reality of the nonhuman animal world, and the reality of our relations with it, which the "Proposal"—before anything else—foregrounds; in short, it eliminates the reality of that text. And of course, by stressing the possibility of reading Swift otherwise, she invites her audience to see a parallel between his modest proposal and her outrageous analogy between the Holocaust and factory farming. What she does not stress is the disanalogy between their approaches. For whereas her alternative reading of Swift depends upon attributing to him the desire that his readers exercise their imaginations, working out his intended moral for themselves rather than having it served up for them on a plate, Costello explicitly draws the moral she has in mind; where Swift invites us to extend our settled moral convictions in a certain way, but risks having his invitation not merely rejected but entirely overlooked, Costello simply tells her audience that we already stand convicted by our convictions, beyond any defence or difference of interpretation. One might say: her literal-mindedness is of a rather different, and potentially less effective, cast than that of Swift. And to that extent, her implicit invocation of his literary authority has its limits.

Nevertheless, the terrain marked out here by both writers concerns what one might describe as stresses and tensions internal to the human form of life: by pointing out ways in which human patterns of thought and action in one context apparently fail to cohere with the patterns characteristic in another context, we enable ourselves to appreciate (for example) how the notion of atrocious behaviour might be extended in new ways. Diamond cites a related strategy for inviting reflection on the human treatment of animals in her essay "Eating Meat and Eating People";[3] and here too it is the perceptions of a poet around which the argument hinges:

LEARNING TO BE A DUTIFUL CARNIVORE

Dogs and cats and goats and cows,
Ducks and chickens, sheep and sows
Woven into tales for tots,
Pictured on their walls and pots.
Time for dinner! Come and eat
All your lovely, juicy meat.
One day ham from Percy Porker
(In the comics he's a corker),
Then the breast from Mrs Cluck
Or the wing from Donald Duck.
Liver next from Clara Cow
(No, it doesn't hurt her now).
Yes, that leg's from Peter Rabbit
Chew it well; make that a habit.
Eat the creatures killed for sale,
But never pull the pussy's tail.
Eat the flesh from "filthy hogs"
But never be unkind to dogs.
Grow up into double-think—
Kiss the hamster; skin the mink.
Never think of slaughter, dear,
That's why animals are here.
They only come on earth to die,
So eat your meat, and don't ask why.
    —Jane Legge (EM, 327)

As Diamond points out, this poem takes a certain range of feeling about animals for granted, and indeed it adopts a canonical linguistic form in which that range of feeling at once finds expression and is designed to elicit it in others who will gradually enter the form of life in which it has its place, along with a range of related practices to some of which it also refers (such as avoiding the gratuitous infliction of pain on animals, or feeding them in winter): the nursery rhyme. The point of the poem is to

---

[3] Hereafter EM. Published in *The Realistic Spirit*. The poem cited from this essay was first published in *The British Vegetarian* (January/February 1969), 59.

bring out a certain kind of double-think—an inconsistency between these aspects of our thought and behaviour with respect to nonhuman animals and others: in particular, our settled habits of eating them, and (lying somewhere in the background) everything that we take to be required in order to continue those habits—not merely slaughter, but its particular industrialized forms. It sees this incoherence as a kind of synthesis of intellectual confusion and moral hypocrisy; and it invites, although it cannot compel, us to see it the same way.

The invitation goes something like this: If we think it right to bring up children so that they will no more maltreat animals than they would other children, and we encourage the development of their imaginations by the construction of worlds in which animals lead lives remarkably like human ones (possessed of names, families, personalities), what do we expect our children to make of the fact that their happy human families dine on those same animals? It remains a nice question exactly how far we can and should interpret the poem's enraged righteousness as an expression of smug moral superiority or as a considered redeployment of the patronising banalities so natural to rhymes made by adults for children. But its expression of rage works, if it works, precisely by exploiting a conflict latent within two closely connected ways in which we forge relations between children and animals, just as Swift's text (on Costello's reading) works, if it works, by emphasizing a discontinuity between our treatment of pigs and of children that might be open for moral rethinking. In both cases, no new achievements of feeling need be conjured out of thin air, whether by the mind or by the heart; rather, thoughtful feeling is invited to go beyond its existing limits in the name of attaining a fuller expression and understanding of itself.

Costello goes on from her contentions about "A Modest Proposal" to contest what she sees as a similarly unrealistic reading of *Gulliver's Travels*, while acknowledging that the realism of this text also has its limits. The basic structure of Swift's fabulous world is tripartite—Yahoos, Houyhnhnms, and Gulliver, who wants to be a Houyhnhnm but knows that he is really a Yahoo. Costello's interlocutor from the literature department, Elaine Marx, interprets the Houyhnhnms as exemplars of pure reason, inhabitants of a rational utopia that Gulliver pines for but whose standards are too demanding for him; and she suggests that we should neither expect nor wish that Gulliver's aspiration should be fulfilled, since it would go against his human nature—against the carnivorous Yahoo within him. Costello argues that this amounts to interpreting both Yahoo and Houyhnhnm entirely in relation to Gulliver, and hence in relation to human beings—the one representing our animality, the other our reason. But what is the Houyhnhnm point of view on Guilliver's aspiration? They expel him, and they say that this is because he is insufficiently rational; in truth, it is because he does not look like a horse, but rather a dressed-up Yahoo. "So: the standard of reason that has been applied by carnivorous bipeds to justify a special status for themselves can equally be applied by herbivorous quadrupeds" (LA, 56). If we have to interpret the Yahoos and Houyhnhnms as something other than the specific living beings they are, Costello prefers the tripartite Aristotelian matrix of god, beast, and man. In this framework, the horses "are gods of a kind, cold, Apollonian. The test they apply to Gulliver is: is he a god or a beast? They feel it is the appropriate test. We, instinctively, don't" (LA, 57). They don't recognize the third Aristotelian category; they see no essential difference between Gulliver and the Yahoos, although we naturally do. Once again, then, these categorizations stand revealed as the conceptual expression of the nature of those constructing them; none is written into the universe, although any might be imposed upon it. Then the question becomes: what ways of imposing such interpretations are available to, within the imaginative and practical compass of, which species?

Here is where Costello sees Swift's fable as reaching the limits of its realism; here is where it is shown to be "somewhat too neat, somewhat too disembodied, somewhat too unhistorical" (LA, 57). For in reality, human beings on voyages of exploration to unknown lands would have come ashore with raiding parties and projects of colonization. What, then, if Gulliver had landed, shot a few Yahoos when they became threatening, and then shot and eaten a horse? It would certainly give a rude shock to the Houyhnhnms, revealing a whole new category of being, and one that stands specifically for physical force. But when Odysseus and his men did exactly this on Thrinacia, slaughtering animals sacred to Apollo, they called down merciless divine punishment upon their heads. If, then, we push Swift's fable to its limits, we must "recognize that, in history, embracing the status of man has entailed slaughtering and enslaving a race of divine or else divinely created beings and bringing down on ourselves a curse thereby" (LA, 57–58). For Costello, then, only the divine inspiration of poetry can counter the divine damnation under which we labour at present; only words of praise can overcome such words of condemnation.

Chapter Eight

ELIZABETH COSTELLO'S SEMINAR:
PRIMATOLOGY AND ANIMAL TRAINING,
PHILOSOPHY AND LITERARY THEORY

COSTELLO'S SEMINAR THUS ADDS new animals to the troop who marched through her lecture: Red Peter, Red Sally, Sultan, and Nagel's bat are joined by a panther, a jaguar or two, some piglets, and some horses. She takes the literary reality of each to be both continuous and discontinuous with that of other literary animals, and with that of real animals; they are neither reducible to nor entirely free from their real-life originals, and always already embedded in a range of intersecting literary genres and the specific predecessors and successors generated within them. Their meaning resides in a complex, open-ended network of associations and contexts—essentially resistant to abstraction and summary. Further dimensions of this network, generating further such resistance, derive from the fact that these literary animals are both created by specific human individuals, and yet always irreducible to the psychic or biographical idiosyncracies of those individuals—in part because they draw upon more general literary traditions and exemplars; in part because all writers teach us more than they know; in part because, insofar as they possess genuine life as literary creations, they result from their authors' willingness to allow the reality of animal life to possess them, to empty themselves out so that the animal's mode of being-in-the-world can inhabit them, and so their words. In this chapter, I propose to explore two pairs of responses to Costello's conjunction of animals and literature: one might say that the first pair concentrate on the animals that literature tries to reveal to us, and the second on literature's distinctive modes of revelation, but in truth both pairs are responsive to both of these conjoined, enigmatic elements.

SMUTS AND HEARNE

In the Tanner Symposium, only the primatologist, Barbara Smuts, really tries to add further animals to the Costello's troop, when she takes up the challenge of Costello's invitation, in response to a question from her lecture audience, to "Open your heart, and listen to what your heart says" (LA, 37). For Smuts's heart lies in her experience of time spent with gorillas, chimpanzees, baboons, dolphins, and dogs, in the course of scientific research—experience of a kind that she finds capable of grounding the use of such terms as friendship, respect, trust, and obstinacy; one might say, she finds ways of projecting such terms into these specific contexts of human interaction with nonhuman animals. I find, however, that I am inclined to resist some of these projections, in ways that lead me to question the degree of conviction that her words might reasonably be expected to elicit from those initially sceptical of her attitude to nonhuman animals, and particularly from those with either a philosophical training or a poetic gift.

Let's set aside for these purposes Smuts's casual endorsement of her fellow symposiasts' perception of Coetzee's lectures as a receptacle for arguments (she talks of wanting to fill a "striking gap in the discourse on animal rights contained in Coetzee's text" [LA, 108]); and let's further bypass her attempts to interpret Costello in terms of a stark opposition between poetry and experience (she talks of rephrasing Costello's point "so that it has less to do with poetic imagination and more to do with real-life encounters with other animals' [LA, 120])—quite as if the poetic imagination were not always ultimately a response to experience (say, of a panther or jaguar in its cage), or as if experience could be properly absorbed without the exercise of the very imaginative faculty upon which poets rely. It will be more to the purpose to focus instead on how she proposes to close the gap she thinks she has found in the text's arguments—on how she brings her own experience of nonhuman animals to linguistic expression.

Smuts begins by noting a specific absence or repression of experience in Costello herself—an absence to which Coetzee's text makes only an oblique reference, when Costello's son says to himself, at the beginning of the Appleton College dinner, "If she wants to open her heart to animals, why can't she stay home and open it to her cats?" (LA, 38). Smuts does not think Costello need have stayed at home; but she does wonder why she should avoid drawing upon her own immediate experience of a shared life with nonhuman animals (as, say, Heidegger does—however briefly and troublingly—in his lectures on animals), and she proposes in her response to do what Costello fails to do.

In so doing, she provides much food for thought; but in inviting us to project a variety of words from their original context, in which they characterize our relations with other human beings, to ones in which they aspire to apply to our relations with nonhuman animals, she makes repeated use of two closely related notions whose aptness to this new context is not earned—that of a person, and that of equality. For Smuts conceives of her time with nonhuman animals as years spent "in the company of 'persons' like you and me, who happen to be nonhuman" (LA, 108), and hence as (in this respect) our equals.

What, then, does Smuts mean by a person?

> [R]elating to other beings as persons has nothing to do with whether or not we attribute human characteristics to them. It has to do, instead, with recognizing that they are social subjects, like us, whose idiosyncratic, subjective experience of us plays the same role in their relations with us that our subjective experience of them plays in our relations with them. If they relate to us as individuals, and we relate to them as individuals, it is possible for us to have a *personal* relationship. If either party fails to take into account the other's social subjectivity, such a relationship is precluded. . . . [P]ersonhood connotes a way of being *in relation to others*, and thus no one other than the subject can give it or take it away. In other words, when a human being relates to an individual nonhuman being as an anonymous object, rather than as a being with its own subjectivity, it is the human, and not the other animal, who relinquishes personhood. (LA, 118).

This chain of reasoning contains some crucial ambiguities, however. For example, while it might make sense to talk of baboons on the one hand, and human beings on the other, as both social subjects, in that both are "vulnerable to the demands and rewards of relationship" (LA, 110), and even constituted as individuals by the structures of their social life, it doesn't follow that these constitutive social structures are sufficiently similar in their complexity (and hence in the opportunities they provide for enacting certain kinds of relationship and so of undergoing certain ranges of experience, whether rewarding or demanding) to engender social subjectivity of a kind that justifies the attribution of personhood to nonhuman animals.

The home of the concept of personhood is that of human intersubjectivity; and the forms of interhuman relationships have a richness and variety that are absent from interbaboon relationships, and so are absent from human-baboon interactions. Human sexual relationships can take a variety of forms, each infused with a certain kind of significance for those participating in them—from one-night stands to lifelong monogamous marriage; the forms in which we can break bread with one another can range from foraging directly from the landscape to sharing a banquet at a three-star restaurant. Interbaboon forms of sexuality and consumption do not take such forms; and human-baboon relationships certainly do not do so either. Hence, any conception of personhood that we find ourselves willing to extend into the context of interbaboon and human-baboon relationships can at best be a pared-down analogue of the original concept.

None of this amounts to a rejection of the idea that direct experience of and interaction with baboon societies, as opposed to fixated a priori conceptions of that aspect of reality, ought to determine the precise extent, and the particular ways, in which the concept of personhood must be inflected to fit that new context. Neither does it entail that we cannot relate to gorillas as individuals, or that they cannot relate to us as individuals; what it does entail is that the most we can achieve in so doing is to relate to a given gorilla as an individual *gorilla*, and that the most any gorilla can do is relate to us as an individual gorilla of a peculiar kind.

All these points, but particularly the last, are in fact underlined by Smuts's own anecdotes, despite her best intentions.

> [T]he baboons stubbornly resisted my feeble but sincere attempts to convince them that I was nothing more than a detached observer, a neutral object they could ignore. . . . Since I was in their world, they determined the rules of the game, and I was thus compelled to explore the unknown terrain of human–baboon intersubjectivity. Through trial and embarrassing error, I gradually mastered at least the rudiments of baboon propriety. I learned much through observation, but the deepest lessons came when I found myself sharing the being of a baboon because other baboons were treating me like one. (LA, 109–10)

According to this passage, human–baboon intersubjectivity consists of the baboon relating to the human being as another baboon, and the human being learning to slough off the distinctive modes of human interaction with the world and other beings in it (including that of the neutral detached observer) in favour of the prevailing modes of baboon–baboon interactions. But of course, a human being could adopt the role of detached observer in relation to the baboons, as the history of animal studies attests; whereas no baboon shows itself capable of doing any such thing to Smuts, or indeed to any other being of its acquaintance. Attending to such differences is not a way of avoiding baboon individuality; it is part of thinking one's way into the distinctive responding refusal of nonhuman animal life.

If a more productive use of direct experience of human–animal relations is really needed to fill the gap created by Costello's apparently wilful omission of her life with cats, then the writings of Vicki Hearne would be one place to look. For she is a poet who is also an animal trainer and a philosopher. Her most famous book, *Adam's Task: Calling Animals by Name*, contains a number of portraits of animals that might usefully be added to Costello's troop, as part of understanding the particular opportunities and constraints afforded by a distinctively literary mode of access to nonhuman animal life.[1]

Where Smuts seems tempted by a misconception of personhood as somehow prior to and independent of our concept of a human being, in something like McMahan's and Singer's manner, Hearne sternly resists. Her view is that there are certain things

---

[1] (New York: Harper Perennial, 1994); hereafter AT.

we have to notice when we project the incredibly complex syntax of rights, duties and the like into our various ways of discoursing with and about animals. The trainer welcomes the attempt to make the notion of "speciesism" coherent but wants impatiently to say something like "Look! When the logician has said 'for all x such that P, where P is the ability to feel physical pain, etc., etc.', and goes on from there to propose a theory of animal rights and consciousness, s/he has said virtually nothing, has not taken the tiniest step towards imagining the personhood of any animal." (AT, 62)

Note first that Hearne is imagining a use that this trainer might have for the very term about which I expressed grave suspicions when Smuts used it. This allows me to emphasize that my suspicions were directed not at the word "person" but at the way in which it was being put to use, at what its user wanted to mean by it.

In fact, in many ways Hearne's ways with words are far more extravagant to a philosophical eye than are Smuts's. For the collage of anecdote and aphorism that she offers in place of what we might have expected (namely, a body of principles or theory making up the dog trainer's expertise) is shot through with ideas of community, loyalty, awe and honour, the sacred and the profane—what one might call a mythology of human–animal relations that she is as fully prepared to attribute to the animal being trained as to the trainer.

Take, for example, Hearne's description of her training of a year-old pointer bitch named Salty. She describes the dog as confounded by her trainer's response to her refusal to stay close when walking together on a long training lead (Hearne runs as hard as possible in the opposite direction to Salty's own unlicensed pursuit of anything huntable, thereby ensuring that the dog hits the end of the line with some force and travels head over heels back in the direction of her trainer).

> The third or fourth time she gets dumped in this way, it dawns on Salty that there is a consistency in my inconsiderate and apparently heedless plunges. She sits down in order to think this over, cocking her head in puzzlement, trying to work out the implications of my behaviour. She suspects, correctly, that they are cosmic. . . . Then the sight of the gate standing there in such an *opened* way tempts her and, forgetting the new cosmology, she charges for it. (AT, 52)

Why, then, do I feel far less suspicious about the spirit in which Hearne constructs this element of her collage? In part, of course, because whereas Smuts attempts in effect to regard her own use of such terms as "person" and "equal" as literal, merely unobvious reiterations of the familiar uses of those terms, Hearne takes a poet's delight in rising above any such flat-footed claim to literal meaning, together with a poet's desire to emphasize the legitimacy of other modes of projection of words. The impression is thereby created in the reader that her right to use such language must be earned, and that she is going to do so.

Another part of the answer is given in the chapter on Salty's training:

> I should notice at this or some point that one of the things that might lead someone to wonder about what looks like the wildest sort of anthropomorphizing is the sketchiness of the tokens of this language game. One thing I should say is, I'm not filling in all of the details (this isn't a language primer). More to the point, a reason for trying to get a feel for a dog–human language-game is that it sharpens one's awareness of the sketchiness of the tokens of English. Wittgenstein says: "It is as if a snapshot of a scene had been taken but only a few scattered details of it were to be seen: here a hand, there a bit of a face or a hat—the rest is dark. And now it is as if we know quite certainly what the whole picture represented. As if I could read the darkness." When we learn a language game, we learn to read the darkness. (AT, 71–72)

The true force of this remark depends upon the fact that it comes after fully thirty pages of very detailed description of the first stages of training Salty, to the point at which she has become genuinely responsive to just two orders: "Sit!" and "Fetch!" Hearne's primary point is an echo of one made by Wittgenstein, in his famous tale of the builders. In an early section of the *Philosophical Investigations*, he imagines two human beings building with four kinds of stones, and employing a language with just four words (one for each kind of stone) in such a way that one builder might bring the other whatever is needed to continue the project.[2] In this tale, insofar as we think we have the right to regard the utterance of "Slab!" and "Pillar!" as the issuing of orders, what earns us that right is the broader context of practical activity within which those utterances fit. In just the same way, Hearne portrays herself as having the right to regard "Sit!" and "Fetch!" as commands in a dog–human language game only insofar as they can be seen to have a place in the far broader context of the particular form of life she shares with Salty.

Salty first learns to respond to the command "Sit!" by repeatedly being placed in an approximation to a sitting position by her trainer as she utters the word; we might feel confident in seeing no meaning in that utterance as yet. Then they progress to Hearne giving the command without placing her, and responding to any failure to sit by a harsh, emphatic correction—thereby transforming "Sit!" into what we might call a highly primitive form of imperative. Salty obeys her, we might think; she is certainly now sitting in response to her recognition of Hearne's intention that she do so. Does this make "Salty, sit!" a piece of language? But then, one day, Salty spontaneously sits, in just the clean-edged formal way she

[2] Cf. PI, section 2.

has learnt, only now in the house not the training yard. This may have a number of meanings, ranging from "please feed me" (performed next to the cupboard with the cans) to "this mess wasn't my fault" (performed next to the overturned garbage can). In each case, it is now Hearne's responsibility to respond appropriately. Now the loop of intention is two-way, and it is Salty who has enlarged the context of projection; now both players of this proto-language game can be obedient to each other, and to their common language (or can disobey).

Many more complexities and elaborations need to be worked out—among them the geographical boundaries of the command's legitimacy (does it hold good in the yard as a whole, or only in certain parts of it? Is sitting-on-grass the same as sitting-on-carpet?), the effect of the introduction of new commands, with their own distinctive content, form, and styles of projection, and so on. The important question here is not to identify the exact point at which what is going on deserves at last to be called the development of a language; it is to see that what determines where one draws the line is not the particular noise uttered, or even the immediate correlation of a noise and a piece of behaviour, but rather the establishment of a particular place for that utterance in a broader context of interaction in a common world. The noise and the response are the sketchiest of tokens; to imagine them as the bearers of meaning is to imagine a highly complex and specific form of life.

In other words, Hearne attempts to justify even her most extravagant uses of words by illuminating what is usually left dark in any account of language use. Her account of Salty's training is in fact an account of the construction, the maintenance, and the increasing elaboration of a relationship between a particular dog and a particular woman, in a context that is itself determined by (among other things) their individual histories (of abuse on the one hand and experience on the other), and what the woman knows of the joint collective history of dogs and human beings, as expressed in the anecdotes and aphorisms trainers tell one another, as well as in more canonical works of literature (such as the writings of Xenophon). What Hearne's use of mythological language more specifically brings out is the extent to which the woman understands her relationship to the dog in fundamentally moral terms, and finds the dog to be responsive to that understanding.

To put this moral myth in its most general terms, it is one that discovers freedom in wholehearted submission to necessity. This myth understands training as involving an ineliminable authoritarian moment (the moment of correction and command), the justification for which is that it enables the animal to fulfil its own nature—to develop the idiosyncratic powers that its nature bequeaths it by making it possible for the animal to enter into a particular universe of understanding (or a particular understanding of the universe) together with its trainer, who herself understands her authority as a form of submission to a good that is external both to her and to the individual animal she is training: the good of continuing and enhancing the distinctive human and canine excellences that can be achieved only in the context of certain kinds of shared forms of canine–human life. This is what Heidegger has in mind when he talks of the animal's encircling ring intersecting with the human world. Hearne puts it differently: "What gives us the right to say 'Fetch!'? Something very like reverence, humility and obedience of course. We can follow, understand, only things and people we can command, and we can command only whom and what we can follow" (AT, 76). In effect, then, Hearne's mythopoetics aims to express a reverence for the reality of animal nature, both nonhuman and human, as her life with those animals has revealed it to her. And the paradoxes involved in its articulation are not merely apparent, or to be eventually dissipated; they are internal to her sense of the enigmatic, mutually educative marvel of kinship between the human animal and her fellow creatures.

SINGER AND GARBER

So much for another poet's attempts to articulate the otherness of animals. But of course, Costello's seminar was just as much designed to underline the mysteriousness of literature as that of animality. She persistently pictures its manifestations in poetry as fundamentally obscure phenomena—ones that depend upon an enigmatic capacity to understand nonexistent beings, and to understand their nonexistence as internally related to real beings, and in particular to the real being of their authors, and of the literary, cultural, social, and historical contexts within which they are all embedded. Appreciating the contours of her lecture and seminar from this perspective thus returns us to one of the examples she deploys in her lecture to illustrate the incomprehensible comprehensibility of animal modes of being—her comparison between thinking one's way into the being of fictional characters, and thinking one's way into the being of other living creatures.

It is worth recalling that this is a point that Singer's central character, Peter, cites only in order to dismiss, in his fictional response to Costello's lecture. The dismissal occurs towards the end of the tale in which he stars, immediately after he has used the example of the Kahlua bottle to criticise Costello's talk of fullness of animal being:

> That's not the worst argument, either. Listen to this. Costello is talking about a book she has written in which she thinks herself into the character of Joyce's

Marion Bloom, and then she says,

"If I can think my way into the existence of a being who has never existed, then I can think my way into the existence of a bat or a chimpanzee or an oyster, any being with whom I share the substrate of life."

Naomi is glad to leave the topic of Kahlua: "You don't have to be a philosopher to see what is wrong with that. The fact that a character doesn't exist isn't something that makes it hard to imagine yourself as that character. You can imagine someone very like yourself, or like someone else you know. Then it is easy to think your way into the existence of that being. But a bat, or an oyster? Who knows? If that's the best argument Coetzee can put up for his radical egalitarianism, you won't have any trouble showing how weak it is. (LA, 90–91)

One should not ignore the fact that this objection is in fact voiced by Peter's daughter rather than Peter himself; but since he offers no explicit disagreement with it, and since she herself is shown to offer it in a spirit of mingled propitiation and distraction (eager to shift the focus of the discussion, and well aware that she can most effectively do so by pandering to her father's sense of his own unquestionable authority and rectitude), we can, I think, safely assume that we are hearing Peter speak through her mouth (the father's voice inhabiting the daughter's body). It is as if Peter the author regards this argument as so transparently simple that even his unduly emotional, immature female offspring might safely be licensed to articulate it.

It's a shame, then, that Peter's ventriloquized counterargument is so transparently question-begging. For Naomi's claim is that if you can imagine another real human being (either very like yourself or at least well known to you), then it is easy to think your way from there into the existence of a fictional human being. But that claim patently presupposes what it purports to demonstrate—namely, that the difference between real human beings and fictional ones is small and easily bridged. She simply takes it for granted that the fictional status of fictional human beings is of vanishing significance in comparison with the fact that they are nonetheless fictional *human beings*. Whereas Costello's contention is precisely that, because fictional human beings do not exist whereas real human beings do, their fictionality is of exorbitant or inordinate significance in comparison with their claim to human status; and so our undeniable and utterly ordinary capacity to comprehend them from within is also utterly mysterious (certainly more mysterious than our capacity to think our way into nonhuman but real, existing animals). For Costello, the fact that Marion Bloom is a figment of James Joyce's imagination sharply distinguishes her from James Joyce himself, because one exists and the other does not and never did. How, then, are we to understand claims to know what she is thinking or feeling, to comprehend her perspective on her world, when she simply does not exist?

It is important to see that Costello is not claiming to possess that understanding: she thinks rather that we have a puzzling phenomenon here—another instance of the combination of the utterly everyday and the essentially incomprehensible to which Diamond gives the label "a difficulty of reality." Costello's talk of the nonexistence of fictional characters does not amount to a denial of the reality of fiction but is rather an attempt to specify the distinctive nature of that particular, enigmatic part of human reality: fiction, and so fictional characters, are, after all, part of our experience of the world. But Peter and Naomi simply deflect themselves, and so encourage us to be deflected, from the real difficulties. For even if we did not share Costello's sense of something constitutively enigmatic here, we can hardly deny that there are a number of hard philosophical questions in this vicinity (to do with our sheer capacity to speak and think about fictional beings).

Furthermore, when Costello emphasizes the peculiar mystery of fictional beings, she is not committed to denying that a certain mystery also inheres in our capacity to think our way into the perspective of other human beings, or other nonhuman animals. For Singer's characters, whereas the reality of nonhuman animal existence may genuinely be beyond our cognitive grasp ("Who knows?"), access to the reality of other human beings is essentially straightforward; it is as if one such task is nothing but mysterious, while the other is nothing but mundane. Costello, by contrast, sees our understanding of both such kinds of being to be at once ordinary and extraordinary—as everyday achievements that nevertheless embody a constitutive mystery.

I am tempted to say that Peter's utter inability to see what Costello sees here is itself an instance of the ways in which (as Wittgenstein puts it) "one human being can be a complete enigma to another. . . . We cannot find our feet with them" (PI, 223), and hence a concrete proof of the preferability of Costello's stance. True, neither Costello nor Peter really exists; but Costello herself never claims that we cannot understand fictional human beings (just that this capacity is mysterious); and of course in this respect the mysteriousness of these fictional beings to one another simply reflects the potentially enigmatic nature of relations between real human beings (for example, between Singer and Coetzee).

Whatever the merits of succumbing to this temptation, however, the enigma inherent in understanding fictional beings has a particular pertinence for us—since it concerns the relationship in which we, as readers of Coetzee, stand to Elizabeth Costello, and so the relationship in which Coetzee himself stands to Elizabeth Costello, and that in which we stand to him. For what, after all, are we doing when we claim to understand, say, Elizabeth Costello's Gates Lecture, or the seminar that follows it, given that it is an entirely fictional event? Can we say instead that we are trying to understand J. M. Coetzee's Tanner Lectures? They certainly happened: we have the textual evidence, as well as a variety of first-person testimony. But everything Coetzee said in his lectures is part of a fictional text; and is it, on reflection, entirely clear what bearing the thoughts and opinions of a set of fictional characters have or can have on the thoughts and opinions of their author? How exactly, if at all, can we come to understand Coetzee by coming to understand Costello? Do we know where we are with any of this?

Since our access to Coetzee is, in the first instance, access to him as the creator of Elizabeth Costello, perhaps we should begin to take our bearings in this area by focusing in the first instance on how our understanding of her is achieved. And here it is important to stress that, as well as the various dialogues with academics that are embedded in and around Costello's sessions of public speaking at Appleton College, Coetzee's two short fictions also embed her in a family context. This is a point noted by Diamond, who reads it as showing that one "difficulty of attempting to bring a difficulty of reality in focus [is] that any such attempt is inextricably intertwined with relations of power between people" (PAL, 55). It is also noted by Marjorie Garber, in her contribution to the Tanner symposium, who asks two questions as a result: "What are the relationships between the sexes, and between family members, in Coetzee's narrative? . . . Why should a classic sexual triangle of the human social and cultural world (mother-son-son's wife) animate an argument about animals?" (LA, 74). In her limited compasss, Garber can barely provide even the beginning of an answer to either question; but unless we try to do so, an important part of the literary force and significance of Coetzee's text will certainly go missing.

Elizabeth Costello stays during her visit with her son and his family. John Bernard is an assistant professor of physics and astronomy; his wife Norma is a philosopher of mind (at present unemployed); their two children appear onstage in only two early sentences, and remain unnamed throughout, but their offstage presence is strongly felt. John, who shares a first name with his author, provides the reader's perspective on the events of his mother's visit throughout the text—more precisely, the third-person narrator never leaves his perch on John's shoulder and only ever enters directly into John's unvoiced thoughts and feelings. His academic profession combines with this fictional function, and with his regularly professed indifference to the central topic of his mother's words, to suggest that he maintains a certain distance above the fray, academic and personal; but that suggestion proves misleading.

The same suggestion is not even floated with respect to his wife. Her professional affiliations align her with the targets of her mother-in-law's lecture, and she (along with O'Hearne) functions as philosophy's representative in the academic context of the story; but she has never liked her mother-in-law, and she particularly resents her attempts to involve their children in what Norma thinks of as power games over food ("I would have more respect for her if she didn't try to undermine me behind my back, with her stories to the children about the poor little veal calves and what the bad men do to them" [LA, 68]). We don't see any direct evidence of this backstabbing, although we did see Costello repeatedly ask why her grandchildren were not having supper with the adults on the night of her arrival, when we are told she already knows that it is Norma's attempt to respect her unwillingness to see meat on the table while continuing to feed meat to the children. Is this a tactless lack of imagination on Costello's part; or the result of her tiredness and jet lag; or of Norma's stubborn unwillingness to alter the children's diet even for two days?

And how far can we trust the authorial claim that Costello "knows the reason" for the children's absence all along? It is, after all, through the perspective of John Bernard that that claim is made; and he is an important element in this familial grid of conflict. Norma remains unemployed because she moved with him to Appleton, where there is no teaching position for her, which we are told is "a cause of bitterness to her, and of conflict between them" (LA, 17); and he tells us that "he and his sister and his late father are written into [his mother's] books in ways that he sometime finds painful. But he is not sure that he wants to hear her once again on the subject of animal rights, particularly when he knows he will afterwards be treated, in bed, to his wife's disparaging commentary" (LA, 17). He is also fairly sure that "his mother would have chosen not to like any woman he married" (LA, 17). And of course, once the family connection that he has so carefully kept hidden from his colleagues is revealed, then everything Costello says and does that is likely to offend or disappoint the officers of Appleton College is likely to make his future there profoundly uncomfortable. She is, after all, his mother.

And, of course, the grandmother of his children—which entails that she must be elderly, in "her declining years" (LA, 17), as John puts it. In fact, at the airport, he is shocked to see how she has aged: "her hair, which had streaks of grey in it, is now entirely white; her shoulders stoop; her flesh has grown flabby" (LA, 15). So why should she subject herself to this gruelling flight, and equally gruelling visit, when it is two years since they last met in the flesh? Is that why? Is her reason for accepting the invitation to give the Gates Lecture, in a medium she so distrusts, and with no need to promote her already-elevated reputation, that it gives her an opportunity to see her only son and his children that may not come again before her death?

But why then choose to talk about animals? The invitation permits her to choose any topic she wishes, and she can hardly be unaware that the issue of human treatment of animals, and the more specific claims she makes about philosophy's implication in those modes of treatment, will profoundly irritate her daughter-in-law, and so deeply unsettle the already-uneasy patterns of their family life. And why make a point of identifying herself with an ape who would be well-advised not to have children, since they could only turn out to be monsters? Is John meant to understand that this is more a matter of accusing herself of monstrosity than of suggesting that he occupies that category? Perhaps it is even a kind of apology for the way writers inevitably treat any children they have—not only by neglecting them in favour of the writing, but also by using them in the writing: allowing them to identify themselves, variously mangled and distorted, in fictional characters whose own life can then seem painfully and humiliatingly inextricable from their own.

Garber's suggestion of an internal relation between the topic of Costello's lecture and the classic sexual triangle of the human world (mother-son-son's wife) provides some orientation here. For of course, while the mother–son tie is one of blood, the son's wife is tied to both by law; her arrival marks the point at which biological reproduction encounters social structure, and distinctively human culture arises from the grafting of each upon the other. What is the difference between being someone's flesh and blood, and becoming one flesh with them—particularly when the latter bond produces two more people who are the flesh and blood of both? And if this endless entangling of nature and culture in the human animal is, as Freud wagered, the primary matrix of our emotional life, then the immensely powerful, unwillingly understood, conflicting impulses of love and hatred that binds this family together represent a kind of ineliminable redoubling of animality in the familial, and hence in even the most sophisticated and abstract domains of culture that grow from it. No wonder Costello's lecture topic engenders such an overdetermined intensity of response from her daughter-in-law, as well as from her son and from herself. Its uncanny power marks the return of the repressed familiar—the rational animal as essentially familial.

Even so, Coetzee's lectures hardly end by resolving the ambiguities and uncertainties they generate, both within the family context in which he embeds Costello's lecture and between the familial and the academic or intellectual contexts themselves. On the one hand, Costello's final reply to Thomas O'Hearne ensures that the whole academic venture ends in "acrimony, hostility, bitterness . . . not what [Dean] Arendt and his committee wanted" (LA, 67), and that Norma is in such a state of fury that she will not even get up to say goodbye to her guest. On the other, it precipitates her final exchange with her son on the way to the airport, where—overcoming her sense that her words are best spoken into a pillow or a hole in the ground—she confesses to her fear that she is herself mad, if the world is not.

> Calm down, I tell myself, you are making a mountain out of a molehill. This is life. Everyone else comes to terms with it, why can't you? *Why can't you?*
>
> She turns on him a tearful face. What does she want, he thinks? Does she want me to answer her question for her?
>
> They are not yet on the expressway. He pulls the car over, switches off the engine, takes his mother in his arms. He inhales the smell of cold cream, of old flesh. "There, there," he whispers in her ear. "There, there. It will soon be over." (LA, 69)

For an undemonstrative family, in which a hug and a few murmured words suffice for a greeting between mother and son after two years, and after a visit throughout which the son has striven to talk with his mother purely as a purveyor of ideas about animals, this scene is unprecedentedly open, emotionally and physically. It is also the point at which the academic and familial contexts of the story explicitly dovetail, in which the most naked intellectual expression of Costello's woundedness takes the form of a direct personal demand. Are we to think that John's subsequent words and actions constitute an answer to her question, or at least his way of answering it, or rather a way of avoiding having to answer it? I am more inclined to view it as both—as Coetzee's way of inviting us to see that Costello has staked out a position that opens onto, and hence requires, both an intellectual and a personal response, and an awareness that each mode of response is internally related to (hence at once deepened and disrupted by) the other.

What, then, are we to make of John's final words to his mother? *What* will soon be over? He begins by addressing her as if she is one of his children—her progress towards the grave or the urn returning her to the condition of childhood, and the need to be mothered by someone she mothered (or failed to). This context suggests that what will soon be over is her need to be so comforted (her childlike, tearful immersion in her overwhelming emotional state). The context provided by his sense of smell—cold cream, old flesh—suggests that what will soon be over is her time in this apparently insane world, a world that is making of her final years a hell on earth. The context of the expressway suggests that it is her visit, and so her audacious, humiliating engagement with the eminences of the academy, that will soon be over. And the context of the fictional tale—that is, the fact that John's claim that "it will soon be over" is the last sentence of the narrative—suggests that it is *The Lives of Animals* that will soon be over: in fact, over immediately, the consummation brought about by the very sentence that announces it, or rather by its author's decision not to affix a further sentence or sentences to it.

I am suggesting that Coetzee intends that we should attempt to regard all of these suggestions as equally relevant interpretations of John's words. It is our job as readers to locate those words within (at least) four different contexts or frames; their significance depends upon the way in which they simultaneously invoke a variety of dimensions of significance, relate each to all the others, and provide no ultimate or final metaframe within which their interrelations can be exhaustively specified. One might say: to aspire to such a reading is what Coetzee offers us as internal to any attempt to read *The Lives of Animals* as a piece of literature. Is such a conception of meaning (as multiple, fractured, interconnected, and always open to further complication) what distinguishes literature from philosophy, and from the reality towards which and from which it turns? Or is it precisely what aligns literature with reality, and so is the necessary focus of any philosophical attempt to comprehend literary interventions into the realm of ideas, and literary conceptions of reality, on their own terms?

PART TWO
ELIZABETH COSTELLO

Chapter Nine

REALISM, MODERNISM, AND THE NOVEL

THE TANNER LECTURES WERE NOT in fact the first occasion on which Coetzee made use of Elizabeth Costello in an honorific academic context. In November 1996, as the Ben Belitt Lecture at Bennington College, Coetzee had presented a short fiction about Costello's visit to Appleton College to receive the Stowe Award (conferred biennially on a major world writer, and involving a purse of fifty thousand dollars as well as a gold medal) and make an acceptance speech. Speech and fiction alike are entitled "What is Realism?" and were published (in the journal *Salmagundi*) before the Tanner Lectures were delivered; accordingly, in her Gates Lecture on "The Philosophers and the Animals," Costello mentions her earlier speech, and Coetzee quietly footnotes the *Salmagundi* text, as something published under his name (thereby inviting us to consider the relation between his and Costello's claims to its authorship).

A lightly revised version of this Belitt Lecture (which, among other things, relocates the acceptance speech to Altona College, Pennsylvania—thus preserving Appleton College for the Gates Lecture—and retitles itself "Realism") constitutes the first chapter, or rather the first lesson, of Coetzee's later book, *Elizabeth Costello: Eight Lessons*.[1] Indeed, all eight lessons represent versions of material Coetzee has presented in a range of academic contexts over something less than a decade, in each case using Elizabeth Costello as their protagonist; versions of the Tanner Lectures (shorn of their original scholarly accompaniments of introduction, footnotes, and commentary) reappear as lessons 3 and 4.[2]

Their central position in this new text, or sequence of texts, therefore amounts to a declaration that the Elizabeth Costello we met at Appleton College has both a past and a future; the Gates Lecture was not her first recorded intervention into matters academic, and more specifically philosophical, and it was not to be her last. And since our reading of the Tanner Lectures made it clear just how far a proper understanding of Coetzee's purposes in presenting certain views and arguments about animals, phi-

---

[1] (London: Secker and Warburg, 2003); hereafter EC.

[2] The epilogue of Derek Attridge's *J. M. Coetzee and the Ethics of Reading* (Chicago: University of Chicago Press, 2004) is an invaluable source of information about many of these original contexts.

losophy, and literature depended upon understanding the character of the person who advanced them, it follows that we are likely to obtain a fuller understanding of those views and arguments by making full use of the further illumination of Elizabeth Costello's character that Coetzee has effected by embedding the narrative of her Gates Lecture within the broader context of her other encounters with the academic world of prize-giving and conference participation.

What, then, would we have known about the Elizabeth Costello who arrives in Appleton College to give the Gates Lecture if we had already been familiar with her acceptance speech for the Stowe Award? That speech is far shorter than her Gates Lecture, but it too takes its initial bearings from Kafka's short story about Red Peter. In this context, how-ever, it allows her to stress above all the ways in which the form of that tale enforces a kind of relation to its readers that breaks decisively with what we are likely to associate with the label of "realism"—the driving desire of a certain strain of literature, which so concerned Plato and is now perhaps primarily associated with the genre of the novel, to create a convincing appearance of reality itself. The problematization of that de-sire—the equal and opposite force of the desire itself and of the difficulties standing in the way of its satisfaction—is itself a primary preoccupation of literary modernism, with which Coetzee's novels have often (although by no means exclusively) been grouped, and with which his critical writ-ings have been centrally (although again, by no means exclusively) con-cerned. In effect, then, the first lesson of *Elizabeth Costello* is that all its later lessons (including those derived from the Tanner Lectures) must be understood as framed by an overarching interest in the literary conjunc-tion of realism and modernism in the genre of the novel. So, before I go on to examine Costello's and Coetzee's particular ways of relating themselves to this conjunction of issues, I first want to delineate the con-junction itself in more general terms.

The (Re)Birth of the Novel

It is notoriously difficult to define the specific literary genre of the novel. Terry Eagleton no sooner offers us an apparently uncontroversial (if triv-ial) specification—"a novel is a piece of prose fiction of a reasonable length"—than he declares that even it is unduly restrictive: for not all novels are written in prose, the distinction between fact and fiction is itself often unclear, and what counts as a reasonable length (what separates a novella from a novel) is open to question.[3] He further suggests that the

[3] *The English Novel: An Introduction* (Oxford: Blackwell, 2005), hereafter EN.

novel as a genre is not just resistant to this kind of precise definition (something true of many concepts), but positively allergic to it—that its nature is best defined as actively subversive of generic distinctions and so of any kind of definition in those familiar terms.

> It is less a genre than an anti-genre. It cannibalizes other literary modes and mixes the bits and pieces promiscuously together. You can find poetry and dramatic dialogue in the novel, along with epic, pastoral, satire, history, elegy, tragedy and any number of other literary modes. . . . The novel quotes, parodies and transforms other genres, converting its literary ancestors into mere components of itself in a kind of Oedipal vengeance on them. . . . The novel is an anarchic genre, since its rule is not to have rules. An anarchist is not just someone who breaks rules, but someone who breaks rules as a rule. (EN, 1–2)

As the concluding image of anarchism suggests, Eagleton's remarks do not amount to acknowledging that he has failed to define the novel; they precisely succeed in specifying something characteristic of it as a genre. An antigenre is certainly one that renders the very idea of genre questionable, but that is not the same as rejecting the idea altogether. On the contrary, one can understand the novel's cannibalizing tendencies with respect to other genres only if one takes it for granted that one can recognize what count as instances of the cannibalized genres within the body of the novel; and to characterize the novelistic operation performed on those genres as anarchistic is to define it in highly specific terms. As Eagleton concludes, breaking generic rules is the presiding rule of this genre.

The essentially parasitic structure of this presiding rule or textual operation immediately suggests that the origins of the novel will necessarily reside in a certain kind of critical relation to a preceding literary genre or genres. Eagleton proposes the romance as the novel's primary generic source: "novels are romances—but romances which have to negotiate the prosaic world of modern civilization . . . [a] place where romantic idealism and disenchanted realism meet" (EN, 2, 3). Hence the temptation to invoke *Don Quixote* as the first novel—a temptation that Eagleton tries to resist. He prefers to say that "it is less the origin of the genre than a novel about the origin of the novel" (EN, 3)—not so much the first literary conjunction of romance and realism, but rather a novel whose topic is what happens, in life and in literature, when romantic idealism collides with the real world.

These last remarks seem hasty. They do not take the time to distinguish the specific literary genre of romance from the contemporary idea of romantic fiction (with its heroes and villains, its fantasies and fairy-tale endings); and if *Don Quixote* does turn the clash between romance and realism into a thematic as well as a formal issue, that can hardly debar it from being the first instance of the genre, for any text that makes a thematic issue of that clash might perfectly well also exemplify it in formal terms. What *Don Quixote* does make clear is how small the step is from exemplifying this formal issue to explicitly reflecting upon it—how little separates the cannibalistic nature of the genre as such from the adoption of a critical, questioning relation to those formal matters in the body of the text. For when Eagleton talks of a clash between romance and realism, he means that the generic conventions of romance appear to the novelist to misrepresent the nature of reality; they no longer facilitate a way of representing the world that has any chance of seeming accurately to capture its nature as opposed to presenting a mere appearance or representation of it, hence a kind of falsification of it. It is precisely the desire to make reality apparent to the reader that forces the novelist to rethink the defining conventions of romance; the novel's endemic questioning of the generic conventions it inherits is in the name of a more faithful representation of the real. In effect, then, Eagleton's discussion suggests that the novel's combination of antigenericism and realism naturally engenders a distinctively modernist relation to itself from the outset. Modernism, realism, and the novel are as if made for one another.

A similar suggestion is developed in more careful and detailed terms in Ian Watt's classic study of the origin of the genre of the novel in the West, *The Rise of the Novel*.[4] He too accepts the common view that realism is the defining feature of the novel form, but he also recognizes that this term needs further explanation, and (in a move that seems highly suggestive in the present context) he proposes that the literary critics and historians should turn to another discipline to provide the resources for so doing. His reasoning is straightforward:

> [There is] an issue which the novel raises more sharply than any other literary form—the problem of the correspondence between the literary work and the reality which it imitates. This is essentially an epistemological problem, and it therefore seems likely that the nature of the novel's realism . . . can best be clarified by the help of those professionally concerned with the analysis of concepts, the philosophers. (RN, 11)

It is not clear why Watt takes this problem to be specifically epistemological, since it does not appear to concern issues of knowledge, certainty, and evidence, but rather what we mean by the concept of representation; but this puzzle does not affect the basic thrust of his analysis, so we can set it aside. In its philosophical context, Watt argues that realism was for a long time understood as the view of the scholastic Realists of the Middle Ages, namely, that the true realities are not the particular, concrete objects of sense perception but universals, classes, or other abstractions. What

---

[4] (London: Pimlico, 2000), hereafter RN. First published in 1957.

happens in the modern period in philosophy, in the defining work of Locke and Descartes, is that this inheritance is rejected. Distinctively modern realism begins from the position that abstract universals are of dubious validity, that truth can be discovered by the individual through the appropriate use of her senses, and that the methods to be employed in the pursuit of truth should be at once critical, antitraditional, and innovating. In all these respects, Watt argues, there are striking analogies between modern philosophical realism and the novel as it originated in the work of Defoe, Richardson, and Fielding.

For example, where Cartesian method embodied the assumption that the pursuit of truth is a wholly individual matter, logically independent of conclusions endorsed on the authority of traditions of past thought, and indeed as more likely to be attained by a departure from those traditions, so the novelists rejected their culture's general tendency to make conformity to traditional literary-generic practice the major test of truth. Whereas literary success was previously a matter of the author's skill in handling the formal conventions of his chosen genre, work in a genre whose avowed goal is that of conveying the impression of fidelity to human experience could only be endangered by attention to any preestablished formal conventions. "What is often felt as the formlessness of the novel, as compared, say, with tragedy or the ode, probably follows from this: the poverty of the novel's formal conventions would seem to be the price it must pay for its realism" (RN, 13). The resulting sense of opposition between convention and originality also affected the novelist's relation to existing plot-structures. Watts claims that Defoe and Richardson were the first great writers in Western literature who did not take their plots from mythology, history, legend, or previous literature. Their predecessors did so, in the last analysis, because they accepted the traditional view that Nature is essentially complete and unchanging, and so could assume that its legendary and historical records constituted a definitive repertoire of human experience. This is in large part why the meaning of "originality" underwent a semantic reversal, in parallel with that of realism, from meaning "having existed from the first" to "underived, independent, first-hand."

In the novel, accordingly, plot-structure was intended to flow purely from the author's sense of what his specific characters might plausibly do next; and those characters were supposed to be particular individuals rather than instantiations of types or archetypes, acting out their lives against culturally and historically specific circumstances. As a result, the representation of time and space took on a distinctively particularistic turn: both individual characters and their environments are rooted in highly specific histories, the narratives of their actions develop increasingly detailed and internally coherent time-schemes, and the settings of those actions take on increasing solidity of specification.

These basically realistic intentions required something rather different from the accepted modes of literary prose. Rather than bestowing beauty on description and action by the resources of rhetoric, which meant the skilful inflection of existing literary forms, Defoe and Richardson aimed exclusively to make their words bring their purported referents home to the reader in all their concrete particularity, and so produced primarily denotative language even at the cost of verboseness, repetition, or parenthesis. They thereby invited criticism from those wedded to prior literary modes for their inelegant, clumsy, and artless incompetence as writers. As Watt summarises it:

> It would appear, then, that the function of the language is much more largely referential in the novel than in other literary forms; that the genre itself works by exhaustive presentation rather than by elegant concentration. This fact would no doubt explain . . . why the novel is the most translatable of the genres; why many undoubtedly great novelists . . . often write gracelessly, and sometimes with downright vulgarity; and why the novel has less need of historical and literary commentary than other genres—its formal convention forces it to supply its own footnotes. (RN, 30)

Watts is, however, careful to bring out the point about this novelistic pursuit of realism that points the genre in the direction of modernist preoccupations: "Formal realism is, of course . . . only a convention; and there is no reason why the report on human life which is presented by it should in fact be any truer than those presented through the very different conventions of other literary genres" (RN, 32–33). Those who preceded the novelists, and operated in other literary genres, not only shared the novelistic desire for a close correspondence between art and life (in the sense of pursuing the truth about that life); they also deployed some of the technical resources of formal realism to do it, even if not in such a total or all-pervading way. For the novelists, then, their unprecedented utilization of those resources amounted to a critical questioning of the other literary conventions they inherited, but in the name of satisfying the same desire as those who employed those conventions. And yet, necessarily, their formal realism could do no more than secure an impression of reality, or create in their readers the conviction that what the text so directly and immediately conveyed to them was a full and authentic report of individual human experience. In truth, however, that text remained a text: the individuals it portrayed did not exist, the specific resources used to create the impression of their reality were no less conventional than those of any other literary genre, and the text as a whole could not but be anything other than a linguistic representation of the real rather than reality itself.

It was not long before the conventionality of the conventions of formal realism became apparent, both to readers and to other novelists, to inevitably subversive effect. By the 1760s, Laurence Sterne was in a position to write a text that simultaneously deploys the resources of formal realism to great effect in creating the impression of reality, but also makes their conventionality a thematic as well as a formal issue, to the point of parody—in *Tristram Shandy*. But precisely by pursuing the latently absurd implications of such conventions, by for example attempting to live up to the requirement that there be a one-to-one temporal correspondence between the novel and the reader's experience of it, Sterne achieves an effect of realism. The reader thinks: if someone really did try to write in accordance with this convention, absurdity of just this kind would really result; and so Sterne manages to recreates the impression of Tristram as a real individual, precisely by allowing him to enact the deconstruction of a preceding convention for the representation of reality—thus showing it to be no more than a convention, and effacing the conventionality of the specific literary means by which this revelation is achieved. In this way, such critical questioning of the novelist's inheritance of convention remains in the service of creating an impression of reality.

The history of the novel since Defoe, Richardson, and Sterne might therefore be written entirely in terms of the ways in which novelists repeatedly subject their inheritance of realistic conventions to critical questioning in order to re-create the impression of reality in their readers (in large part by encouraging those readers to see prior uses of convention to represent the real as merely conventional in contrast with their own, far more convincing ones). This reflexive or deconstructive operation is not something that began with the modernist literary projects of Joyce and T. S. Eliot; it can be traced back through Hardy and Dickens, Austen and Scott, to Swift and Sterne and so to the origin of the genre itself. In effect, then, it is not simply that the novel has a cannibalistic relation to other literary genres; from the outset, its practitioners had a similarly Oedipal relation to prior examples within the genre of the novel, and so to the prior conventions within which they necessarily operated.

The novel's association with originality is thus both external and internal: it endlessly renews its claim to be an unprecedentedly faithful representation of individual human experience of the world in comparison with other literary genres precisely by claiming to be more faithful to that task even than its novelistic predecessors. Only by ceaselessly testing, criticising, and otherwise innovating with respect to the conventions through which it represents reality can the novelist create the impression that, unlike her predecessors' merely conventional efforts, she is conveying reality to her readers as it really is for the first time. And since her best efforts could only result in the recreation of new conventions, they —

and so the impression of reality they make possible—will inevitably be vulnerable to the critical questioning of her own successors.

It is not hard to see the potential open-endedness of this parasitic process; but neither is it hard to see how, sooner or later, the fact that no novel could ultimately be anything other than a convention-bound representation of reality of one kind or another might test the faith of both novelist and reader in the very possibility of an authentic representation of individual human experience. One might think of the difference between the modernist and the postmodernist as determined by whether, in the face of this realization, the novelist can keep his faith in realism, or whether he finds himself forced to abjure it.

Realism and the Realistic Spirit: The Case of Philosophy

As Ian Watt makes clear by implication, realism is both a recognized category of philosophical thought and a contested one. Aiming to be realistic is a central, perhaps even a defining, motivation in philosophy, insofar as it amounts to grasping the truth of things, the way things really are; but no sooner does one philosophical position or approach claim to have achieved that aim than its successors criticise it precisely for failing to have done so, and substitute what they take to be an more authentic form of realism. Watt concentrates on the particularly stark case of the Scholastics, on the one hand, and the early modern Rationalists and Empiricists, on the other; the Scholastic version of realism is not simply criticised but rather inverted or turned inside-out by Descartes and Locke, all in the name of doing philosophy in a genuinely realistic spirit. But of course, Cartesian method and British Empiricist doctrines are by no means the last embodiment of philosophy's aspiration to realism; so anyone who finds at all plausible Watt's guiding intuition that realism in the novel can best be understood in relation to philosophical understandings of realism should recognize that more recent phases of philosophical work on this issue may open up possibilities of understanding that go far beyond early modern conceptions of what realism might be.

As it happens, Cora Diamond traces some of the further history of this dialectic in a paper entitled "Realism and the Realistic Spirit."[5] This essay presents itself as an attempt to understand Wittgenstein's remark, "not empiricism and yet realism in philosophy, that is the hardest thing"; and it takes its preliminary bearings from an understanding of what realism means outside philosophy—most specifically, in the field of literature. In

[5] Included in *The Realistic Spirit*.

short, it seems entirely congruent with the intellectual orientation of Watt's classic work; thus a closer examination of it might help to break up any unquestioned assumption that early modern rationalism and empiricism might remain the best contemporary contenders for embodiments of an authentically realistic spirit in philosophy, and so the most suitable points of comparison for illuminating realist projects in literature such as that of Coetzee.

After first identifying a realistic attitude as a refusal to maintain one's preconceptions in the teeth of the facts, Diamond uses literary realism to flesh out this skeleton definition. She characterises the realist novel as presenting individual characters built out of detailed observations rather than character types whose qualities are determined in advance by labels, as excluding certain kinds of happening (magical, fantastic, fairy-tale) from its narratives, and as placing immense weight on causal connections—on ensuring that plot developments are congruent with the way things (physical, social, and cultural) actually work. These are all features of literary realism underlined in Watt's argument, and they allow Diamond to present Berkeley as an example of another early modern philosopher whose enterprise is both anti-empiricist (or at least hostile to any Lockean variant of empiricism) and nevertheless realistic.

Berkeley freely acknowledges that such an empiricist thinks of himself as a realist; when, for example, he invokes an idea of matter as something essential to our sense of reality as existing independently of us. But his understanding of this idea is such as to subvert his realist enterprise. For if matter is defined as a kind of real existence that is absolutely distinct from and independent of its being perceived—such that if a horse is real, what makes it real is that its sensible appearances to us are caused by qualities inhering in a material body whose existence is absolutely independent of our own—then the reality of that horse is something that necessarily transcends anything we might be made aware of by our senses. After all, no matter how things appear to us to be, how they actually are is surely another, essentially independent matter.

But Berkeley points out that this realist faces a dilemma. Either he can explain to us how we can tell the difference between real and chimerical experience (in which case, his characterisation of real existence as necessarily transcendent of the realm of appearance cannot be right, since any such technique of judgement must be based on perceptible differences between the real and the chimerical); or he cannot, in which case his idea of real existence is revealed to be empty—not a mistake, but a fantasy of what reality might be.

It is critical to Diamond that Berkeley's realistic critique of such "realism" diagnoses their idea of reality as not mistaken (and so at least intelligible, coherent) but rather chimerical or fantastic—as only appearing to make sense or have content. In other words, once our conviction in any such conception of reality and realism falls away, it can seem no more than a naïve illusion: not even mere words, just marks on a page. More specifically, what happens is that the would-be realist is prevented from actually looking to see how we draw the distinction between the real and the chimerical, because he thinks that he knows in advance what reality must amount to; so he knows that it must be there, even if it does not, for all the world, appear to be. The essence of the real is thus always hidden; what is open to sight simply cannot be all that there is to reality. So we refuse to be satisfied with all that there is to see, because we take the essence of what there is to be captured in an idea of the real that turns out to be the mere appearance of an idea—devoid of content, empty of meaning.

This is not to say that the realistic spirit requires us to accept any and all claims about how things are, simply by virtue of the fact that those claims conform to the conventions governing a particular practice of judgement and assertion. Where Watt talks of the conventions of medieval literary rhetoric, Diamond refers to the genre of hagiography. Works in that genre make a variety of claims about their subjects that would normally be subject to certain demands and constraints, such as coherence with the evidence or with other claims in the hagiographic text. Yet the author of a text that claims that "St N. hid the signs of divine favour" while other parts of that same text show or imply that his companions quickly discovered those signs gives no indication of discomfort about this, and neither should any of his readers who understand that such reticence was a generic mark of sainthood, not a historical claim about St. N. in particular. Nevertheless, the historian can come along and ask whether or not St. N. really did hide the signs of divine favour; and it makes perfect sense to think that there is a truth of the matter that is not settled by the existence of these generic conventions, and that might turn out to demonstrate that the hagiography is simply not true in this respect. This reveals no deep flaw in the practice of hagiography; but its internal coherence does not exclude a priori the possibility of revealing, in a realistic spirit, that many of its claims were false.

In this elementary version of realism, we have a perfectly valid contrast between the way things were said to be (even when those remarks adhere to the conventions of a practice) and what the facts really were. The philosophical realists that Berkeley has in his critical sights think that they are taking up an analogous position with respect to our practices of distinguishing the real from the chimerical; but their conviction that there is any such room is itself another fantasy (not a mistake). For they take our genuine scientific discoveries about the dependence of perception on the body and its environment to imply that we never perceive material objects but only their effects; the objects themselves do not and could not have sensible qualities, but only the power to produce certain experiences in us.

> Here the philosophical realist is engaging in the purest fantasy. He *thinks* he thinks of objects with non-sensible properties and unknown natures, he *thinks* he thinks of matter, a substratum of the objects of sense, but all he has is a construction of *words*, linguistic surface, as far removed from any practice of comparison with the world as is the story of St. Columcille. (RS, 58)

For what, after all, is the content of a Lockean idea of matter as "something, I know not what"? How might its use be guided or governed? In truth, the realist's critique of our everyday practices of judging the reality of things is in the name of a fantasy of reality; he is subject to exactly the kind of internal incoherence that he attributes to those practices.

Perhaps unsurprisingly, the philosophical position from which Berkeley criticizes these realists as ultimately irresponsible to the way things really are is itself subject to exactly the same criticism. For example, it relies just as much as its opponents on a notion of what is given, the irreducible basis of our knowledge of the world; Berkeley may think of this given as God's language of signs, but the signs of that language are sense-data—the look of the tree, the taste of the cherry. And this preconception—that there is a given, and what it consists in—doubly disables his own attempt at realism, by licensing him to conclude that when we say that there is a tree, we speak as if we actually saw what is merely suggested to me by the tree-appearance. Once again, the essence of reality seems to be hidden, and our everyday actual practices of judgement about material objects are rejected as irresponsible on the basis of an ultimately empty preconception about what is real.

In Diamond's view, what must be rejected here in a genuinely realistic spirit is not Berkeley's conception of what is given, so much as the very idea of an ultimate, irreducible realm of the given as such. For that idea—with its invocation of an absolute or unconditioned underpinning of reality—in fact encodes an essentially unrealistic conception of what a genuine grasp of our ideas, concepts, or words (of anything whatever) might conceivably amount to.

Suppose, for example, that we are teaching someone how to follow a rule, or engage in any kind of uniform activity. Wittgenstein notoriously points out that some pupils, given exactly the range of ordinary examples that we typically give one another in such teaching contexts, might go on from them in quite different ways, and yet take themselves to be going on in the same way, understanding differently what those examples show. Having received and responded in the usual way to a familiar range of small numbers when being taught how to add two, such a deviant pupil might go on above 1,000 to produce the sequence 1,004, 1,008, and so on—all the while declaring that he is doing exactly what he did before. Suppose we acknowledge this to be possible; what follows?

On one understanding, it shows that any continuation of the number sequence stands in any number of different describable relations to the earlier part of the sequence—that there is no such thing as *the* relation in which each stands to what is already there, and so no prospect of explaining the particular continuation I had in mind to the deviant pupil by defining it as *the* relation in which the continuations I made stand to the earlier sequence I generated. Someone who knew only that there is *some* relation in which all the exemplary continuations he had been shown stood to what went before, and that his continuations should stand in that same relation to what he did before, would not yet know what he was supposed to do. So my own understanding of what he should do cannot reside solely in the sequence of examples of the sort we normally use in teaching. It must reside elsewhere; and then it becomes all-but-impossible to avoid understanding Wittgenstein as saying that this something extra resides in the shared form of life of the rule-following community.

But there is another way of taking Wittgenstein's example of the deviant pupil, and so of taking his claim that the best answer I can give to the question "what do I want him to do?" is an example or set of examples. He is not saying that philosophy can give a better or fuller answer to that question than we can if we restrict ourselves to what we ordinarily say and do. He is rather saying that the inclination to think that there is or could be such a better answer is confused, fantastic, illusory. The fact of the matter is that I can and do explain a particular rule to others by means of examples: he responds to them in a certain way, and I am satisfied. It is also true that in particular cases, with particular others and/or in particular circumstances, *certain* possibilities of misunderstanding may need to be ruled out; and it may even be the case that in certain highly unusual circumstances, the misunderstanding cannot be surmounted, so that I cannot explain to this particular other in those circumstances what rule I mean him to be following. But the reality of these specific possibilities of misunderstanding does not show that outside those circumstances, and indeed across the board, we need an account of what it is to "go on in a particular way" that is entirely independent of the specific uptake or responses of any particular pupil.

It is as if, as philosophers, we think that any adequate elucidation of rule-following, and so conceptual or linguistic meaning, must pick out something in the realm of things-that-might-possibly-be-meant; not possibly-in-human-practice, but in some other sense that is utterly independent of what actually goes on in our lives. The fact that someone very different from us might take an explanation by examples very differently is taken to show that there is a position in an absolute space of things-that-I-might-possibly-mean that must be explicitly excluded if my explanation is adequately to represent what I mean. But the idea of such a space, as opposed to the idea of a real semantic space in which I actually operate in my life with others, is itself a fantasy. And this is why Wittgenstein draws attention to our actual use of examples in real life: not because he hopes that it will reveal the latent inadequacy of what ordinarily counts as an adequate explanation, but rather because he means to let us see that, by contrast, the idea of "explaining what I mean" in its philosophical context is idling, doing no work at all. And yet, cut free from its ordinary functioning, we take it to determine a contentful ideal of what a properly realistic philosophical explanation of anything at all must look like. Philosophy in a truly realistic spirit would refrain from attempting to answer any question that presupposes any such fantastic standard of adequacy for its answers.

On this understanding of realism in philosophy, then, it finds expression in the refusal to ask certain kinds of question, in the recognition that what seems to be an essential underpinning of the real may turn out to be pure illusion, and in the willingness to recognise that what might seem like the record of a few details scattered across the darkness (hence essentially in need of supplementation) is in fact a snapshot of the scene as a whole, human life as it really is. As Vicki Hearne earlier expressed the situation: what may seem like darkness can be read, and what appear to be gaps are nothing of the kind. As we shall see, the refusal to give us what we feel that we need may turn out to be the purest kind of fidelity to reality in the genre of the novel as well; in our present circumstances, Coetzee's apparent austerity of style and content may in fact contain all the richness that realism could conceivably provide. Less may not be more; but it may nevertheless (despite the convictions of his realist predecessors in the genre) be enough.

MODERNISM, REALISM, AND CRITICISM: THE CASE OF PAINTING

It might also help to clarify the dialectical interplay of realism and modernism in the context of the novel (this time focusing more on the concept of modernism) by examining the way in which it worked itself out in a cognate artistic field—that of modern painting. This historical development has been traced out in compelling detail by the art historian and critic Michael Fried, in a mighty trilogy of texts devoted to exploring the roots and genesis of pictorial modernism: *Absorption and Theatrical-*

ity (1980), *Courbet's Realism* (1990), and *Manet's Modernism* (1996).[6] And what he claims to find is an accelerating process of the critical questioning of realist conventions that is strikingly analogous to the one we have identified in the history of the novel, and occurs at roughly the same historical epoch.

First, however, it is important to emphasise that Fried understands that much-contested term, "modernism," in what he thinks of as an antireductionist or anti-essentialist way.[7] For him, modernist painters can no longer rely on agreed upon conventions inherited from the past to establish that what they are producing is indeed painting—a contribution to that same tradition of artistic endeavour. Instead, they must test those conventions by testing which can be discarded or modified in their work without damaging that work's capacity to bear comparison with the indisputably great work previously produced in the tradition. The issue of what is to count as a painting is therefore at stake in each painting, and each painting can alter our conception of what a painting is; accordingly, a painting's success or failure puts in question its representation of the living present of the tradition it aims to inherit.

Fried thus rejects two key assumptions lying behind Clement Greenberg's notorious assertion that, by the early 1960s, modernist painters had established that "the observance of [flatness and the delimitation of flatness] is enough to create an object which can be experienced as a picture; thus a stretched or tacked-up canvas already exists as a picture—though not necessarily a successful one." For Fried does not assume either that what modernist painters discover in their work is the irreducible essence of all painting, or that any such discovery might be establishable independently of establishing the value of their paintings as works of art. On his view, what modernist painters discover in their work is that which, at the relevant moment in painting's history, is capable of establishing their work's identity as painting by providing artistic solutions to problems posed in and by the development of their art—something Fried thinks of as a matter of producing work that stands up to comparison with the great art of the past (both modernist and premodernist) by acknowledging the conditions of that art.

The purpose of Fried's trilogy is to demonstrate how Manet's work might be characterised as modernist in this sense, by locating his achievement in relation to the history of French, and so European, painting; and

---

[6] *Absorption and Theatricality: Painting and Beholder in the Age of Diderot* (Chicago: University of Chicago Press, 1980), hereafter AAT; *Courbet's Realism* (Chicago: University of Chicago Press, 1990); *Manet's Modernism* (Chicago: University of Chicago Press, 1996).

[7] he highly influential series of articles in which Fried developed his understanding of modernism in the 1960s and 1970s was collected and republished under the title *Art and Objecthood* (Chicago: University of Chicago Press, 1998).

that demonstration takes off from a particular reading of the way in which Diderot (among others) understood the contemporary condition of that enterprise. Diderot recognised the primordial convention that paintings are made to be beheld, but he felt that the presence of a beholder was not any longer something that a painter could simply take for granted; it must rather be earned, accomplished, or at least powerfully affirmed by the painting itself. In short, paintings must attract, arrest, and enthrall the beholder, hold him there as if spellbound. But Diderot further argued that if, in doing so, the painting betrayed too blatant an awareness of the beholder's presence, it would thereby court theatricality, making the beholder aware of the illusion of reality by means of which he had been halted in front of the painting, and so breaking its spell. The tension could be resolved only if a means could be found of securing the behold-er's presence by establishing the fiction of his absence; hence Diderot's particular advocacy of history painting. The inherent drama of the scenes represented in such paintings could match the beholder's increasingly de-manding need to be enthralled; and its orientation to past events made more plausible the illusion that the *dramatis personae* had determined their own positions and groupings (critical to what Diderot calls the paint-ing's success as a dramatically unified composition or "tableau"), unlike work in such genres as landscape and still-life painting.

Fried comments as follows:

> This paradox directs attention to the problematic character not only of the painting-beholder relationship but of something still more fundamental—the *object*-beholder (one is tempted to say object-"subject") relationship which the painting-beholder relationship epitomizes. In Diderot's writings on painting and drama, the object-beholder relationship as such, the very condition of spec-tatordom, stands indicted as theatrical, a medium of dislocation and estrange-ment rather than of absorption, sympathy, self-transcendence; and the success of both arts, in fact their continued functioning as major expressions of the human spirit, are held to depend on whether or not painter and dramatist are able to undo that state of affairs, to *de-theatricalize beholding* and so make it once again a mode of access to truth and conviction. . . . What is called for, in other words, is at one and the same time the creation of a new sort of object—the fully realized *tableau*—and the constitution of a new sort of beholder—a new "subject"—whose innermost nature would consist in the conviction of his absence from the scene of representation. (AAT, 103–4)

The inherent ambiguity of Fried's reference here to "the scene of represen-tation" is pivotal to his analysis. It might most naturally be taken to refer to the scene represented or depicted in the painting; but it also refers to the literal scene within which such representational fictions are achieved, the situation of the beholder standing before a painted canvas in order to see the scene it depicts. On Fried's analysis, painting's power to create convincingly realistic fictional scenes of representation was now seen as threatened by its embeddedness in the literal scene of representation; the beholder's absorption in the fictional scene could now be achieved only by somehow negating or neutralizing his presence before the canvas depicting that scene.

The critical point for Fried, however, is that any such achievement could itself only be a supreme fiction. For of course, the dramatic illusion of reality in painting can operate only in the context of the literal scene of representation, so the beholder's existence before the canvas could no more be negated or denied in any literal or straightforward sense than could the canvas's existence before the beholder; indeed, to aim for the one is to aim for the other. Consequently, the antitheatrical tradition Fried sees as emerging with Diderot and the painters who share his understanding of their situation in effect commits itself to the entirely incoherent aim of denying the material reality of its own works as well as the material reality of those who behold them.

Nevertheless, the proponents of this tradition were responding to a real problem. They sensed that the beholders of paintings were becoming alienated from the objects of their beholding—no longer absorbed or enthralled by canvasses *qua* paintings, *qua* fictional scenes of representation; and they rightly saw such alienation as a sceptical threat to painting's capacity to maintain its status as a major art form. Their (metaphysical) error was to attribute this scepticism to spectatordom as such, rather than to the increasingly exhausted powers of traditional modes of creating absorption in the dramatic illusions of painting. For they assumed that what was undermining the beholder's capacity to be absorbed by the dramatic illusion of any painting was the ineluctable fact of his existence as an embodied being standing before a pigment-smeared canvas, rather than some developing loss of conviction in a prevailing system of painterly conventions for creating this illusion. Consequently, they took their painting's continued capacity to create dramatic illusion as dependent upon those works embodying denials of the literal or physical reality of both beholder and painting—strategies of negation that became increasingly extreme as previous ones necessarily failed to achieve their incoherent purpose, and thus ironically contributed by their resultant theatricality to the beholder's intensifying loss of conviction in the dramatic illusions of painting.

An alternative antitheatrical strategy, which Fried primarily associates with Manet, would be to accommodate or defuse the threat of scepticism by acknowledging the metaphysical constraints of the literal scene of representation—by producing work that is able to find a source of new artistic convention in taking cognizance of the necessary physicality or embodiedness of painting and beholder, of the fact that (if not above all then at least before all) the two face one another in space and time, and that any fictive or dramatic encounter they facilitate depends upon that fact and its implications. Both antitheatrical strategies would then be responding to the same metaphysical fact about both painting and beholder. Since a painting is both canvas and depiction, its beholder is at once the beholder of a physical object and of a fictional scene of representation: in this sense, beholding is an inherently doubled or dual mode of subject/object relations. One mode of antitheatricality interprets this duality as self-cancelling: either literal beholding negates its fictional counterpart or vice versa, so painting must commit itself to the production of works that deny their own literality and thereby attempt to constitute a beholder whose literality is negated. The other interprets the duality as ineliminable and therefore aims to produce convincing representational works that simultaneously acknowledge their own literality and thereby construct a beholder capable of acknowledging his own literal presence.

The further development of such antitheatrical painting (particularly in the work of Courbet) is shown by Fried to reveal a further internal complexity in this evolving concept of the beholder—one that emerges once one finds oneself asking whether, and in what ways, the painter of a given painting is merely one more beholder of it. In one sense, the painter is simply the first beholder of a finished painting, the first to see it after the last brushstroke is applied; his priority is purely temporal, and to this extent the beholding position he occupies by virtue of his status as the painting's creator is identical with that of any other beholder of that painting. On the other hand, the painter necessarily also beholds the process of creating the painting, and that privilege—of beholding the application of every one of its brushstrokes, the painting of the painting—belongs to no other beholder (except by accident, as it were). And yet, even though these two beholding functions (that of the painter-beholder and that of the beholder *tout court*) diverge in their relation or access to the process or act of painting the painting, there is no reason why any beholder of a finished painting cannot view it as the product of a process—that is, incorporate into his encounter with the painting an understanding that it is essentially the result of human labour, the trace or remainder of an act of painting. He can, in short, acknowledge the paintedness of the painting, its having been painted.

We might think of this as a third dimension or level of the painting–beholder relationship. The painting exists not just as physical object and as fictional scene of representation, but as product—as the result of meaningful human activity; the beholder not only perceives an object and is absorbed in a dramatic illusion, but confronts the work of another human being. Fried's talk of "the scene of representation" thereby acquires or

reveals a further significance. As well as referring to the painting understood as representing a scene, and to the scene of the beholder's literal
confrontation with the representational canvas, the phrase can also refer
to the scene in the artist's studio, the scene of his representational efforts.
And just as Fried earlier distinguishes painterly attempts to negate the fact
that paintings are made to be beheld from attempts to acknowledge it,
so he now distinguishes what he sees as Courbet's ultimately incoherent
attempt to negate the fact that paintings are the intentional product of
human activity (in what he calls his project of quasi-corporeal merger
with the painting—Courbet's attempts to incorporate himself into the
depicted scene) from an alternative antitheatrical possibility: that of producing work that might acknowledge its origins in human action, and
thereby make it possible for a beholder to acknowledge his role as beholder of an intentional or worked object. This latter possibility, of producing paintings in which the act of painting is prolonged within the work
itself by acknowledgment rather than denial, and without denying its representational powers, is one that Fried attributes to Manet.

Take, for example, Manet's use of the model. The issues arising from
this fact about the production of paintings threatened to destabilize realism in the Diderotian tradition. For on the one hand, verisimilitude
seemed to require that the painter admit to his reliance upon a real human
being in the production of his painting; but on the other, someone holding
a stationary pose under the artist's gaze for long stretches of time introduced the threat of theatricality. According to Fried, Manet confronts
this issue by directing his viewers' attention to the relationships between
painter, painting, and model with unprecedented force, and he does so
precisely in order to acknowledge the divisions Courbet's work helped to
identify within the beholding function *tout court*.

For by emphasising the literal reality of the model over the fictional
reality of the depicted person for which she is the model, Manet's paintings direct attention to the painter's privileged capacity to behold the
model while she is being painted, and thereby to the beholder of the finished painting's exclusion from that position; the beholder *tout court*
just is someone to whom the painting, but not the model, is present. Nevertheless, the beholder can and does behold the figures in the painting,
the people it depicts or represents; indeed, it is only through his perception
of these figures that the painting can insist on his exclusion from the
presence of the models on which they are based. So that very insistence
reinforces the beholder's awareness of himself before the representational
canvas. Furthermore, the painting's insistence on the model's absence
from the beholder questions the finality of the split between the beholder
and the painter-beholder. For a painting can insist on the painter's
privileged access to the process of painting the painting, and so to the

scene of representation that is the artist's studio, only by prolonging the act of painting within the painting itself; and this prolongation offers the beholder the opportunity to acknowledge the paintedness of the painting, the fact of its having been painted. In this sense, the difference between the painter-beholder and the beholder is that between seeing a painting's being painted and seeing a painting's having been painted; and although this difference might seem infinitely large, it can also seem vanishingly small. For one cannot acknowledge a painting as a product of human intentional action without acknowledging the process of which it is the product.

This is how Fried sees Manet as addressing rather than seeking to negate the beholder *qua* beholder of a humanly worked object. But the beholder is also the beholder of a physical object and a representation; how does Manet's art acknowledge those facets of the beholder? Here, the notion of the tableau becomes central.

In Diderot's writing and afterwards, the notion picks out an effect of unity, autonomy, and absorptive closure achieved by the painting *qua* dramatic illusion or depiction, whether by the dynamics of human action (as in history painting) or otherwise. In so doing, it effects an instantaneous and enduring enthralment in the viewer—offering immediate access to the depicted scene and holding the viewer indefinitely before the canvas depicting it. However, the tableau thereby also effectively keys itself to two distinct properties of easel paintings *qua* physical objects—that they are all surface, every element of which faces the beholder and can therefore be taken in all at once, and that they persist over time.

Since Manet is committed to liquidating the antitheatrical tradition that aimed at denying the beholder's existence by attempting to absolutize his absorption in the depicted scene, his work inevitably avoided the paradigm of the tableau, absorptively understood. Instead, he developed a new conception in which what Fried calls "facing" rather than absorptive closure would be the tableau's operative principle—in which the instantaneity and strikingness that most contemporary critics saw as achievable only through absorptive closure would be achieved instead through representational strategies of a fundamentally opposing kind (ones that some of his colleagues were beginning to associate with the portrait and its tendency to turn the faces of its figures towards the viewer). Thus, Manet systematically avoids depictions of people absorbed in what they are doing, tending rather to depict figures gazing directly out of the painting; he makes use of unintelligible subject matter and internally disparate *mise-en-scene*; he combines strong figural gestalts with abrupt tonal contrasts in a way that stamps out the depicted image; he executes his paintings with a marked lack of finish, and so on. In general terms, he does all he can to dramatize or underscore, and thereby to acknowledge, the primordial convention that paintings are made to be beheld, that they face their viewers with a representation. In so doing, he emphasizes the temporal instantaneity of his paintings, which in turn underscores the fact that, qua material objects, they are all surface and so can be taken in as a whole by those beholding them.

Manet's enterprise thus involves the simultaneous acknowledgment of the three dimensions of beholding or of the scene of representation, each keyed to the painting *qua* physical object, painted object, and/or depiction. Unlike the antitheatrical tradition he opposes, Manet's work does not presuppose that these elements necessarily eclipse or negate one another; but neither does it assume that they form self-contained parts of a self-sufficient whole. In that sense, where absorptive tableaus aim for a mode of closure that stands opposed to the fragmentary (to *morceaux*), Manet's anti-absorptive tableaus might also be called assemblages of *morceaux*—or better, as placing the *tableau/morceau* contrast in question. Fried's Manet rather sees the three conditions or dimensions of painting as engaged in a constant mutual confrontation or facing-off, each constraining and being constrained by the others, and each standing in need of acknowledgment by and through the others in a kind of productive and open-ended dialogue that can be brought to a provisional conclusion in particular works of painting, but for which no final, totalizing closure can ultimately be imagined.

Fried's third volume has a further, controversial story to tell about the complex historical developments that connect Manet's achievements to those of American and European painting and sculpture of the 1950s and 1960s, via the development of Impressionism; but the part of it that I have attempted to summarise is, I hope, enough to suggest some striking similarities between the project of modernism as it evolves in painting and as it evolves in the novel. For what we see in Fried's Manet is someone whose work is in continuous critical dialogue with work of the past (his own and others), with each new work casting a new light on that past and each new conception of the past helping to bring about further work, with its own new historical perspective, and so endlessly on. In Manet's case, that critical dialogue is empowered by a sense that the beholders of painting are no longer gripped by its dramatic illusions of reality, no longer able simply to take it for granted that the canvasses before which they stand are (as it were) transparent windows through which one sees reality. And this loss of conviction in prevailing representational conventions is seen as threatening a far more serious loss of conviction in the practice of painting as such—in the very idea that pictorial representations might create an impression of reality whatever conventions they employ. But whereas one antitheatrical tradition takes it to be possible to re-create that impression of reality only by somehow denying or repressing the inherently conventional nature of the medium of painting as such, the other (with which Manet aligns himself) sees the incoherence of any such project, and proposes in turn to reconstruct its specific representational conventions in such a way as to acknowledge those apparently ineliminable conditions of pictorial representation of any kind.

What thereby finds acknowledgment is a threefold complexity inherent in anything Manet finds recognizable as a painting—its material reality as pigment on canvas, its capacity to generate fictional pictorial space (which relates it to a beholder), and its createdness (which relates its to a maker or producer). In other words, Manet paints out of the conviction that the inherent reliance of painting upon the work of the painter, a historical inheritance of representational conventions, and the engagement of the viewer can be acknowledged without giving up on the idea of (re-)creating in both viewer and painter alike the conviction that a particular work gives us access to important and valuable truths about human experience of the world that might stand comparison with great painting of the past. But the mode of that acknowledgment is not such as to engender an illusion of totality or coherence; rather, these mutually determining conditions are placed in a kind of open-ended dialogue or confrontation, without any sense that this conversation must or even will resolve itself into a synthesis beyond any further question. Indeed, any such sense would preclude future work in painting that might put this conception of what is essential to painting as such in question, and would itself be inconsistent with the historically questioning way in which this body of painterly work was itself begun and maintained.

One can see, I hope, how this modernist response to the history of painting as an undismissable problem might have its parallels in the field of literature in general, and the novel in particular. The modernist novelist will find himself unable simply to take for granted the prevailing conventions for the representation of reality as capable of engendering conviction in his readers, and yet unwilling to regard the impotence of those specific representational conventions, or the inherent conventionality of the representational enterprise as such, as a ground for giving up on the novel's characteristic commitment to represent reality. For why should the fact that any representation of reality is nevertheless and necessarily a representation of it and not the thing itself be a ground for giving up on the project of creating convincing representations *of reality*? This sounds rather like denying that photographs could possibly present us with nothing less than reality (could possibly be of real persons, objects, and environments) solely on the grounds that they are photographs. If the appropriate standard of realism in literature were that the text actually become or *be* that which it aims to represent, it could never be met; but that is because such a goal is incoherent or unintelligible, not because the novel is fated to fail to achieve a condition it could intelligibly satisfy. There is nothing here—no specific state or condition or achievement—that the realist novelist cannot attain, and hence no inherent contradiction in his project. What would truly be incoherent would be to define realism as successful only when the representation of reality is indistinguishable from the reality itself.

All novels deploy the inherently conventional medium of language, and the more specific conventions of a particular genre or medium of literature; all have authors and readers, makers and consumers of these textual productions. If they did not, they would not and could not be novels at all. So one cannot intelligibly reject realistic novels as necessarily failures simply on the grounds that they rely on representational conventions of some kind, any more than one can subvert the realistic power of a particular Rembrandt portrait by pointing out that it consists of pigment on canvas. These representational conditions cannot be transcended; but that is precisely why their sheer presence cannot constitute a reason for abandoning the very idea of a realistic representation. It may, however, be the case that at certain points in the history of the realist project in the genre of the novel, those conditions can no longer simply be taken for granted; they must rather be acknowledged in and by the novel itself, if the genre of the novel as such is to maintain its capacity to find acknowledgment by author and reader alike as conveying an authentic impression of reality. And as we shall see in the following chapter, Costello's and Coetzee's ways of attempting to effect such an acknowledgment exemplify a Manet-like refusal of totality, coherence, and frictionless synthesis.

In this understanding of modernism, then, there is no inherent opposition between modernism and realism; on the contrary, faithfulness to the realist impulse that is so deeply embedded in the genre of the novel may be precisely what pushes a writer into the condition of modernism. As Toril Moi has recently argued, elaborating Fried's basic conceptual matrix in the context of nineteenth-century literature, the modernist's true opposite is rather the idealist—understood as the representative of an approach to aesthetics that regards truth, beauty, and goodness as inextricably intertwined, and that can accordingly legitimate literary realism only on condition that it finds beauty and goodness to be the underlying truth about reality.[8] Cora Diamond would think of this as a fundamental betrayal of the realist impulse, insofar as it amounts to the refusal to accept as real

---

[8] See the opening chapters of her *Henrik Ibsen and the Birth of Modernism* (Oxford: Oxford University Press, 2006).

anything that does not fit a predetermined set of ideals. Genuine realism must therefore oppose idealism, thus understood; and it may feel that the most effective way to do so would be to portray the necessary embeddedness of any set of ideals in reality—in the complex, multifaceted contexts of material, social, and cultural conditions. As we shall see, Coetzee appears to be one such modernist realist.

Chapter Ten

COSTELLO'S REALIST MODERNISM,
AND COETZEE'S

I N THE PREVIOUS CHAPTER, I portrayed interrelated elements of work by Eagleton, Watt, Diamond, and Fried in order to articulate a general context (Fried himself might think of it as a nonabsorptive tableau of intellectual *morceaux*) embodying the thought that the genre of the novel is inherently implicated in the projects of realism and modernism. In this chapter, I want to trace out in some detail the way in which Costello's Stowe acceptance speech utilizes Kafka's "Report to an Academy" in order to specify her particular relation to this nest of problems, and so helps to specify our understanding of Coetzee's relation to that same conceptual nexus.

COSTELLO: REALISM AS EMBEDDING

Costello begins by pointing out that, because Kafka's canonically modernist tale consists of a monologue by Red Peter, there is no means for either speaker or audience to be inspected with an outsider's eye. The speaker may be an ape, or a human being deluded into thinking that he is an ape, or a human being presenting himself as an ape for rhetorical purposes. The audience may be a collection of bewhiskered red-faced gentlemen-explorers, or Red Peter's fellow apes, either trained up so as to be capable at least of listening, even if not of speaking, or else simply chained to their seats.

> We don't know. We don't know and will never know, with certainty, what is really going on in this story: whether it is about a man speaking to men or an ape speaking to apes or an ape speaking to men or a man speaking to apes (though the last is, I think, unlikely) or even just a parrot speaking to parrots.
>
> There used to be a time when we knew. We used to believe that when the text said, "On the table stood a glass of water," there was indeed a table, and a glass of water on it, and we had only to look in the word-mirror of the text to see them.
>
> But all that has ended. The word-mirror is broken, irreparably, it seems. About what is really going on in the lecture hall your guess is as good as mine:

men and men, men and apes, apes and men, apes and apes. The lecture hall itself may be nothing but a zoo. The words on the page will no longer stand up and be counted, each proclaiming "I mean what I mean!" The dictionary that used to stand beside the Bible and the works of Shakespeare above the fireplace, where in pious Roman homes the household gods were kept, has become just one code book among many. . . .

We could think of this as a tragic turn of events, were it not that it is hard to have respect for whatever was the bottom that dropped out—it looks to us like an illusion now, one of those illusions sustained only by the concentrated gaze of everyone in the room. Remove your gaze for but an instant, and the mirror falls to the floor and shatters. (EC, 19–20)

This way of presenting the threatened exhaustion of literary realism is more complex than it may appear. At first glance, it seems that Costello is simply endorsing the conclusion that the very idea of a project of representing reality in modern literature has ended, that the ideal of the word-mirror has shattered irreparably, and that it has done so because words can no longer be regarded as responsible to their referents, no longer willing or able to go proxy for what they claim to represent. Indeed, she seems to think that any sense of tragic loss attending this realization is itself illusory; for the very idea that representations might embody reality seems naïve and jejune, evincing a hopeless failure to appreciate the obvious and inexpungeable difference between words and world—between the phrase "a glass of water" and a glass of water. Once we admit that novels are made of words, the pious idea that they might give access to a reality beyond themselves will inevitably dissipate, leaving behind the realization that literature is only a world of words, an endlessly receding horizon of texts.

But to settle for this reading of her speech, one must repress the fact that Costello continues to think of the dictionary as one kind of code book, and so of words as capable of being decoded or deciphered, hence as having sense and reference. What she actually says is rather that the dictionary has lost a certain kind of pious preeminence, one that embodied an inappropriate attempt to divinize or transcendentalize what is ultimately a wholly natural, merely human capacity for representation. And more importantly, what prepares the way for her image of the broken word-mirror—her interpretation of Kafka's tale—does not exemplify an idle nihilism about meaning. The tale allows for a certain undecidable, open-ended multiplicity of interpretative possibilities precisely because it is composed of specific words whose individual referents and collective ordering at once deprive us of certain dimensions of evidence (via the monologue form) and condition the interpretative possibilities that remain open (men and men or apes and apes, maybe, but a man talking to apes is highly unlikely—to say the least—and parrot to parrot lies beyond the bounds of plausibility). Ultimately, the limits here are the limits of one's ability to imagine a broader context within which any such possibility could intelligibly be embedded, and thus motivate its realization; but any such context must respect the multiple but individually precise valencies of the words that make up the text (the complex and competing ways in which they can conjoin with other words to generate significance).

By initially placing the dictionary on the same shelf as the Bible and Shakespeare, Costello further suggests that our notions of a literary canon or tradition, and of individual literary genius, both set within broader cultural frameworks and assumptions, live under the threat of irreparable de-divinization. But once again, that need not (and should not) be viewed as equivalent to their suffering a total loss of relevance or authority. For they constitute another set of ways in which a literary text further opens itself to multiplicities of sense while acknowledging further kinds of constraints upon that multiplicity. The more these overlapping frames of genre, style, mode, and canon engage and reengage the semantic and syntactic frames we mentioned earlier, the harder it becomes to regard the text as magically transparent. But one can acknowledge the highly textured nature of literary texts without picturing them as absolutely opaque, as essentially capable only of giving onto other texts; there are ways of envisioning access to reality that are not inconsistent with acknowledging texts as palimpsests.

So when Costello talks of us no longer being able to see what previous generations took to be a mirroring of reality as anything other than a collective hallucination, while nevertheless respecting the limits of intelligible and plausible interpretation set by Kafka's words in so doing, she is giving expression to the perennial literary effect we identified in the previous chapter—that of previous exercises in literary realism coming to appear merely illusory from the perspective established by a critical reformulation of representational conventions. The bottom has not dropped out of realism, but out of a particular, quasi-theological understanding of what it is for a work of literature to be realist. So Costello's invocation of the shattered word-mirror is not necessarily a denial of the possibility of continuing the realist project of the novel. On the contrary: she wants to interpret Kafka's modernist fables as essentially realist in inspiration, and this becomes clear precisely (if paradoxically) in the way she denies any straightforward relation between Kafka's tale and the reality of her own, present situation.

For example, she denies that she means her claims about the indeterminate creaturehood of Kafka's speaker and audience to apply straightforwardly to herself and her audience: "I am not, I hope, abusing the privilege of this platform to make idle, nihilistic jokes about what I am, ape or woman, and what you are, my auditors. That is not the point of the story, say I, who am, however, in no position to dictate what the point of the story is" (EC, 19). But she immediately goes on to assert that "There used to be a time, we believe, when we could say who we were. Now we are just performers speaking our parts. The bottom has dropped out" (EC, 19).

In other words, the recent shattering of the literary word-mirror in fact mirrors, or at least bears upon, the recent shattering of contemporary human confidence in one's identity—not only one's knowledge of what it is, but one's ability to make it fully manifest in (some conjunction of) one's social roles. So a text such as Kafka's, which develops itself in such a way as to foreground its own distance from any simple correspondence to reality, might thereby find a way to reconnect with that reality—its very opacity making one aspect of that reality more transparent to us. And we might begin to wonder whether Coetzee's novelistic presentation of Costello herself over eight lessons and a postscript may share this aim of reflecting the notion of human identity as shattered by adopting an overall form that does not even try to function as a composite sequence of word-mirrors in which a pure, self-sufficient, and unitary individual might be reflected, but rather as a collection of shards whose refusal of overall co-herence and individual transparency in fact mirrors the contemporary con-dition of both the idea and the reality of human character as such.

Similarly, Costello takes the trouble to deny or at least fend off (and so, of course, to air) an interpretation of her invocation of Kafka that she leaves tellingly unchallenged in her Gates Lecture—namely, that she wishes to pretend that she too is an ape, torn away from her natural surroundings and forced to perform in front of a gathering of critical strangers, with a view to demonstrating her mastery of their manners and conventions. "I hope not. I am one of you, I am not of a different species" (EC, 18). But of course, the direction of this denial presupposes that Cos-tello is assuming that Kafka's tale is, in the first place, about an ape, a particular kind of real, nonhuman creature with a specific nature.

It is this aspect of her realist reading of Kafka that she develops later in Coetzee's story, in response to her son's query about her use of Red Peter in her speech.

> "When I think of realism," he goes on, "I think of peasants frozen in blocks of ice. I think of Norwegians in smelly underwear . . . people picking their noses. You don't write about that kind of thing. Kafka didn't write about it."
>
> "No, Kafka didn't write about people picking their noses. But Kafka had time to wonder where and how his poor educated ape was going to find a mate. And what it was going to be like when he was left in the dark with the bewil-dered, half-tamed female that his keepers eventually produced for his use. Kaf-ka's ape is embedded in life. It is the embeddedness that is important, not the

life itself. His ape is embedded as we are embedded, you in me, I in you. That ape is followed through to the end, to the bitter, unsayable end, whether or not there are traces left on the page. Kafka stays awake during the gaps when we are sleeping, that is where Kafka fits in." (EC, 32)

Kafka's ape is not in a realistic situation; no real ape has been, or (we think) could possibly be educated to the cultural level of an average European. Nevertheless, having fantastically embedded his ape in European culture, Kafka develops its consequences with a rigorous attention to the real nature of the ape and of the culture he (impossibly) inhabits. A real ape will have sexual and emotional needs; real human beings would try to satisfy them, in order to maintain their profits, and would care little about the sanity of the mate they procure, or the potentially monstrous consequences of their congress. True, the tale that results from its author's unrelenting immersion in the reality upon which he is drawing to construct the fictional reality he has imagined does not dwell upon this aspect of Red Peter's situation, or upon his experience in the dark with his chimpanzee companion. But it is mentioned briefly, at the very end of the tale; so it would be more accurate to say that Kafka thereby leaves it to his readers to develop for themselves (as Costello has, as Coetzee has) the full fictional reality of his ape from this barest of textual traces, and thereby to acknowledge the mutual implication of author and reader in the construction of fictional reality.

One might think of Costello's characterization of Kafka as a realist on these particular grounds as a kind of inversion of Diamond's conception of difficulties of reality. Here, it is not that we encounter phenomena of ordinary experience that can nevertheless confound the mind's capacity to encompass them in thought, and so can be acknowledged in all their reality only by texts willing to maintain themselves within the impression of obscurity they prompt. Rather, she is arguing that even a tale that takes its starting point from a sheer impossibility (beyond anything to be encountered in reality) might nevertheless count as a contribution to the project of literary realism, insofar as the development of that tale can be seen as a logically and emotionally rigorous unfolding of the consequences of that unintelligible origin—an unsentimental articulation of what the impossible embedding of one reality into another might reveal about both.

Costello's key notion of embedding is itself embedded in a context that associates it with two other notions, and thereby confirms our earlier suspicion of a reflexive aspect of the discussion—the sense in which, as her son's question presupposes, her description of Kafka's realism is also a self-description. First, she compares Red Peter's embeddedness in life with her son's embeddedness in her and hers in her son's. This gives a particular twist to the familiar comparison of literary creativity and vitality with that of human flesh and blood: for her analogy is not simply between authorial creation and human procreation, but (insofar as both Costello and her son function as the term analogous to life on the ape side of the metaphorical equation) further suggests that the fictional creation endows its creator with life as much as the creator her creation. It might also imply that both children and parents constitute the primary structures of reality for each other, and in that sense embed each other in life. And of course, it recalls us to the specific, mutually life-determining ways in which Costello's own characters relate to their creator and are at once rooted in and essentially distinct from—even competitors with—her flesh-and-blood progeny.

For we learnt earlier, in one of the many interviews Costello gives during her visit, that she has a specific view of the human impulse to relate fictional creations to the biography of their author. When asked whether her most recent novel is autobiographical to any extent, she has this to say: "Of course we draw upon our own lives all the time—they are our main resource, in a sense our only resource. But no, *Fire and Ice* isn't autobiography. It is a work of fiction. I made it up" (EC, 12). This is the analogue in Costello to Manet's acknowledgment of his paintings as both conditioned by, and yet not reducible to, the fact of their being painted, and painted by one particular, historically situated individual. In both cases, to deny any relation between creator and creation would be as foolish as to identify the two. The reality is, one might say, that they are embedded in one another. And it follows, first, that the real people in Costello's life will find themselves embedded in her novels (as we saw earlier, John notes during her Gates Lecture that he finds that fact personally painful), and second, that the two modes of life will rub painfully against one another. John remembers her seclusion every morning to do her writing, when he and his sister would often slump melodramatically outside the locked door and whine, until they forgot their sense of forsakenness; but he also recalls his mother storming "around the house in Melbourne, hair flying in all directions, screaming at her children, 'You are killing me! You are tearing the flesh from my body!' (He lay in the dark with his sister afterwards, comforting her while she sobbed; he was seven; it was his first taste of fathering)" (EC, 30).

These screams may express the intimacy between Costello's sense of her mode of embeddedness in life and that of Red Peter, both feeling the touch of madness, of self-willed self-destruction; but such self-destruction inevitably threatens harm to the others embedded in that life with her. And of course, given that Costello's equation of human procreation with literary creation works both ways, one might equally well hear in her screams her sense of what is involved in giving birth to and nurturing fictional characters—the way in which the reality of their existence requires that she allow herself, as well as her family, to be consumed by them.

The second notion she associates with that of realism in her discussion with her son is that of Kafka as staying awake when we are sleeping. This partly specifies her sense of the realist author as having a commitment to the real and its ineluctable consequences that most human beings most of the time can neither desire nor bear; but it also invokes a canonical cultural image of philosophy—that of Socrates still awake, when all the other winers and diners have collapsed into unconsciousness, as dawn breaks at the end of Plato's *Symposium*. Even at this early stage, then, Costello has a sense of literature's uncanny intimacy with philosophy, sharing its interest in moral edification and in a genuine apprehension of the real (as the format of a lesson, with its suggestion of taking instruction, already implies).

The reflexivity of Costello's conception of realism is prepared for in other ways by the issues that arise in her interviews. In particular, the idea of her fiction as both determined and emancipated in its relation to reality by its relation with the canonical, with literary and cultural tradition, is underscored. For her interviewers not only emphasize the fact that her most famous creation is in truth a re-creation, of Joyce's Molly Bloom; she responds to that emphasis by herself emphasizing that her attempt to make something new from the material left over from Joyce's prodigal inventiveness was itself conditioned by a desire to relocate her from Joyce's realistically imagined bedroom ("with the bed with the creaking springs") to the real sights and smells of the streets of Dublin in 1904, as well as the particular cultural possibilities actually open to Molly and Leopold alike at that historical moment. She does not quite accede to her interviewer's suggestion that she showed how Joyce's liberation of the sensual reality of women from its prior literary confinement was itself confined, that Molly could "equally well be an intelligent woman with an interest in music and a circle of friends of her own and a daughter with whom she shared confidences" (EC, 14), but neither does she actually deny it.

One might, therefore, say that she plays off one kind of embeddedness against another: by exploiting the indebtedness of any literary creation to its antecedents, she tries to embed the wholly fictional and yet vitally real Molly more deeply into nonfictional human reality. She tries to stay awake during the gaps when Joyce was sleeping—or rather, she brings us to see his apparently seamless creation (its successful creation of an impression of real femaleness in his Molly) as actually having gaps in the light of her own, apparently more successful, fictional representation of real femaleness. Insofar as a prior fictional representation has any reality to it—insofar as it aspires to, or anyway succeeds in, apprehending something about reality—then attending properly to it in all its fictionality, even if that process takes the form of creating another fiction, may nevertheless bring us closer to what is real.

At the same time, however, Costello is well aware of the risks attendant upon pursuing such a vision of simultaneously weaving oneself into the canon and bringing oneself closer to reality—the risk of that vision coming closer to fantasy than reality. She cannot deny that the vision grips her, that it holds out a possibility worth pursuing; but neither can she deny its vulnerability to failure—more specifically, to various failures of realism. This is why she cites another member of the literary canon in her acceptance speech—Jorge Luis Borges and his tale of the Library of Babel. That fable envisions a library in which all conceivable books, past, present, and future, coexist; and Costello acknowledges the magnetic force of that image, its driving role in the life of the imagination of any writer, and in particular the way in which it might work to allow the writer to deny a fundamental aspect of her own human reality, by acknowledging her own obsessive concern for the deposit copy of her first novel, and the wish it encoded that her literary creation might outlive her: "if I, this mortal shell, am going to die, let me at least live on through my creations" (EC, 17). But she also knows that no real library could conceivably assuage her desire: the British Library will crumble into dust and elude living memory, as will the books on its shelves—if the ones deemed ugly, unread, and so unwanted are not tossed into a furnace long before in order to make space for the new and newly wanted.

This realism (about her own motives for writing, and about the concrete, historical reality of books, the institutions that house them, and the societies that determine their fate) engenders a countervision to the Library of Babel—a library "from which books that were really conceived, written and published are absent, absent even from the memory of the librarians" (EC, 18). It is through the conjunction of these paired and contrary visions that Costello introduces her remarks on realism and Kafka's ape; and they return to haunt the conclusion of her remarks:

> Despite this splendid award, for which I am deeply grateful, despite the promise it makes that, gathered into the illustrious company of those who have won it before me, I am beyond time's envious grasp, we all know, if we are being realistic, that it is only a matter of time before the books which you honour, and with whose genesis I have had something to do, will cease to be read and eventually cease to be remembered. And properly so. There must be some limit to the burden of remembering that we impose on our children and grandchildren. They will have a world of their own, of which we should be less and less part. (EC, 20)

This is not simply an acknowledgment of the way fantasy and reality are embedded in one another in the very idea of the literary canon, and so of literary value, as essentially timeless or eternal, as if capable of floating free of the human reality that engenders and informs the literary enterprise. It also suggests a realistic appraisal of the ways in which a writer's necessary indebtedness to the past can be as much a burden as an empowerment; as Costello puts it in an earlier interview, "we can't go on parasitizing the classics for ever. I am not excluding myself from the charge. We've got to start doing some inventing of our own" (EC, 14–15). Here, we encounter another aspect of her comparison between fictional creativity and human procreation. Just as fictional characters inhabit a world of their own to just the extent that their authors remove themselves from it, coming to allow or think of their creations as having a life of their own, so each new human generation will be able to come into its own only insofar as its predecessors do not seek to overcome their own supersession by determining the terms of the future—by turning the future into something that is merely remembered, an act of domestic piety.

There is no question that, as acceptance speeches go, this one might seem tactless or grudging; on the other hand, Costello is well aware that the ways in which such literary committees think exhibit a tendency to overlook altogether the genuine significance of the idea of a literary canon, in favour of an essentially political evenhandedness between generations, genres, genders, and nationalities. As John sees it, his mother "will be disappointed . . . if she learns that the Stowe award is hers only because 1995 has been decreed to be the year of Australasia. [She wants to be] the best . . . not the best Australian, not the best Australian woman, just the best" (EC, 8). But the reply by the chairman of the committee is hardly reassuring on this front; and more broadly, John suspects that even the most intelligent of Costello's critics and admirers are not fully prepared to allow that her literary achievement can ever escape determination by her biography, her gender, or her cultural and historical location. He wants to affirm her aspiration to transcend such factors, and in terms that might have been drawn directly from Fried's characterization of the modernist painter: he presents her as "measuring herself against the illustrious dead . . . paying tribute to the powers that animate her . . . measuring herself against the masters" (EC, 26). In fact, John takes a rather old-fashioned view of these animating powers, as he explains to one of the academics at Altona.

> I think you are baffled, even if you won't admit it, by the mystery of the divine in the human. You know there is something special about my mother—that is what draws you to her—yet when you meet her she turns out to be just an ordinary old woman. You can't square the two. You want an explanation. You want a clue, a sign, if not from her then from me. (EC, 28)

Since these words are a way of warding off explanation, I take it that this astrophysicist is invoking the divine not as a causal factor in literary creation, but as a way of underlining the mysteriousness of such creativity. It is offered not as an alternative to the reductionisms of gender and nationality, but as a way of seeing that they repress or displace something—namely, a proper acknowledgment of something that is essentially beyond our grasp.

On the other hand, we must take seriously the context in which this gesture towards mystery is placed. First of all, the words are those of Costello's son, not Costello herself—even though in the view of his interlocutor, their utterance shows that he is his mother's son; and he is speaking to a woman—the literary critic and scholar Susan Moebius—with whom he has just had sex, whom he suspects of using him as a conduit to his mother, and more fundamentally whom he now (the morning after) fears may have understood him and his motives rather better than he had thought or hoped. So this speech may serve purposes other than the articulation of his deepest belief about his mother—although, given that he has earlier, in less charged contexts, articulated something like those beliefs (describing the striking impression his first reading of his mother's books gave him, and describing a line from Shakespeare as "out of the dark emerging, out of nowhere: first not there, then there, like a newborn child, heart working, brain working, all the processes of that intricate electrochemical labyrinth working. A miracle" [EC, 27]), we need not deny that it also serves that purpose. But more importantly, having happily characterized himself to Moebius as Costello's son ("not a foundling, not an adoptee. Out of her very body I came, caterwauling . . . flesh of her flesh, blood of her blood" [EC, 28]), he ends the story—sitting beside his sleeping mother on their return flight to Australia—by rejecting such a tale of his origins:

> He can see up her nostrils, into her mouth, down the back of her throat. And what he cannot see he can imagine: the gullet, pink and ugly, contracting as it swallows, like a python, drawing things down to the pear-shaped belly-sac. He draws away, tightens his own belt, sits up, facing forward. No, he tells himself, that is not where I come from, that is not it. (EC, 34)

In other words, his reaching towards the idea of divine inspiration, in a context that links literary creation with human procreation, now takes on an aspect of disavowal. Just as his sense of the creation of new human life as an incomprehensible miracle is here undercut by the thought that the idea of the miraculous is a cover for a certain disgust at one's fleshly origins, so the idea of fictional creation as divine retrospectively appears as a refusal properly to acknowledge the concrete reality of literature's origins—in the chaotic intermingling of psychic, familial, cultural, and historical matrices. In both cases, the creature's genuinely independent existence seems threatened by any acknowledgment of its createdness—as if to do so would be to submit to being engulfed by the life of one's creator, no more than a way of sustaining her own autonomous existence. Once again, it seems, we must not allow our denials of the reductionist impulse to lead us into a straightforward counterdenial of the way literary originality is always already embedded in the contexts that condition it. One can be realistic about (say, acknowledge) that embeddedness without thinking that one has thereby dissipated the essentially enigmatic nature of creation.

COETZEE: REALISM AS EMBODYING

Since John is his mother's son, we might think of this concluding emphasis upon the concrete reality of human flesh and blood as reflecting his mother's way of seeing things (as manifest in her admiring acknowledgement of Kafka's emphasis upon the sexuality and fertility of his ape) as much as his own; and we might similarly connect his persistent picturing of his mother in animal terms (as a seal and a cat, as fish and as fowl) with her ways of picturing herself (as, for example, an ape, or a whale surrounded by nibbling goldfish [EC, 6]). In other words, a profound sense of the animality of the human being, its internal relation to other species of animal and its embeddedness in flesh, joins them together—as if their relatedness is fleshed out or animated by such commonalities of vision. And this commonality is of course taken up and foregrounded in lessons 3 and 4 of *Elizabeth Costello*, devoted to her Gates Lecture and its aftermath, where the theme of animality is unmissable, and equally persistently reflected in the pervasiveness of animal imagery throughout the text.

But one might equally well take the centrality of this issue as reflecting an aspect of Coetzee's way of looking at the world: after all, the genesis of characters and events that so foreground this matter is something with which the author of the Tanner Lectures, the Belitt Lecture, and *Elizabeth Costello* itself has something to do (cf. EC, 20). And this in turn should lead us to ask how much further the commonalities or mutual embeddings between Elizabeth and John extend to their author. In particular, how far does Costello's conception of literary realism—as manifest in Kafka's work as well as her own—apply to the mode of writing in which she appears? In short, is "Realism" (not to mention the book of which it is the first lesson) to be understood as a realist work in Costello's sense of the term? Since, however, Costello's view is that the relation between author and character is one of embedding (as opposed to identity or difference), then if in this respect her creator mirrors his creation, he will do so precisely by not precisely mirroring her—that is, by showing that his views are neither simply continuous nor simply discontinuous with her conception of the theory and practice of realistic writing.

On the one hand, in a variety of ways, Coetzee's position as a writer mirrors that of Costello. His reputation was first cemented by a critical appropriation of a canonical author's fictional creations (in the novel *Foe*); his critics have persistently attempted to understand him in relation to the specificities of his own cultural, national, and historical contexts (as South African, as white, as supporting or disdaining certain political issues and movements) as well as in relation to certain literary categories and genres (as modernist and postmodernist, colonial and postcolonial, as creator of fable or allegory, not to mention realism). A further, more specific point of correlation with Costello lies in her willingness to write from the point of view of men, just as Coetzee—not only with respect to Costello herself but throughout his writing—attempts to write from the point of view of women.

Costello's version of this task, and the critical opprobrium it can generate, is thematic in "Realism." Moebius presses her in a radio interview on the difficulties inherent in the task, as attempted in *Fire and Ice*. Whereas Costello herself argues that "it is the otherness that is the challenge. Making up someone other than yourself," and that "if it were easy it wouldn't be worth doing" (EC, 12)—thereby implying that it can be done—Moebius later argues that "whatever [Costello] does, she does as a woman. She inhabits her characters as a woman does, not a man. . . . If her men are believable, good . . . but finally it is just mimicry" (EC, 23). Determining who is right is beyond the reader; for quite apart from the unavailability to us of *Fire and Ice*, it is part of Moebius's argument that what a man can see in a literary creation of a man is not what a woman sees; and this presents discussion about the possibilities of representing other genders as itself limited by the gender of the participants, and in a way that blocks the possibility of progress.

Coetzee relates this argument about the genuineness of Costello's literary inhabitation of otherness to the matter of his namesake John's one-night stand with Susan Moebius, and the ways in which each of them understands that experience, and so each other. Does the straightforwardly realised possibility of their mutual desire, its mutual recognition and its consenting consummation, show that men and women can do more than lead parallel lives, that they can really meet or encounter one another? Each claims to know what the other is thinking, not only about each other's desires and their satisfaction, but about literature and about Costello in particular; and each proves better able to ground that claim than the other expects. When John concludes that Susan is "an unexplored continent" (EC, 27), does that mean that he cannot fully under-

stand her, or that given enough time he could explore anything and everything that he does not at present understand about her? And does his
predilection for metaphors of exploration, which invoke colonial ventures
into putatively virgin territory, bespeak a decisively male perspective on
women that is bound to misrepresent her otherness, or simply a personal
limitation that might submit to further interaction? Either way, Coetzee
implies that the literary and the personal dimensions of this question of
gender otherness must be seen as embedded in one another, and so as
distinct but internally related.

The triangle of John, Susan, and Elizabeth Costello also provides a
certain perspective on understanding another kind of otherness—the otherness of fictional human beings. Within the story, John claims to Susan
that "my mother has been a man. . . . She has also been a dog. She can
think her way into other people, into other existences. I have read her; I
know. It is within her powers. Isn't that what is most important about
fiction: that it takes us out of ourselves, into other lives?" (EC, 22–23).
But this returns us to a question we broached earlier: what exactly is the
relation between fictional characters and real human beings? How does
the ability to understand one relate to the ability to understand the other?
John thinks that he understands, recognizes and is convinced by, his mother's fictional men and women and dogs; but he does not think that he
understands Susan Moebius, and he is by no means certain that he understands his mother—if only because her ability to create fictional characters is itself beyond his understanding. Susan thinks she understands Costello's male creations, but what she understands is that they are mere
imitations or parodies of real men (the women are another matter)—not
real at all; and she is similarly inclined to claim a fullness of knowledge
of Costello herself and of John that is fundamentally reductive of them
both, and that John at least is inclined to judge as to that extent indicative
of a failure to understand either. Costello thinks she understands both
Susan and John: "You're the one she was really after, not me" (EC, 30)—
exactly what both John and Susan would deny. How, then, should we
take her claim to have understood Molly Bloom better than Joyce himself?

Of course, in making these various claims, I am claiming to understand
three fictional characters, and so, to that extent, to understand their creator. And yet their creator is insistent upon what one might call a constitutive resistance to understanding that they all embody, each in a different
though related way. By her very name, Susan Moebius declares herself to
be all surface, or more precisely a two-dimensional form so arranged that
what appears to be its inner surface is simply a continuation of its outer,
just more externality; she is always elegant and well-dressed, and when
her clothes are removed, John finds her body "handsome in every detail
. . . but in a blank way" (EC, 26)—not so much an unexplored continent,

then, but the illusion of an interior. Costello herself is present in the story purely from the third person, solely in terms of appearance, deeds, and words: the narrative voice never penetrates to her consciousness, content merely to record her utterances and the impressions she makes on others. And of course, at the story's end, she too appears as a creature whose interior is a continuation of her exterior: her digestive tract appears not as part of what is inside her, but as a passage linking the outside (breathed in or ingested) with the outside (excreted). In this sense, even what seems to be her physical interior is just another surface; everything pertaining to her sustenance and her fertility—to her identity—is open to the invasive air. And of course, this vision of the human body as always already penetrated, as if constructed around a core of emptiness, is our concluding impression of a purely fictional individual—one with (one wants to say) no body at all.

What of John Bernard? As with the Tanner Lectures, Coetzee locates the narrative voice of his tale firmly on his namesake's shoulder, so that everything we see of its events is from the perspective of his experience of them; and we also encounter elements of his inner life—unarticulated thoughts, memories, and judgements. Nevertheless, this is not a first-person but a third-person narrative; even John is in this sense other to the narrator, not simply to be identified with him, even if uniquely privileged (and so uniquely vulnerable) in relation to him. But Coetzee is careful to ensure that John too foregrounds his purely fictional status: for even with the opportunity created by the publication of *Elizabeth Costello* to render consistent his initially discrepant portraits of John in the Belitt Lecture and in the Tanner Lectures, he refrains from so doing. The only trace of the family who will appear in lessons 3 and 4 is his mysterious description of himself as "Married and unmarried" (EC, 28), and the love that here leads him to accompany his mother around the world, to the point at which he imagines himself as her trainer, has almost entirely dissipated in those later lessons. In other words, the John Bernard of lesson 1 both is and is not the John Bernard of lessons 3 and 4. These rough edges can of course be smoothed out with some imaginative effort on our part; but the need to do it, and so the author's apparent unwillingness to do it for us, is pressing, and it suggests a certain desire on Coetzee's part to demonstrate how far we are prepared to go as readers to confer coherence and plausibility on fictional creations even when their author chooses not to do so.

In these ways, the three main characters in Coetzee's story not only point us towards their own mysterious status; they also recall us to those critical moments in the text at which the narrative voice speaks from somewhere entirely other than John's shoulder and thereby foregrounds not so much the tale to be told but rather the teller of it and those to whom it is told. For example, this is how the lesson, and so the book, begins:

> There is first of all the problem of the opening, namely, how to get us from where we are, which is, as yet, nowhere, to the far bank. It is a simple bridging problem, a problem of knocking together a bridge. People solve such problems every day. They solve them, and having solved them push on.
>
> Let us assume that, however it may have been done, it is done. Let us take it that the bridge is built and crossed, that we can put it out of our mind. We have left behind the territory in which we were. We are in the far territory, where we want to be. (EC, 1)

In what kind of space can one build a bridge from nowhere to the far bank, let alone do so simply, time and time again? Well, in what kind of world can one knock together such a bridge merely by assuming or taking it that it has been done? Exercises of the imagination can make things so in literature: if the author tells us that our hero has built a bridge, then he has built a bridge. But this does not mean that, in the story, our hero can build a bridge simply by imagining that he has built a bridge; and neither does it mean that any old way in which the author tells of the bridge-building will create it in our imaginations, and so in the world of the story. On the contrary, unless the author can tell us how his hero might have done so (whether because of his years in engineering school, or because of his possession of a genie), then the reader will not credit it. And yet, over the years, authors have found an indefinite number of ways of convincing their readers that these bridges have been built.

But Coetzee's words refer to the problem of the opening of his story, and indeed of any story: the bridge he speaks of is not a bridge in any particular story, but the bridge into a story—the means by which he and his readers enter into its world. So the mystery of that bridge's construction is an aspect of something real and everyday—of the humdrum acts of writing and reading, telling and hearing, stories, and not of the often far from humdrum things that go on in the worlds of those stories.

Making things up is one of the things that real human beings do; more precisely, according to Coetzee, we regard it as always already done, something that can be put out of our minds in favour of imaginatively inhabiting the particular far territory to which it conveys us. How so? Coetzee tells us that this far territory is where we want to be; so perhaps we find it so easy to pass over the building of the bridge because we are so eager to pass over it into the world we desire, a world that can satisfy our desires, give us what we deeply, even desperately want (whether that is something given to a character in the fictional world with whose satisfied desires we identify, or simply the imaginative inhabitation of a fictional world). But what we want is not always good for us—not always what we really want, or should really want; perhaps it merely satisfies our desire for fantasy and so distracts us from reality. And sometimes we find ourselves no longer able simply to put things out of our minds—simply to assume that something is done despite the fact that we have no idea exactly how it has been done, or even how it so much as could have been done (how, exactly, does one build a bridge from nowhere to the far bank?). Such a world would be one in which the opening of a story, of any story, is a problem: it is the world of literary modernism, the world in which Coetzee locates himself and us by opening his story in the way he does.

And yet he solves the problem he has identified simply by inviting us to assume that it is solved; even when he explicitly refuses to pass over the building of this bridge, or to let us pass over it, we barely need an invitation before we hasten to do so anyway, that is, to pass into his far territory, and to pass over the means by which we pass into it. In this way, the true, unfathomable depth of our desire for that far territory, and for pushing on within it, comes out; and so does another reason for regarding the bridge as always already built, despite or beyond anything the bridge-builder can do. For when we read the first two paragraphs of Coetzee's book, are we already within his fictional world or not?

We do not seem to be within the world of the story he is about to tell, which seems to begin only in the third paragraph, when the familiar God-like authorial voice creates Elizabeth Costello by stipulating her date of birth, profession, and body of work. But if that is so, then the first two paragraphs are not part of the story at all; they might simply have been omitted, and in beginning with what is now the third paragraph, we would already have crossed the bridge. But if the first two paragraphs are part of Coetzee's fictional world—and they are, after all the first two paragraphs of the first lesson of the book—then they do not contain the act of bridge-building (for the first paragraph presents it as a problem to solve and the second as a problem solved, but neither presents the solving of it—that appears to occur in the space between the two paragraphs); and in fact they could not so contain it, for if we are already within the fictional world at the beginning of the first paragraph, then the bridge to it must already have been built and crossed.

In short, a work of fiction cannot contain or embody the problem of the opening as a problem, even in its opening sentence; for it must already have opened in order to do so, and so must already have relied upon our willingness to pass over the bridge and its building. It can only, therefore, gesture towards a mystery of its own constitution as something essentially mysterious—at once mundane and miraculous, and always already beyond its grasp.

If the far territory is the world of the story, the near must be the real world; but why, then, does the real world becomes a genuine territory, as opposed to nowhere, only in retrospect—after the bridge to the fictional world has been built and crossed? In part, because reality can appear to us as such only by contrast with something which is not real—the imaginary, the fantastic, the fictional; for example, the reality of our desires may be revealed by our dissatisfaction with the fictional world that satisfies our present, actual desires. In part, because it is only after the fictional world has been built and inhabited that its creation can be seen to have a location or context in reality, in which it can be said to have been embedded or from which it can be said to have grown: at the moment of its creation, it is as if it came from nowhere, from divine inspiration. In part, because this bridge can always be built again, whenever anyone picks up the text in and through which it was built, and allows it to be built again, in her imagination; and each such reading will itself be retrospectively revealed as having a particular location in space and time, in culture and history. And yet, despite all this, we know that the act of bridge-building does occur in the real world; we do it every day. In other words, literary creation both has and does not have a place in reality, a real location: it is both nowhere and somewhere in particular. And so, of course, is the fictional world thereby created, the world of the narrative. This (nowhere and somewhere) is where we are, as author and readers, not only at the opening of the text, but at every point within it.

Coetzee further emphasizes the opacity of our location as readers, and hence his own unlocatability as author, by embedding a series of interruptions of the narrative into his narrative. One kind involves references to scenes that take place in the world of the story, but which are not simply omitted but positively skipped; and the skips are not merely made, they are made by means of a sentence that describes the speech-act it is performing, and in the technical terms of the literary (or perhaps the screenwriter's) trade: "There is a scene in the restaurant, mainly dialogue, which we will skip. We resume back at the hotel" (EC, 7). Another, closely related, involves the creation of a gap in the narrative, one that is represented not by a literal gap but by the insertion of the words themselves ("A gap" [EC, 27, 28]), between two sentences that are straightforwardly part of the narrative. After one such skip or gap, he comments on this strategy and its risks:

> It is not a good idea to interrupt the narrative too often, since storytelling works by lulling the reader or listener into a dreamlike state in which the time and space of the real world fade away, superseded by the time and space of the fiction. Breaking into the dream draws attention to the constructedness of the story, and plays havoc with the realist illusion. However, unless certain scenes

are skipped over, we will be here all afternoon. The skips are not part of the text, they are part of the performance. (EC, 16)

If skipping risks breaking into the dream, then skipping conjoined with a discussion of its costs and benefits hardly reduces the risk: and yet we continue with the story (if we do), accepting the idea and the fact of Coetzee's skips without losing our interest in Costello and her visit. What kind of havoc does an author have to create to stop us getting, and staying, where we want to be, in the far territory?

But the form of this metatextual discussion emphasizes other paradoxes internal to the nature of this particular text. First, it encodes an awareness of its own origins in a talk or lecture—something already implicit in its formal status as a lesson, with that term's suggestion of a text meant to be read aloud: it adverts to its "reader or listener," talks of being here all afternoon (not the more natural "all day"), which suggests to my mind the familiar time of a lecture, and it introduces a distinction between the text and the performance (not its performance). The idea of a lecture text naturally suggests such a distinction, although on a certain understanding of performance, it might also apply to individual acts of reading; but since the distinction is being drawn here, in the text that records that performance for posterity, it seems hard to deny that the skips to which it refers are in fact part of the text. After all, can we simply say of a skipped scene either that it is, or that it is not, part of the story? Is it not, far from simply, both? When he skips, or hurdles a gap, is Coetzee sleeping, or rather staying awake while we sleep?

But it is not as if Coetzee sticks to his initial claim that skips as such are assignable to performance as opposed to text. For at the only other point at which the distinction is drawn, the narrator refers to a skip he is making as "a skip this time in the text rather than the performance" (EC, 24). Does it matter that what is being skipped is a scene of sexual intercourse between John and Susan, and one preceded by an expression of disorientation ("Where is [room] 1307 in relation to 1254: north, south, west, east?" [EC, 24]), more specifically an expression of John's inability to relate Susan's room to his mother's, in part because Susan's room appears to be on a floor that real hotels generally omit (the thirteenth)? Is it also significant that the paragraph immediately following offers us a single moment in place of the skipped scene, as its monument in John's memory, as well as a mnemonic for what happens after that scene, and is subsequently recorded within the terms of the realist illusion?

> When he thinks back over those hours, one moment returns with sudden force, the moment when her knee slips under his arm and folds into his armpit. Curious that the memory of an entire scene should be dominated by one moment, not obviously significant, yet so vivid that he can still almost feel the ghostly

> thigh against his skin. Does the mind by nature prefer sensations to ideas, the
> tangible to the abstract? Or is the folding of the woman's knee just a mnemonic,
> from which will unfold the rest of the night? (EC, 24)

This is not just a mechanism of John's memory: it is a variant of a central
mechanism in the articulation of Coetzee's story. For, as if to confirm or
perform the dreamlike nature of the realist illusion, the chronology of the
story is irregularly studded with images whose significance seems both
intense and occluded, and that appear to interlink with one another. Quite
apart from the opening image of the bridge, I would pick out three: Moebius's folding knee, Costello's pythonlike gullet and belly-sac, and between them both, John's vision of his mother

> in her big double bed, crouched, her knees drawn up, her back bared. Out of
> her back, out of the waxy, old person's flesh, protrude three needles: not the
> tiny needles of the acupuncturist or the voodoo doctor but thick, grey needles,
> steel or plastic: knitting needles. The needles have not killed her, there is no
> need to worry about that, she breathes regularly in her sleep. Nevertheless, she
> lies impaled. (EC, 26)

This vision comes as he wakes next to Moebius and her handsome, blank
body; and it is succeeded by his recollection of Shakespeare's line about
"sleep that knits up the ravelled sleeve of care" (beyond the capacity of
any monkey with a typewriter to produce); so the context gives us two
ways in dream-logic of accounting for that impalement. But one might
also think of the image itself as one of three such images that protrude
from the text of "Realism"—as indicating Coetzee's desire to bring realism into conjunction with other modes or dimensions of meaning, or
rather to show that realism demands the recognition of such modes of
meaning in human reality.

   Coetzee's narrator talks twice of the relation between his enterprise and
more familiar modes of realism much earlier in the story, or at least the
text. The first such interruption comes early, after a paragraph describing
Costello's appearance:

> The blue costume, the greasy hair, are details, signs of a moderate realism. Sup-
> ply the particulars, allow the significations to emerge of themselves. A proce-
> dure pioneered by Daniel Defoe. Robinson Crusoe, cast up on the beach, looks
> around for his shipmates. But there are none. "I never saw them afterwards, or
> any sign of them," says he, "except three of their hats, one cap, and two shoes
> that were not fellows." Two shoes, not fellows: by not being fellows, the shoes
> have ceased to be footwear and become proofs of death, torn by the foaming
> seas off the feet of drowning men and tossed ashore. No large words, no despair,
> just hats and caps and shoes. (EC, 4)

On the one hand, Coetzee is associating his enterprise with that of Defoe's plainly denotative realism: supply some small and plain particulars, and the significations will emerge by themselves (and so implicitly dissociating himself from Costello's later association of herself with Swift's hyperbolic modes of satirical realism). On the other hand, he is also dissociating himself from what will appear from the perspective of the text before us to be Defoe's prolixity—his sense that an unending profusion of such plain particulars is essential if the illusion of reality is to be successfully created. For where Robinson Crusoe's life is conjured from a vast terrain of textual detail concerning his life on the island, Elizabeth Costello comes to life for us (if she does) from a comparatively meagre diet: the colour of her clothes and the greasiness of her hair constitute Coetzee's entire expenditure of particularity upon her. This idea of moderation would seem exiguous even to Defoe's Puritanism of prose.

Beyond this matter of adopting and (or by) testing the generic conventions of the realist literary heritage, certain other, more complicated, significations emerge of themselves from the particulars of this passage. To begin with, Defoe's exemplary restriction of his prose to the barest of bare denotations (emphasized by Watt) cannot prevent the efflorescence of figurative significance even there. For when he says that the two shoes were not fellows, does he mean that they do not form a pair with each other, or that they are not identical with the human fellows whose shoes they are? Both dimensions of descriptive meaning seem equally available; and each, in its own way, points towards the emergence of symbolic truth from the notation of literal truth, and so to language's refusal to restrict itself to the purely or absolutely literal—its revelation of the true emptiness or irreality of any such notion of literality.

Furthermore, Coetzee doesn't allow the significations implicit in Defoe's hats and cap and shoes to emerge of themselves, but rather articulates them for us; he enacts their emergence in his reader's imagination and thereby preempts us from so doing (as I am about to preempt Coetzee's readers—does any reader have an alternative?). But by choosing just these particulars from this text, Coetzee not only implicitly acknowledges an aspect of his own literary reputation as a contester of canonical texts (the text of *Foe* being the prime example) and prepares the ground for a theme in his story about Costello. He also allows us a premonition of her later, central claim that realism of the familiar, Defoe-like kind has itself suffered shipwreck—individual elements of its textual constructions might be reclaimed and embodied in new reconstructions, but the central illusion on which it is based has been shattered and so can only survive in a radically revised form (such as Kafka's, such as Costello's, such as Coetzee's). And yet, behind or before it all, readers continue to believe in the drowning men and the foaming seas, in the man and woman having sex and arguing about literature; even when these lines from Crusoe are quoted in another story altogether, the lost sailors revive in our imaginations, just as Costello takes life through the perfunctory notation of her blue dress and greasy hair. One might well wonder whether there is a conventional minimum below which the impression of reality simply will not be conveyed—a degree zero of formal realism that stops short of the utterly blank page.

The second interruption about realism occurs a little later, after John's discussion with the chairman of the Stowe committee about literary merit:

> Realism has never been comfortable with ideas. It could not be otherwise: realism is premised on the idea that ideas have no autonomous existence, can exist only in things. So when it needs to debate ideas, as here, realism is driven to invent situations—walks in the countryside, conversations—in which characters give voice to contending idea and thereby in a certain sense embody them. The notion of *embodying* turns out to be pivotal. In such debates ideas do not and indeed cannot float free: they are tied to the speakers by whom they are enounced, and generated from the matrix of individual interests out of which their speakers act in the world—for instance, the son's concern that his mother not be treated as a Mickey Mouse post-colonial writer, or Wheatley's concern not to seem an old-fashioned absolutist. (EC, 9)

One might say: where Costello sees embeddedness as pivotal for realism after the shipwreck of realism, Coetzee's narrator sees embodiedness. This is the point at which author and character converge and diverge—since embeddedness and embodiedness can be seen as variations or inflections of each other, the same and different (just like the individuals by whom they are enounced). As we have seen in the themes and the spine of imagery in his story, Coetzee takes the premise that ideas cannot float free from the individuals who articulate them (a premise that Plato's choice of dialogue form appears to acknowledge, even if so many of his dialogues variously aspire to reorient our attention to a realm of pure ideas or Forms), and then he pushes it further, by emphasizing their rootedness in the animality of the human animal, its flesh and blood and all that it generates or engenders. He literalizes the realist idea of embodiedness—sees the concrete reality of living human bodies and freights images of the human body in all its concreteness (folding around another body, pierced by needles, swallowing air and food into its pear-shaped belly-sac) with a range of more or less abstract, obscure, and ultimately unsynthesized significations. And he claims that this is how realism can and must accommodate ideas, be—as it were—realistic about them.

This is not the same as being comfortable with them: but perhaps discomfort with ideas is precisely what their real nature demands. Perhaps his point is precisely that ideas discomfort us: they demand a degree of abstraction from reality that challenges us, although in a way that we—as genuinely rational animals—cannot dismiss; and their fleshly origins—their rootedness in the particularities of individual cultures, minds, and bodies—revolt us, as they revolted Plato and continue to revolt the philosopher in every rational animal, at least some of the time. Accordingly, any mode of realism that engages with ideas must do so in a way that embodies that very discomfort, and so transmits it to its readers. It must allow itself to run the risk of formal shipwreck—leaving gaps and skipping scenes, interrupting text and performance with reflections on itself, and images that are embedded in the text without exactly being embodied in it. It thereby delineates, by embodying, a mode of evaluating ideas that runs contrary to our sense that such evaluation can only take the form of impersonal, internally coherent lines of argument and criticism that result in definitive conclusions of universal application. That there are such arguments, and that they are worthy of respect, is not to be denied; but all such arguments are also embedded or embodied in a variety of ways to which they should not be reduced, but by which they are significantly conditioned, and often in tangled, mutually conflicting ways that complicate evaluation to the point of putting definitive conclusions beyond our reach—asking of us a willingness to contemplate or suffer the difficulty rather than attempting to solve or resolve it. To deny the relevance of such embeddedness to any assessment of the significance of lines of reasoning and the ideas they support would be as unrealistic as to reduce such assessment to an exclusive concern with their various embodiments. It is not hard to see why such a conclusion is one with which philosophy might well be discomfited; but is it one that it can ignore?

Chapter Eleven

THE BODY IN AFRICA

I
N THE TERMS PROVIDED BY the first lesson of *Elizabeth Costello*, a moderate realist who cannot honestly pretend that the word-mirror of literature is still intact might nevertheless find that it can continue to reflect reality if one reconstitutes it from its own shards. Such a mirror would no longer present a single, coherent image to those looking into it, and so would no longer be in a position to deny its own reality as a medium or intermediary; it would rather declare its reflective nature by virtue of the fact that each constituent shard would at best fit imperfectly with its fellows, forming a necessarily crazed surface. But the resultant mosaic could still be said to display an image of reality, whose elements might each accurately reflect an aspect of the reflected object in accordance with the specific orientation of each mirror-shard towards it; it is just that this image would be as crazed as the surface that presents it, ultimately failing to resolve into a unitary, sharply focused reflection of the object as a whole.

If we think of the individual lessons of *Elizabeth Costello* as shards in such a reconstituted word-mirror, then we should expect that the overall image of Elizabeth Costello it imparts to us will be a mosaic of related but unsynthesized reflections of different aspects of her identity, and so a portrait of her identity as essentially an assemblage of elements whose overarching unity is always in question—open to the interpretative stance of the reader. More specifically, it will be open to the reader or viewer so to position herself in relation to certain mirror-shards that she will take the elements they contribute to the overall image as central, and interpret other elements as variously related to them—as extending, complicating, or otherwise supplementing the impression those central elements convey in their own internally coherent visual space.

The structure of this book should make it clear that I am taking lessons 3 and 4 of *Elizabeth Costello* as the central shards of the word-mirror it constitutes, and reading the other lessons primarily as relating to them. But although some shards or other must necessarily acquire a certain centrality for the viewer of any such mirror, insofar as any such viewer must take up a specific position in relation to the mirror, the relativity of that attribution of centrality is equally necessary (because just as much a function of the embodiedness of viewing and reading alike), and so equally merits acknowledgment. To shift my figurative terms from one set provided by the first lesson to another, we might say that I am committed to regarding the Tanner Lectures (which appear as lessons 3 and 4) as the centre of the book; but I am equally committed to acknowledging that their reappearance in this book decentres them by embedding them in contexts or frames that complicate in various ways the internal coherence that they might have seemed to possess when viewed on their own. I have already examined the ways in which the first lesson's focus on realism alters our impression of lessons 3 and 4; in the following chapters, I want to explore the parallel impact of the other lessons, beginning in the present chapter with the African context provided by lessons 2 and 5, within which the Tanner Lectures are most immediately embedded.

THE BREATH OF THE POET

Lesson 2, entitled "The Novel in Africa," reproduces the text of Coetzee's 1998 Una's Lecture at the University of California (which therefore postdates the delivery of the Tanner Lectures, which it nevertheless precedes in the book); and lesson 5, entitled "The Humanities in Africa," reprints his 2001 lecture at the Carl Friedrich von Siemens Stiftung in Munich. These connections and discontinuities between performance and text are themselves thematized in the first of the Africa lessons, which takes as a central concern the relation between oral and written language, and thereby foregrounds another aspect of literature's interest in the body— its dependence upon an idea of the human voice, and its ambivalence about that dependence, about whether to celebrate or resent and deny it. It is an interest that Plato shared, and that philosophy ever since has inherited.

In "The Novel in Africa," Costello once again gives a talk—this time, as one of a number of speakers invited to entertain the passengers on a luxury cruise to Antarctica. But hers, on "The Future of the Novel," is paired with another, much longer one given by a Nigerian writer named Emmanuel Egudu, the title of which is also the title of the lesson that contains it. That eponymy, taken together with the fact that, whereas the lesson directly reproduces every word of Egudu's talk, it resorts to a brief summary of most of Costello's (reproducing only its opening paragraphs), might suggest that Coetzee's focus has been displaced onto another character. But matters are not so simple—in part because Costello's thinking is far more stimulated by, and so stimulating about, Egudu's claims than those of her own talk, in part because the latter play a more important structural role than we are at first encouraged to see, and in part because this story's narrative viewpoint is throughout (for the first, but not the last, time in this book) tethered to that of Costello herself, and even more tightly than the narrative viewpoint of lessons 1, 3, and 4 is tied to that of her son. By eliminating his namesake's intermediary presence in this way, Coetzee also at once simplifies and intensifies the question of his relation to Costello.

Costello's talk comes first and concerns the relations between literature, history, and the historicality of human experience. She pictures the future as merely a structure of hopes and expectations, a fiction of the mind; but although the same is true of the past—"a story made of air that we tell ourselves" (EC, 38)—it has the further miraculous property (unshared by our sketchy and bloodless imaginings of the future, even when they take the form of visions of heaven and hell) of being shared: "in making thousands and millions of individual fictions, fictions created by individual human beings, lock well enough into one another to give us what looks like a common past" (EC, 38). The novel is an attempt to understand the human fate one case at a time, and in essentially historical sequence: how X got from A through B, C and D, to Z. "Like history, the novel is thus an exercise in making the past coherent. Like history, it explores the respective contributions of character and circumstance to forming the present" (EC, 39) and its power to produce the future. This, she claims, is the point of the novel, its reason for existing; and in so doing, she once again locates herself firmly within the tradition of realism as understood by Ian Watt.

The core of Egudu's talk is the following claim, which recasts a thought familiar to Western philosophy since Plato characterized writing as mere inert matter (a corpse from which the living spirit of speech has always already departed), so as to reopen the question of its cultural affinity: "The African novel, the true African novel, is an oral novel. On the page it is inert, only half alive; it wakes up when the voice, from deep in the body, breathes life into the words, speaks them aloud" (EC, 45).

African writers, he claims, are heirs to an oral tradition. By this he means a culture in which the alphabet is a recent affair, in which reading is not a typically African recreation although talking certainly is, in which writing books can provide no indigenous livelihood because it lacks an indigenous audience (and so African writers earn their living primarily through a variety of primarily oral activities that spin off from their achievements on the page—teaching, lecturing, addressing those on cruises). This makes it possible for the sensitivities, rhythms, and styles of African prose to stay in touch with the way its culture inhabits and finds expression in the bodies of its members—the way they live their bodies in dance, music, and eating, but also in the way they smile or frown, the way they sleep. And in so doing, the African novel constitutes a critique of the Western novel, which has gone far down the road of disembodiment, and thereby engendered a culture of reading in silence and solitude. African writing is, in effect, a form of writing that aims to overcome the privileging of writing—to be most fully itself when read aloud.

Costello is having nothing of this quasi-Platonic "pseudo-philosophy" (EC, 46), which disparages writing not by relating its mere materiality to that of the body, but by associating the vivacity of speech with the vitality of animate, bodily being. In a dinner-table conversation with Egudu, she argues that his aspiration runs contrary to the essence of the novel: while being perfectly capable of giving expression to an individual voice, it was never intended to be the script of a performance by a living actor, and its nature as a handy, pocket-sized, and so easily distributable block of paper militates against any such function. The real problem for the African novel, she claims, is rather that those who attempt to write such novels are (as Egudu has already pointed out) doing so with an eye to their reception by Westerners; they have accepted the role of interpreting Africa to foreigners rather than attempting to explore African experiences and African worlds to and for fellow Africans. In short, they end up performing their Africanness, understood as a species of the exotic, as they write, rather than exploring it in their writing as a species of the familiar, the common, the everyday. And finally, she thinks but does not say, a novel about people who live in an oral culture is not an oral novel, any more than a novel about women is a women's novel: in other words, Egudu is conflating an object or subject of inquiry with the form and nature of the inquiry itself.

Recalling the fact that lesson 2 is embedded within the context provided by lesson 1, a reader might be inclined to say that, taken in terms of their internal logic, Egudu's and Costello's critiques of one another are both offered in the name of realism. In Costello's case this is obvious: in effect, she accuses Egudu of romanticising himself and his culture—of failing to be realistic about either the material basis of the literary medium of the novel or the economic, cultural, and political conditions of contemporary African writing. Egudu might at first be taken to be rejecting the realistic aspirations of the Western novel altogether; but in fact, he criticizes the genre's development in the West precisely because it amounts (in his view) to a denial of the reality of human embodiment, and more specifically of the ultimate embodiment of such literary functions as style and tone in the bodily reality of the human voice. If Egudu emphasises an idea of performing oneself in his lecture, does that not amount to a more realistic acknowledgment of his present circumstances, particularly his immediate task of performing for an audience of passengers on a cruise, than Costello's high-minded account of the writer's vocation in exactly the same performative, even vaudevillean, context? And if Costello seems strangely wedded to an idea of the novel as possessed of an essence, when (as we have already seen, and Egudu points out) one might define the novel as "the form of writing that was formless, that had no rules, that made up its rules as it went along" (EC, 44–45), is not Egudu equally wedded to an idea of the body as possessed of an essence (i.e., the voice)? If so, should we not conclude that they are both insufficiently thoroughgoing in their attempts to define a realistic version of realism?

Coetzee does not, however, offer these, or indeed any other, explicit attempts to adjudicate between this pair of opposed and complementary positions. Instead, he juxtaposes them and allows them to rub against each other as the story progresses; and he explores the way in which they are embodied (emerging from a complex matrix of interests constituting the individuality of those who enounce them), and the ways in which this embodiment modifies the degree of our conviction in their validity as ideas, as well as our understanding of the individuals who profess them.

Most immediately, there are the performative differences between Costello and Egudu. Because Costello is no longer sure that she believes what she is saying in her lecture, and is incapable of preventing that absence of conviction from emerging in her voice, she generates little enthusiasm, and even less conviction, in her audience; and her performance in the after-dinner conversation with Egudu is variously hampered by the desire to preserve a façade of civility with a fellow entertainer. Egudu, by contrast, has the audience of his talk in the palm of his hand: his natural, physical charm, his effortlessly booming voice, the force and passion of his performance, all contribute to his rhetorical success; and they continue to carry him past Costello's more forcefully enunciated personal objections around the dinner table.

This contrast returns us to the distinction between text and performance introduced in lesson 1 from a different angle—one that aligns it with a distinction between rhetoric and substance, charisma and content. But matters are more complicated. To begin with, Costello's failure to achieve rhetorical conviction in her performance is partly a matter of her not really believing in her text—more precisely, it has to do with her no longer being sure whether or not she believes what she is saying.

> Ideas like these must have had some grip on her when years ago she wrote them down, but after so many repetitions they have taken on a worn, unconvincing air. On the other hand, she no longer believes very strongly in belief. Things can be true, she now thinks, even if one does not believe in them, and conversely. Belief may be no more, in the end, than a source of energy, like a battery which one clips into an idea to make it run. As happens when one writes: believing whatever has to be believed to get the job done. (EC, 39)

Costello suspects that Egudu is in a rather similar condition. She cannot believe that his big, engaging smile is genuinely spontaneous, or indeed genuine at all; she feels that he is in fact as bored with the sound of his own voice on the topic of the African novel as she is with hers, and she knows that what he describes as a spin-off from his primary task of writing—such performances as this talk—has in fact become his primary mode of life. It is not that either of them is insincere, as if offering what they know to be false as true: it is that both, in their different ways, are operating in a domain where the distinction between rhetoric and substance, appearance and reality, no longer has a grip. The passage embodies a dialectic whose starting point is that ideas or beliefs begin by taking a grip on us, by our being convinced of their truth, and our understanding their truth as something that holds independently of whether or not we believe in them; but their endless reiteration wears away our conviction, or more precisely leads us to the view that our belief in the truth of something might become, and so be, a matter entirely unconnected with its truth. In other words, it is the very idea of truth as independent of our beliefs that creates the logical space for a phenomenon of belief that is entirely independent of truth—a domain in which belief is no longer inherently truth-oriented but is ultimately reducible to a matter of energy or mere utility.

One might think of this situation as one in which belief becomes opaque to reality—in which the medium of thought is losing its capacity to render what exists independently of us nonetheless graspable by us, and becoming rather an impenetrable barrier between us and what is really the case. Costello is, in effect, picturing the medium of philosophy in precisely the terms in which she previously pictured the medium of contemporary literary realism—as no longer capable of allowing us to see straight through it to reality, and as threatening to convince us that it was always an illusion to think that either medium could ever do so.

There certainly do seem to be certain ways of life in which such a threat is realized. For example, the career of a politician—from youthful idealism, through years of engaging again and again in debates and declarations of the truth and validity of one's conviction, to the wholly professionalized condition in which ministers can produce opinions and arguments in favour of any given government policy to any interviewer they meet while neither believing nor disbelieving what they are saying—might be thought to follow the dialectic Costello lays out with perfect fidelity. The condition of an experienced novelist, who has endlessly devoted her life to the creation of credible characters who are nevertheless always and necessarily mere appearance, might also be thought to match the concluding stage of that dialectic; although here we need to remember that the novelist's job can be done well or badly, and that part of doing it well may be learning how to acknowledge the unreality of one's creations without losing faith in their ability to unveil reality. And any philosopher will recognize in Costello's anxiety about the reality of the distinction between appearance and reality, between pure rhetoric and truth-oriented discourse, as taking her to the verge of endorsing the sophist's view of human reason as simply one more power game with representations. The sophist has been philosophy's most intimate enemy since Plato's founding of the subject; and what Costello is pointing towards is the possibility that, in the domain of everyday life, sophistry is winning.

The phenomenon Costello describes might in fact be thought to have at least one other important manifestation in modern life—a phenomenon she indicates at the beginning of the tale, again picking up a theme from lesson 1, which connected realism with individuals' inhabitations of social roles: "[A] poseur, she now wonders: what is that? Someone who seems to be what he is not? Which of us is what he seems to be, she seems to be?" (EC, 36). This social world is not one of insincerity: it is one in which the idea of sincerity, and so of insincerity, has increasingly restricted application. And what effects will that have on the task of apprehending reality as it truly is, whether in literature's way or philosophy's?

A second contextual level or layer for the ideas in play here emerges through the differences of perspective engendered by Costello's and Egudu's rather different kinds of non-European cultural contexts. Costello has visited parts of Africa and so can test Egudu's claims against that experience. But she primarily understands his position as an African writer in terms of her experience as an Australian writer; and it is the terms provided by that experience that condition her advice to Egudu to cultivate a domestic audience, to turn away from foreign eyes and focus on exploring a world common to both reader and author. What she offers may or may not be good advice; but it is one that wagers on exactly the ideas of cross-cultural reach and commonality that Egudu, from his particular Nigerian perspective, wants to put in question. More specifically, from his point of view, Costello's suspicion of particularity and instinct for universality locates her as a representative not of Australian cultural difference but of Western cultural imperialism. The charge will not be unfamiliar to her white South African creator.

The third framework provided for these ideas is the very one outlined by Costello's talk on the novel's inherently historical mode of understanding its individual human cases. For Costello and Egudu have a history: in their progress from A to Z, they encountered one another many years before their meeting on the cruise ship, at a PEN conference in Kuala Lumpur. But it is only at the very end of the story that we learn how close that encounter was.

> Her thoughts go back to Kuala Lumpur, when she was young, or nearly young, when she spent three nights in a row with Emmanuel Egudu, also young then. "The oral poet," she said to him teasingly. "Show me what an oral poet can do." And he laid her out, lay upon her, put his lips to her ears, opened them, breathed his breath into her, showed her. (EC, 58)

What prompts this recollection is a conversation with another ship's entertainer with whom Egudu is having sex; when asked what she sees in him, this woman mentions his generosity and manliness, but particularly his voice, and the way it makes one shudder; and she makes Costello realize that, if she is not exactly jealous, she is certainly mourning her retirement or exile from "the game. Like being a child again, with a child's bedtime" (EC, 58). So what is the connection between her hostility to Egudu's idea of orality, of "the voice, dark essence of the body, welling up from within it: (EC, 46), and her knowledge of the way Egudu's real, physical voice participates in, emblematizes or embodies, the sexual charisma of his body, as well as of the way her body responded to it? Does the relation undermine Egudu's advocacy of the idea of literary orality, revealing it to be merely one more, sublimated expression of his overwhelmingly oral mode of being? Or does it undermine Costello's resistance to that idea, by showing not only that in reality she responds ecstatically to the living presence of this voice, but also that her rejection of the idea might be rooted in her sense of having been seduced and then discarded by its owner—that abandoning herself to the voice will result in being abandoned by it? Can anyone sincerely declare that their evaluations of ideas always, or ever could, float free from their experiences of their referents, or from the ways in which they are embodied in flesh-and-blood individual advocates?

This image of the oral poet interestingly crosses ideas of the sexual with that of literary creativity, with Costello's invitation to Egudu to show what he can do; and Egudu's response furthers this crossing, by avoiding the obvious sexual connotations of oral activity, and substituting for them a more barely linguistic deed. But he does not, in the end, actually whisper words into her ear, or at least we are not told that he does so; rather, he breathes his breath into her ear—the irreducible vehicle or medium of speech, an essential element of what Costello earlier called the mingling of breath and sense in great poetry, and a literalization of literature's most familiar story of its own origination, in inspiration (a word embarrassingly advanced by one of those listening to the after-dinner debate, and glossed—although not clearly by any character, not even Costello—as "receiving the spirit into oneself" [EC, 52]). In effect, then, Coetzee pushes the Freudian plotting of relations between artistic and sexual energy further, by relating both to bare breath, to the sheer physicality of the voice beyond or beneath sexual purpose or semantic message.

Two other details of this final passage, one of content and one of form, further complicate the picture. The first emerges if one feels, as I do, that to talk of Egudu as having "laid [Costello] out" is to employ a phrase more suited to a funeral director's presentation of a corpse than a sexual encounter with another living body. Take this intimation of death together with the idea of introducing something into someone's ear, and with the fact that what Egudu shows her is revealed by breath without speech—call it a dumb-show; then one might wonder whether one way in which this lesson aspires to be a palimpsest as well as a mirror lies in its invocation of Hamlet, and specifically his play-within-the-play, the one designed to catch the conscience of the king.

Within that doubled but initially dumb-show, Hamlet apparently intends to represent Claudius as murdering Hamlet's father by pouring poison into his ear. Are we, then, to think of Costello as intending to represent her poet's breath as poisonous? If so, is this because the deed poisons Costello and Egudu's relationship for the future, or because poetic orality, with its synthesis of sense with breath, taints the essence of the novel, and so the essence of realism, as Costello understands it? But if Egudu stands in Claudius's place, then Claudius's failure to recognize himself in Hamlet's dumb-show until that representation is supplemented with unambiguous words might suggest that Egudu would fail to recognize Costello's account as accurate. Would this be because he does not think of their relationship as poisoned, or of the novel as tainted by orality (as Claudius might deny that he poisoned old Hamlet in this particular way, without denying that he murdered him); or would it be because he would deny that the represented event ever happened (as Claudius might deny murder, perhaps by arguing that the blame lay rather with Gertrude)?[1]

Coetzee's relation to this particular question might best be assessed by bringing into the picture the second, formal detail that I mentioned earlier. For the final sentence of the lesson—with its six clauses, each taking off from a word in the previous clause, and each contributing beats to a hypnotic overall rhythm in which sense and sound are complicatedly and yet smoothly married—enacts what it describes: the fusion of poetic breath into the body of language, and so the capacity of the novel form to acknowledge the embodied orality of the human voice without failing in its task of showing the real (even if the form of that showing is not what the traditional realist might previously have expected, addressing as it does

---

[1] Stanley Cavell's essay "Hamlet's Burden of Proof," included in his *Disowning Knowledge: In Seven Plays of Shakespeare* (Cambridge: Cambridge University Press, 2003), explores some of the uncertainties surrounding this play-within-a-play.

the ear as much as the eye). One might say: just as the fourth clause of this sentence simultaneously says that Egudu opens his lips and (thereby) opens Costello's ears, so Coetzee aims to open our ears to the full range of his voice.

This complex embedding of literary, linguistic, sexual, and physical registers is also furthered by the fourth and final framing of the Costello–Egudu intellectual exchanges—one that presages the theme of lessons 3 and 4 and amounts to a displaced representation of the third talk arranged for the cruise passengers, one on "The Lives of Whales" (with sound recordings). For those passengers are headed to Antarctica—a domain bereft of human life and so of history; and the discussion with the Russian woman that ends the lesson takes place on Macquarie Island, on the edge of that extrahuman continent. But of course, it is an environment teeming with nonhuman life—with fish, penguins, and albatrosses in particular. It is also an environment into which humans have made violent inroads: in the nineteenth century, Costello recalls, hundreds of thousands of penguins were "clubbed to death here and flung into cast-iron steam boilers to be broken down into useful oil and useless residue" (EC, 55). And yet even this near-psychotic vision of animal life as merely physical, as either resources or remains, has left that life essentially untouched—prelapsarian; the penguins still innocently swim out to welcome visitors, to be touched and stroked by them, or simply to be contemplated as fellow creatures.

There is ample evidence here that Costello's woundedness by our treatment of nonhuman animals is not reflected only in the mirror-shards of lessons 3 and 4. For she experiences a strong sense of identity with the albatross and its fledgling (giving its "long, soundless cry of warning") that she encounters on the island before encountering the Russian: "*Before the fall*, she thinks. *This is how it must have been before the fall. I could miss the boat, stay here. Ask God to take care of me*" (EC, 56). To stay with these creatures would be to take on their vulnerability, and the apparent invulnerability of their innocence. More specifically, it would be to acknowledge a certain kinship between their unknowing performance of themselves before the cruise-liner's passengers and her earlier all-too-knowing performance of herself as a writer before that same audience. But to become like the albatrosses would be to recover Adam's ability to name the animals, which Costello (following many philosophers since Plato) fantasizes as a matter of being able to represent and replicate cries without sound, that is, to enact meaning without material embodiment. To miss the boat would therefore amount to missing the boat as a writer, and so as a human being—that species complex enough to be burdened by language. It would amount to the denial of one aspect of human embodiment in the name of another, as if our animality could be acknowledged without acknowledging what differentiates us from our fellow creatures. It is, perhaps, no accident that the Russian woman's arrival interrupts this fantasy and recalls Costello to her earlier experience of the embodiedness of Egudu's voice.

Indeed, for Costello, contemplating the albatrosses also offers a further, and possibly competing, perspective on the embodiedness of the human voice:

> The Southern Ocean, Poe never laid eyes on it, Edgar Allen, but criss-crossed it in his mind. Boatloads of dark islanders paddled out to meet him. They seemed ordinary folk *just like us*, but when they smiled and showed their teeth the teeth were not white but black. It sent a shiver down his spine, and rightly so. The seas full of things that seem like us but are not. Sea-flowers that gape and devour. Eels, each a barbed maw with a gut hanging from it. Teeth are for tearing, the tongue is for churning the swill around: that is the truth of the oral. Someone should tell Emmanuel. Only by an ingenious economy, an accident of evolution, does the organ of ingestions sometimes get to be used for song. (EC, 54)

Is this the truth of the oral, or just of the nonhuman oral? If an eel is essentially a barbed maw with a gut hanging from it, does that make Elizabeth Costello (earlier described in terms of a mouth leading to a pythonlike swallowing gullet leading to a pear-shaped belly-sac) just like the eel, or not at all like the eel (since she can grasp the eel in these terms, and it cannot so grasp her)? The vision of this paragraph is not single, but double; and so are its sources. We have a concluding evocation of the evolutionary point of view, but in a paragraph that begins from a purely literary perspective. The literary imagination sees fellow human beings as essentially not like us, simply because their teeth are a different colour; even when that colour is black, why is the shiver it might induce rightly induced and suffered—as opposed to something to be overcome? Is this because our sense of other humans as not like us ultimately resolves itself into a visceral disgust at physical otherness? And does the evolutionary imagination demonstrate a continuity or a discontinuity between humans and nonhuman animals?

The idea of humans as one more species subject to evolutionary processes, and so as having evolved from nonhuman animal forms, would suggest continuity, and so would suggest that the sea is full of things that not only seem but are like us. But at the same time, it suggests that accidents of evolution can have a fateful significance for any given species—so that, for example, the use of organs of ingestion for song amounts to a re-creation of those organs as something else entirely, and so engenders a qualitative difference between our own and other species (so that those who can tell stories with their mouths are not at all like those who cannot).

Once again, Coetzee does not advance an opinion or an argument about these matters, and the ways in which they might either threaten to eviscerate human life of genuine meaning or rather provide ways of resisting that threat. Instead, he offers a way of seeing each perspective, and each way of thinking within each perspective, as related to—and hence something that should be embedded or embodied within, that is, acknowledged by—every other.

THE BODY OF CHRIST

The second African lesson is set in South Africa, and it foregrounds an issue that the format of a lesson (with its suggestion of the liturgical) anyway invokes, and that has left its traces in every preceding tale, through their brief references to divine inspiration, prelapsarian states, and the nature of God and his creation: distinctively religious belief. The narrative viewpoint remains tethered to Elizabeth Costello's consciousness, and a speech is once again central to the narrative itself; but this time it is given by Costello's sister, Blanche, better known as Sister Bridget of the Sisters of Mary, a Catholic nun whose work for children infected by the AIDS virus in a Zululand hospital has led to the award of an honourary degree from the University of Johannesburg. Blanche's speech at the ceremony to which she invites her sister presses Elizabeth, and us, to consider whether these sisters in blood are, or are not, sisters in spirit (as lesson 2 invited us to consider how different Costello's and Egudu's realisms really are beneath the skin).

The university has awarded Blanche a doctorate in *literae humaniores*, human letters or the humanities; and in her address to all the humanities graduates of that year, Blanche argues that the humanities are at once indebted and hostile to religion. Indebted, because their central concern with textual scholarship originally arose from a desire to recover the true message of the Bible; it was in seeing that such a recovery presupposed powers of translation, interpretation, and understanding of that book's cultural and historical matrix that the core subjects of the humanities came to be bound together. But the more specific need to command New Testament Greek led scholars to immerse themselves in the pre-Christian texts of antiquity, and understanding them and their culture became an end in itself. What started as a way of understanding humans in their unredeemed state, and so of understanding redemption, then became a way of advocating an alternative conception of how to live well. What was supposed to be a means of access to ultimately religious reality became the sole reality with which we concerned ourselves, as if we saw no way of acknowledging its reality other than by denying the reality it originally mediated.

According to Blanche, that vision also ultimately failed, so the study of the classics (rather than the classics themselves) was offered as a way of living well instead—another medium becoming the sole putative substance of reality, a second deferral or detour of the realist project; but that too failed. Now the humanities can offer no view of redemption, of the good life for humans, whatever: they are simply an array of desiccated techniques in the service of no particular end, having definitively lost touch with their original, animating, edificatory purpose. The humanities are on their deathbed; and what has brought about this death is "the monster enthroned by those very studies as first and animating principle of the universe: the monster of reason, mechanical reason" (EC, 123).

One can see the family resemblance, particularly against the background of Elizabeth's Gates Lecture. Blanche patently shares her sister's willingness to venture fearlessly into the realms of complex historical scholarship, to tell a story about the whole sweep of modern Western culture, and to locate the core of our contemporary malaise in a certain (mis)conception of reason. She also possesses her sister's capacity to confound expectations, and to risk giving deep offence to those wanting only to honour her good works. Like Elizabeth in her animadversions on animals, Blanche's concern is with saving souls: not simply her own, but those of all human beings.

Nevertheless, Blanche later explicitly includes the novel, or at least a certain humanistic understanding of it, among the creations of humanistic study to which she takes exception: "I do not need to consult novels . . . to know what pettiness, what baseness, what cruelty human beings are capable of. That is where we start, all of us. We are fallen creatures. If the study of mankind amounts to no more than picturing to us our darker potential, I have better things to spend my time on" (EC, 128). Where in lesson 2 Elizabeth had seen the myth of the fall as facilitating a prelapsarian vision, and even an invitation to make that vision a reality, Blanche takes it to show that any representation of the real must be a representation of fallenness, of our darker potential realized, and hence a misrepresentation of true humanity. And insofar as the novel is inherently realist, so much the worse for it. For in its hands, unredeemed human nature (whether in its classical, its academic, or its contemporary forms) is not merely a distracting obstacle to the study of reality, something we attend to instead of attending to the real; it will positively misrepresent that reality as a childish illusion (which is all that religion could be if the reality of our nature were what religion knows as fallenness).

Even though Blanche also recognizes that the form has other, more redemptive, possibilities, with which she is more in sympathy, Elizabeth

is unsettled by these apparently pointed remarks; and her initial inclination to support her sister's position mutates over the time of her visit to
a more settled opposition, one that is provoked by something she encounters on a short visit to her sister's hospital, in its chapel:

> [S]he is struck at once by the carved wooden crucifix behind the altar, showing
> an emaciated Christ with a mask-like face crowned with a wreath of real acacia
> thorns, his hands and feet pierced not by nails but by steel bolts. The figure
> itself is of near life size; the cross reaches up to the bare rafters; the whole
> construction dominates the chapel, overbears it. (EC, 134)

The station is full of such crucifixes, of varying sizes but all reproducing
the same agonized human figure, and all carved by one local man, Joseph,
who has devoted his life to their production. Elizabeth finds this construction repellent in a number of overlapping ways: it represents the order's
willingness to tether a local person's talents and life to a single, unvarying
rut of activity, denying him a fuller life both as an artist and as a man;
and it embodies a specific kind of representation of Christ, one that is not
only European but Gothic, essentially masochistic and imbued with hatred of the human body, hostile to any mode of affirming embodiment,
and particularly to artistic representations of it as beautiful:

> Why should people not be able to look at a work of art and think to themselves,
> *That is what we as a species are capable of being, that is what I am capable of
> being*, rather than looking at it and thinking to themselves, *My God, I am going
> to die, I am going to be eaten by worms*? (EC, 139)

Blanche is unmoved. She denies that Joseph was either dragooned into
piety, or into this particular mode of its artistic expression, which is anyway utterly faithful to the reality of one human being's suffering and
death and utterly without the importation of fashion or the artist's individual ego. It is, in short, a mode of artistic self-abnegation that is entirely
in tune with the extremity of self-emptying that it represents. And the
ideals of the beautiful human form to which Elizabeth opposes the Gothic
crucifixional tradition—rooted ultimately in that of the Greeks—is in fact
one that the colonial rulers of Zululand explicitly offered to their charges,
and which those charges rejected in favour of a Christianity that offers
instead a god who suffers with them, who thereby acknowledges the reality of their lives by acknowledging the reality of their suffering, and gives
them a way of finding comfort or succour in that suffering. Blanche offers
her congregations no talk of a better life after death; she offers only to
help them bear the cross of their mortal lives, in all its embodied reality.

At the end of Elizabeth's visit, Blanche modifies or complicates the preceding opposition between Christian and Hellenic aesthetic, moral, and
metaphysical values. She tells Elizabeth that, even within the Greek tradi-

tion, there is more to be found than the Apollonian ideals of harmony, formal beauty, and rational intelligibility. There is Orpheus:

> The ecstatic instead of the rational. Someone who changes form, changes colour, according to his surroundings. Someone who can die but then come back. A chameleon. A phoenix. Someone who appeals to women. Because it is women who live closest to the ground. Someone who moves among the people, whom they can touch—put their hand into the side of, feel the wound, smell the blood. . . . You went for the wrong Greeks, Elizabeth. (EC, 145)

The opposition between Orpheus and Apollo is not exactly Nietzsche's famous opposition between Dionysus and Apollo, but it is close enough to recall the way this dispute is articulated in philosophical terms (going right back to Plato), and to suggest that Blanche is in effect turning Nietzsche against himself. For she is claiming that what he saw as the founding Western repression of the ecstatic and irrational is not something that Christianity continued but rather something that it contests—that Christ is best understood not as a successor to Socrates and Euripides, but as a version of the understanding of the world they mean to annihilate. It is not that Hellenistic versions of redemption must necessarily oppose themselves to Christian ones: everything depends on which Hellenistic version of redemption we choose. The humanities chose Apollo; they went for the wrong Greeks, and they lost.

The published version of Coetzee's oral presentation of this material in Munich stops here—with what at the very least gives Blanche the last word over her sister, and a resulting sense that the resources of Christianity are intellectually and emotionally formidable (certainly far more capable of providing a nuanced understanding of Hellenistic humanism than it is of understanding Christianity). But lesson 5 of *Elizabeth Costello* gives Blanche's sister the right of reply—first in a letter that she composes but does not send, then in a continuation of the story begun in that unsent letter but not includable within it.

The letter tells of Elizabeth's visits to an old man in her mother's nursing home, for whom she acts as a model. When he expresses regret at not being able to paint her nude, she removes her blouse and bra and allows him to have his wish. Elizabeth connects her choice, and the pose she adopts in following it through, not with the Greeks but with a figure central to the Christian tradition and a certain mode of her artistic representation—Mary, the Mother of God, breast-feeding the infant Christ, as painted by Correggio and other Renaissance artists. Costello emphasizes the mutually determining relations here between Mary, Correggio's image of her, and the relation of Correggio's actual model to himself and his assistants in their studio; she thereby activates a version of Fried's sense of the mutually implicating fictional, real, and actional scenes of representation in painting. And in so doing, Costello sees an acknowledgment of what she wants to call, not humanism or the humanities, but humanity:

> When Mary blessed among women smiles her remote angelic smile and tips her sweet pink nipple up before our gaze, when I, imitating her, uncover my breasts for old Mr. Phillips, we perform acts of humanity. Acts like that are not available to animals, who cannot uncover themselves because they do not cover themselves. Nothing compels us to do it, Mary or me. But out of the overflow, the outflow of our human hearts we do it nevertheless: drop our robes, reveal ourselves, reveal the life and beauty we are blessed with. (EC, 150)

Coming upon this passage in its new context, after lessons 3 and 4, the reader will particularly be struck by Costello's untroubled acknowledgment of a fundamental difference between human and nonhuman animals; and it aligns interestingly with Stanley Cavell's sense that this difference was always already expressed (in lessons 3 and 4) by the hiddenness of Costello's wound, which he understood as figuring the clothedness of the human body (hence its possible unclothedness). But in the present context, that acknowledgment is embedded within a complex consideration of religion's understanding of the body.

For Costello, the beauty of the female breast is not just an aspect of the beauty of the human form: it reorients the Incarnation towards life rather than death, and towards the body as the bearer of life and giver of sustenance, as essentially fertile and creative. If one wishes to overturn the "centuries-long Christian night" of Gothic masochism, self-denial, and denial of life, one need not go to the Greeks, but to a particular synthesis of Greek and Christian culture, and thence to a particular element within Christian culture as such—its sense of the significance of Mary in particular, and femaleness in general, that is ineliminable from the scandalous notion that God becomes man. One might say: if Orpheus is Elizabeth's overlooked Greek, Mary is Blanche's overlooked Christian.

Costello cannot write even this unless she thinks of it as a letter to Blanche: but we are not told that she ever sends it, or that she has any intention of so doing; and primarily she thinks of herself as "writing to herself, that is, to whoever is with her in the room when she is the only one there" (EC, 145). Does this mean that writing is always writing to oneself as well as, even before, it is writing to another, and hence that the writing self (perhaps the self as such) is always another to itself? Or does it mean that the writing self is always already constituted by others—in particular by intimate familial others, brothers and sisters of the flesh becoming part of its spirit or soul? This letter begins to seem like an expression of resistance to a rigorous, unyielding aspect of herself that both is and is not her.

If so, then the story this writer is telling itself overflows what she can write, even to her sister (even to herself)—just as Coetzee seems to have found that his story about these sisters overflows itself, proceeding beyond any due, decorous limits of form or time and place. What she cannot write, he can include in his writing—the story of how Costello visits Mr. Phillips again, and uncovers herself again, not in order to be painted but as a treat to brighten up his Saturday; and of how she also stays long enough to perform an act of fellatio upon him, or at least to mimic the reality of such an act: "to loosen the cord of Mr. Phillips' pyjamas . . . and open up the front and plant a kiss on the entirely flaccid little thing, and take it in her mouth and mumble it until it stirs faintly with life" (EC, 154).

It is quite as if Coetzee finally satisfies the expectation aroused by Costello's teasing of Egudu, when her talk of oral poetry in a sexual context brings forth only breath in her ear. But if this constitutes a scene of deferred representation in the context of the book as a whole, it poses a rather different representational problem for Costello in its more immediate context of an unwritten letter. For she declares that she cannot write this account, and only in part because it is indecent; the more important obstacle is in fact the particular name she would give to what she did:

> Not *eros*, certainly—too grotesque for that? *Agape*? Again, perhaps not. Does that mean the Greeks would have no word for it? Would one have to wait for the Christians to come along with the right word: *caritas*?
>
> For that, in the end, is what she is convinced it is. From the swelling of her heart she knows it, from the utter illimitable difference between what is in her heart and what Nurse Naidoo would see, if by some mischance Nurse Naidoo, using her pass key, were to fling open the door and stride in. (EC, 154)

This passage circles around a problem of translation that is also one of interpretation, and of properly locating the cultural matrix of what is there to be seen and understood: it is, in other words, a problem of and for the humanities. But the redemptive word for this redemptive deed is one that Costello—perhaps because of her historical position—can only find in Christianity; it is not even a matter of finding the right Greek, for there is no such Greek to be found. But is it a use of this Christian word— one which embodies their notion of what redemption must be—that a Christian can accept? Can this way of acknowledging the body, of honouring its reality and the reality of its mortality by activating at least a memory of its capacity for sexual pleasure and its various sublimations and transformations, be part of any understanding of what it is to be part of the body of Christ?

In the end, then, the human body—call it the spirit's necessary embodiment in flesh and blood—may pose an insuperable problem for both Hellenism and Christianity, for humanism and religion alike; and if for them, why not for any cultural system of sense-making? Perhaps that is the truth about the body: it is both the origin of human ways of making sense of things, and that which exceeds any such sense-making system. No way of seeing it can incorporate all there is to see, and to say, about it, and yet no doubt about our ways of articulating the reality of things can stand in the face of its reality. Perhaps this is what Coetzee has in mind when, speaking as a critic about his own novels, he offers the following account of his interest in the body:

> If I look back over my own fiction, I see a simple (simple-minded?) standard erected. That standard is the body. Whatever else, the body is not "that which is not," and the proof that it *is* is the pain that it feels. The body with its pain becomes a counter to the endless trials of doubt. (One can get away with such crudeness in fiction; one can't in philosophy, I'm sure.)
>
> Not grace, then, but at least the body. Let me put it baldly: in South Africa it is not possible to deny the authority of suffering and therefore of the body. It is not possible, not for logical reasons, not for ethical reasons (I would not assert the ethical superiority of pain over pleasure), but for political reasons, for reasons of power. And let me again be unambiguous: it is not that one *grants* the authority of the suffering body: the suffering body *takes* this authority: that is its power. To use other words: its power is undeniable.
>
> (Let me add, *entirely* parenthetically, that I, as a person, as a personality, am overwhelmed, that my thinking is thrown into confusion and helplessness, by the fact of suffering in the world, and not only human suffering. These fictional constructions of mine are paltry, ludicrous defenses against that being-over-whelmed, and, to me, transparently so.) (DP, 248)

It would be easier to accept Coetzee's description of his position as crude in comparison to philosophy, if the manner of its articulation did not imply an ironic awareness on his part of the fact that philosophy has persistently regarded pain, and so the body's being in pain, as one possibly decisive counter to the endless trials of sceptical doubt (Wittgenstein's remarks on the pseudo-topic of a private language being the most pertinent contemporary example). Moreover, his worry about crudeness is far from crudely expressed, from (let us call it) a literary point of view—given, for example, its constituent idea of erecting the human body (with its distinctively erect carriage) as a standard for conviction. We might further wonder whether Coetzee's apparent confirmation that he is as haunted as Costello by the difficulties of reality surrounding the suffering animal body is really *entirely* parenthetical. It would surely be at least as unrealistic to regard thesis and parenthesis here as entirely unrelated as it would to think of them as collapsing into one another. Setting these complications aside, however, we might still ask whether Costello's act of charity reflects the authority that Mr. Phillip's suffering body takes over her own, or whether the fact that this act is fictional (certainly a fiction of Coetzee's, possibly an incommunicable fiction of Costello's produced by the authority that her sister's understanding of the body takes over her mind) really makes it no more than a transparent admission of fiction's paltry inadequacy, *qua* that which is not, in the face of that which most undeniably is.

To be sure, Costello herself does not exactly claim to understand what she did, and what it meant; she is clear that it would resist the understanding of others (the difference between what she is doing and what she means to be doing is utterly illimitable), and she is equally clear that the doing of it makes her a puzzle or a mystery to herself. "What can one make of episodes like this, unforeseen, unplanned, out of character? Are they just holes, holes in the heart, into which one steps and falls and then goes on falling?" (EC, 155). If *caritas* is nonetheless the word for what was in her heart, then it must be a word for a hole, an abyss—for the possibility of a human being acting out of character, flowing illimitably out or over herself; it is as if the redemptive word of Christianity does not so much save one from falling (from the Fall) or simply transcend our fallenness, but rather presents salvation as lying in an endless inner fall through oneself and beyond oneself as fallen, an ability to inhabit an absence internal to oneself.

Can literature capture this hole in the human heart? Can a character act out of character; or is it that whatever a character does will inevitably form one more shard of her character—not a hole, but part of a larger whole? Could anything Coetzee adds to this lesson, or any lesson he adds to the ones already present, be out of character for Elizabeth Costello? If human embodiment exceeds the grasp and the (un)certainty of all human sense-making systems, it must exceed that of literature; how, then, can literature properly represent this excess, if not by enacting it—by exceeding its own limits?

Chapter Twelve

EVIL AS OBSCENITY

I N JUNE 2002, COETZEE participated in a Nexus Conference on "Evil," in Tilburg, Holland, by giving a fictional account of Elizabeth Costello's participation in a conference on the question of evil in Holland. His presentation, announced as a "reading" rather than a lecture, was under the heading "The Possessed; Crime and Punishment; Guilt and Atonement" and appears as lesson 6 of *Elizabeth Costello*; Costello's talk is entitled "Witness, Silence and Censorship" and was advertised under the heading "Silence, Complicity, Guilt."

Rather than give her routine talk about censorship, Costello chooses instead to explore an experience that has recently led her to change her views about the reach of literature, and its capacity to bring certain experiences to words; and in portraying that exploration, Coetzee chooses to engineer a situation of Kafaesque realism, an occasion for the rigorous thinking through of an impossible intersection—here, between a fictional world and the real one. For what motivates Costello is her response to reading a (real) novel, Paul West's *The Very Rich Hours of Count von Stauffenberg*, which gives an account of the plot by a number of *Wehrmacht* officers to kill Hitler, and its aftermath. One chapter in particular, in which West re-creates the execution of the plotters in graphic detail, sickens Costello to the point at which she questions the morality of West's decision to imagine the scene, and to invite his readers to do likewise.

> She is no longer sure that people are always improved by what they read. Furthermore, she is not sure that writers who venture into the darker territories of the soul always return unscathed. She has begun to wonder whether writing what one desires, any more than reading what one desires, is in itself a good thing. (EC, 160)

Accordingly, having conjured up at the beginning of her talk the familiar, particularly Romantic, image of the author as brave explorer in search of a higher truth, and with a duty to venture into forbidden places— "to emerge from the cave with reeking sword in one hand and the head of the monster in the other" (EC, 172)—she cites West's book, but she refuses to quote from it. She argues, in strongly Platonic vein, that the cellar in which the plotters were executed is a forbidden place, into which authors as well as readers risk a great deal—perhaps all—by going.

"What arrogance, to lay claim to the suffering and death of those pitiful men! Their last hours belong to them alone, they are not ours to enter and possess" (EC, 174).

Costello's talk ends rather abruptly soon after this point, in part because her spirit fails her ("a limit has been reached, the limit of what can be achieved with a body of well-balanced, well-informed modern folk in a clean, well-lit lecture venue in a well-ordered, well-run European city in the dawn of the twenty-first century" [EC, 175]), but mainly because—as she learnt soon after her arrival in Holland—Paul West is participating in the conference and is a member of her audience. She has, in fact, spent much of the story trying to decide whether to give the talk at all, given West's presence—whether it might be altered so as to omit its key example, whether she really believes what she has written in her text, whether she knows exactly what it is that she believes and wants to say, what exactly it is about her reading experience that has led her to this change of heart. In the end, however, she decides to give the talk largely unaltered, having warned West in advance of its contents and attempted to explain her choice of example. How, then, does this shard of Coetzee's word-mirror supplement and complicate the images relayed by its fellows?

As always, Coetzee provides a number of overlapping contexts for Costello's stance. The first is the aftermath of her lecture and seminar at Appleton College on the lives of animals, which—we hear at the outset of this lesson—has led to accusations of anti-Semitism and of belittling the Holocaust, as well as support from people whose goodwill embarrasses her; one aspect of these consequences is, she suspects, her invitation to this conference. To choose an aspect of the Second World War, and the moral squalor of Nazism, as her theme in Holland thereby both fulfils and defies the expectations of the organizers and the audience. But in the book, it is not the Gates Lecture but her visit to Blanche in South Africa that provides the immediate context within which her thinking is embedded: and the stance she presents is in fact highly reminiscent of that of her sister (quite as if Costello's gift as a novelist is a species of negative capability, a capacity to inhabit and—at least for a time—incorporate the beliefs of each person she encounters). It involves taking not only evil but the devil seriously; it offers a variation on Blanche's charge that novels describing human fallenness (as opposed to the possibility of redemption) are futile or worse; and it invokes an idea of the absolute as opposed to the merely relative, in favour of the former. It is not just that the events West depicts exhibit an extremity of moral squalor; Costello also argues—in response to a questioner who suggests that reading West's text may be bad for some (weaker vessels, he calls them) but good for others—that the experience offered by real writing . . . , real reading, is not a relative one, relative to the writer and his capacities, relative to the reader. . . . Mr. West, when he wrote those chapters, came in touch with something absolute. Absolute evil. His blessing and his curse, I would say. Through reading him that touch of evil was passed on to me. Like a shock. Like electricity. (EC, 176)

I take it to be no accident that what Costello understands as absolutely evil is closely related to Coetzee's recognition (cited in chapter 11) of the suffering human body as functioning in his fiction as an ultimate standard, one that stands firm even in the face of global sceptical doubt about morality or indeed about human judgement and sense-making of any kind. However that may be, this sudden introduction of a conception of evil as absolute rather than relative is plainly as much the articulation of a view of morality as it is of literature; and it thereby suggests a further connection between Costello and Coetzee and the philosopher Rai Gaita, whose writings on animals I had occasion to quote in an earlier chapter. For Gaita is also the author of a book entitled *Good and Evil: An Absolute Conception*—a text that acknowledges the sheer difficulty of making sense of ideas of absolute value in contemporary cultural circumstances (in which the multiple conditionedness of all judgements and concepts seems self-evident), but wishes nevertheless to articulate a conception of absolute good and evil that makes mysteriousness internal to its nature.[1]

To condense a long and complex argument: Gaita attempts to elaborate a conception of human beings as absolutely or unconditionally precious or valuable in the sense that, no matter how profoundly evil their actions and character may be, they may never be killed in the spirit of ridding the world of vermin. This view can be taken to be morally serious only if it embodies an acknowledgment of just how deeply, even absolutely, evil human beings can be; in this sense, to think of some things as unconditionally good is not inconsistent with, but rather hangs together with, a preparedness to regard some actions and dispositions as absolutely evil. Even in the light of that acknowledgment, however, the holder of Gaita's conception would say that no human being (not even the most apparently unregenerate) is beyond the reach of a sober remorse. No one can or should be deemed necessarily incapable of coming to see the evil of what he did, and of that in his character which allowed him to do it; and no one who is capable of experiencing such remorse need think of himself as essentially filth or vermin. In other words, even in the light of a genuine remorse, which fully illuminates the evil of what he did, he will not be compelled to regard himself as utterly worthless, deserving only destruction.

---

[1] (London: Macmillan, 1991; second edition 2005).

He will, however, think of what he did as essentially mysterious: for the characteristic cry of such remorse is "My God! What have I done!"—an expression of absolute incomprehension that might also be expressed by asking "How is it possible for me, for anyone, to have done such things?" This is not a question in search of an answer—as if further information (whether psychological, autobiographical. or cultural) might dissipate this sense of puzzlement. It is an expression of a sense of such evil as both undeniable and yet inherently beyond our comprehension, of the incomprehensible truth that it nevertheless exists in the world and so is something with which we can and do make contact in our experience.

And in Gaita's view (which here runs parallel with Milosz's view of beauty), it is internal to the companion conception of absolute goodness that one regard it as essentially mysterious that there should be anything of unconditional value in the world, and as equally incomprehensible that there be people capable of elaborating and sustaining such a way of perceiving the world—which means people capable of resisting the all-too-natural thought that some human actions place their agents decisively beyond the pale, as if removing them from the moral field as necessary limits on our actions (beings to whom certain things simply must not be done).

It is not obvious that Costello's sense of some forms of evil as absolute is paired with a sense that even its practitioners retain absolute worth, and so impose a limit on our actions in response to their evil deeds. It would certainly seem all too apt to characterise the Nazi torturers of West's account as executing their victims in the spirit of ridding the world of vermin; but Costello herself is rather too happy to talk of the torturers as creatures or monsters for us to be confident that she would reject any attempts to execute them in turn in the same spirit. (She might also question Gaita's unqualified use of this idea of vermin in his articulation of this idea of absolute good and evil, with its suggestion that nonhuman animals are our best image of utter moral worthlessness—and in fact Gaita himself elsewhere reports one of his students as suggesting that we should not even destroy vermin in the spirit of ridding the world of vermin.) Nevertheless, Costello's sense of absolute evil does plainly involve a sense of its intrinsic mysteriousness: making contact with it is like receiving an electric shock of the kind dispensed by those who perform such deeds of absolute evil, and so appears as something that incomprehensibly violates her sense that the world makes sense, something that denies her confidence in her own moral standing and the moral coherence of human experience.

So much for the moral dimension of her encounter with West's book; what of its literary dimension? Most immediately, it serves to put in question a central assumption of the project of modernist realism as Costello and Coetzee have thus far developed it; for it leads Costello to reject the suggestion that readings, and so the texts being read, are always relative to writer and reader, who therefore constitute conditions (of production and consumption) that any genuinely realistic novelist must acknowledge. One might say: the view that all writing is so conditioned is itself conditioned—by a rejection of the idea of the unconditioned or absolute; and this too requires acknowledgment by any modernist writer.

But Costello's experience also reframes the view of imaginative activity around which her entire critique of philosophy in the Gates Lecture is based—the capacity of the writer and reader imaginatively to enter other modes of being and other individual consciousnesses, as well as one another's consciousness. For it is this very capacity that is at the root of her discomfort with West's book.

> Word by word, step by step, heartbeat by heartbeat, I accompany him into the darkness. *No one has been here before,* I hear him whisper, and so I whisper too; our breath is as one. *No one has been in this place since the men who died and the man who killed them. Ours is the death that will be died, ours the hand that will knot the rope.* ("Use thin cord," Hitler commanded his man. "Strangle them. I want them to feel themselves dying." And his man, his creature, his monster, obeyed.) (EC, 174)

By writing his book so well, West allows himself and his readers to feel these old men dying, hence to feel themselves dying, hence to re-create the absolute evil that Hitler and his monstrous creature brought about— which means that writer and reader come to occupy Hitler's position with respect to this evil, becoming not only its victim but its source. As Costello puts it directly to West, just before delivering her talk: "I was deeply impressed by your book. That is to say, it made an impress on me the way a branding iron does. Certain pages burn with the fires of hell" (EC, 171).

This is in part an attempt to recover the original experience behind a "dead" metaphor—an exercise just as much relevant to philosophy (with its familiar empiricist concern for the basis of ideas in sense-impressions) as to literature, and vital to her whole project of trying to understand her revulsion at West's book ("Hold fast to the word, then reach for the experience behind it: that has always been her rule for when she feels herself slipping into abstraction" [EC, 177]). But Costello also means what she says: it is not that his book represents something that is burning with the fires of hell, or that it represents those fires; the pages themselves are burning, and both author and readers are being consumed.

She is thereby giving expression to an impression of representations (and so, creators and consumers of such representations) and what they represent collapsing into one another; Costello reacts as if the evil that so incomprehensibly took up residence in northern Europe in the 1930s has now, through the power of literature, been incomprehensibly re-created, first in a novelist's comfortable living room in Australia, and then again in a clean, well-lit venue in a well-ordered, well-run European city at the dawn of the twenty-first century. This annihilation of temporal and spatial distance, this conjunction of the impossible with the real, this sense of fires of hell burning not in torture chambers but in the pages of a book, thereby exemplify once more that collapse of all our systems of knowledge that Costello's earlier Gates Lecture associated with our unwilling attempts to understand death.

As this particular association confirms, to put things in this way is not to claim that these ways of putting things are straightforwardly intelligible: how exactly is it that, through literature, we can die another's death, let alone kill another whom we have not killed? But to say that imagining something and actually doing it are two different things is precisely to miss the nature of Costello's experience of reading this book, and hence of reading books (of literature) in general. For it is words that imply direct participation in that which is being imaginatively represented that bring her as close as she can come to finding adequate expression for her experience. As she puts it later: "It is not something that can be demonstrated. It is something that can only be experienced" (EC, 176). And it is of the nature of this experience that it disturbs Costello in ways that she finds difficult to comprehend, and hence for the expression of which only words that resist understanding are appropriate—words such as her own reference to "the madness of my reading" (EC, 174). In short, what finds expression here is a fundamental resistance of literature and the literary imagination to the understanding—a difficulty of literary as well as moral reality.

This resistance is represented in Coetzee's story in various ways. The structural irony of Costello's unwillingness to embarrass a man whom she accuses of a kind of moral monstrosity, her self-bewildering anxiety about the etiquette of one's relation to absolute evil, is perhaps the most obvious reflection of her moral confusion. Such questions of tact and common politeness were hardly matters with which she seemed very concerned at Appleton College when delivering her Gates Lecture. Beyond this, however, Costello is driven by the knowledge that West will be in her audience to reexamine her relation to her own ideas, as expressed in the text she actually delivers, which was composed in the immediate aftermath of reading West's book.

She tries twice to retrace her steps to that original experience, and thus to avoid the simultaneously literary and moral threat of succumbing to abstractness in her thinking, once before and once after delivering the talk. The first appears more decisive in its conclusions. Beginning from the memory of her own brush with evil—a sexual assault from which she suffered broken bones—and her refusal ever to draw upon this episode in any of her writing (a refusal that she rather smugly contrasts with West's refusal of any analogous restraint), she eventually reaches the following perception:

> *Obscene.* That is the word, a word of contested etymology, that she must hold on to as talisman. She chooses to believe that *obscene* means *offstage.* To save our humanity, certain things that we may want to see (*may want to see because we are human!*) must remain off-stage. Paul West has written an obscene book, he has shown what ought not to be shown. That must be the thread of her talk. (EC, 168–89)

Once again, a word is traced back through its history to its origins, and so to the egg or seed from which its meaning grows; and it appears to generate an imperative. On the face of it, however, that imperative is moral: it is not that one could not show such things, could not bring what is offstage onto the stage, but rather that one should not. There may be a link here between Costello's thinking and the phenomenon I mentioned in chapter 2—that of the morally unthinkable. Such a conception is explicitly invoked in Gaita's book; and it fits neatly with broader conceptions of good and evil as absolute, insofar as it involves the thought that even to contemplate certain possible scenes and scenarios of what one knows to be moral evil is itself to succumb to evil by establishing the kind of contact with it that can taint and corrupt one's mind and heart. The question is: would the recognition that there is such a thing as the morally unrepresentable amount to the imposition of an external limit to the project of literary realism, a subjection of literature and its internal drives to the imperatives of morality; or would it rather amount to recognising that this project always already had a moral dimension—that the impulse to see things as they really are is in fact part of a drive towards self-improvement, a refusal to live in the realm of fantasy? Such an avowedly moral version of realism might well have to think of the morally unthinkable as essentially beyond representation.

However this may be, it is worth emphasizing that the tracking back by means of which Costello tries to stabilize her thinking is itself contestable; it entails that Costello chooses to believe something, thereby undermining the sense in which we think of belief as compelled by the nature of its subject matter rather than as an expression of the autonomy of our will; and what she chooses to believe is that human beings must be saved from their own humanity—a vision of human nature as compelled to undermine itself that matches Blanche's vision of originally sinful mankind in its pessimism and in its blatant air of self-contradiction.

Little wonder that she finds herself needing to rethink her relation to this belief in the aftermath of the talk itself. True: she continues to hold on to her guiding thread, her compulsion to use the word "obscene." But here, the issue at stake is more overtly incoherent or internally riven—she describes it now as "an obsession that is hers alone and that she clearly does not understand" (EC, 177), saying further that "you cannot exchange thoughts when you do not know what you think" (EC, 181)—and hence in a certain sense inconclusive. On one level, she pictures her experience as a kind of sense-impression: "that Saturday morning when she felt, she could have sworn, the brush of Satan's hot, leathery wing" (EC, 178). But of course, this manifestation of her literary literal-mindedness does not exactly look like a possible sense-impression, given its mixing of supernatural and natural registers—evil as embodied in a non-human animal (she later compares Satan to a liver fluke or pinworm) or monster. And the same resistance to comprehension is repeatedly returned to at a more abstract level: "It is like a wall that she comes up against time and again. She did not want to read but she read; a violence was done to her but she conspired in the violation. *He made me do it*, she says, yet she makes others do it" (EC, 181).

Implicit here is a further connection between what she feels that West did to her, and what the docker did to her years ago when she at first agreed and then refused to have sex with him: a violation of her being, a kind of glee in hurting her. It was West who excited her to read. To the obscene energy with which the hangman of the plotters exceeded even his commission from Hitler, West added his own—to use one of Costello's own earlier metaphors, he clipped in his imaginative belief in his characters like a battery to make the story run: "It was West who invented the gibes . . . , put them in the hangman's mouth" (EC, 177). But she recognizes in herself a degree, even a kind, of complicity in this literary violation that was absent from the real assault. To begin with, she already knows most if not all of what he has to teach her about the Nazis; and "what right had she not to know what, in all too clear a sense, she already knew?" (EC, 178). Is this split or incoherent state not exactly what she condemned, in the Ukrainians and Poles and ordinary Germans of the Nazi period, not to mention her fellow human beings in the era of the industrial production of animals for food, in her Gates Lecture?

Moreover, the techniques that West deploys to this effect are simply those that she has deployed, both generally and specifically: "Fitting speech to character: what is satanic about that?" (EC, 178). When the topic was what went on in abattoirs, a place in which she continues to think Satan is rampant, "[s]he, no less than Paul West, knew how to play with words until she got them right, the words that would send an electric shock down the spine of the reader. *Butcherfolk in our own way*" (EC, 179). And if she has now changed her mind, then how is she to understand her own previous, qualmless stance? Is she to forgo the literary powers with which she might awake people to the abyssal cruelty of the abattoirs that still maddens her, or is she rather to deploy them in ways that she knows will place her readers under the malign spell, the bottomless depression, of imaginative consorting with the morally insane?

We leave Costello at the end of the story having failed to engineer a moment of direct confrontation with West, in which their encounter might have been given shape and meaning, some final word or exchange "sudden as lightning, that will illuminate the landscape for her, even if afterward it returns to its native darkness" (EC, 182). And Coetzee? His alignment with Costello seems particularly salient in this chapter, with its opening delineation of an aftermath to lecture-giving that seems remarkably similar to his own experience with the Tanner Lectures. And the notion of obscenity that she embodies in her thinking seems particularly pertinent to his writing—not only in its engagement (via Costello) with the Holocaust in relation to nonhuman animals, but also in his representations of those stages in Costello's relation with Mr. Phillips that she cannot imagine writing down, even to Blanche, not to mention the variety of scenes of brutal violence and moral squalor to be found in his other works of fiction. But perhaps this only means that he is as much the victim as the prosecutor in Costello's confrontation with West—that author whose willingness to engage to his imaginative limits with human possibilities in his writing is matched only by his refusal to say a word in his own name and voice in academic contexts that deliberately, even offensively, invite it.

Part of what further appears to distinguish Coetzee from Costello in this context is the fact that everything Costello characterises as obscene, whose representation she condemns as absolutely evil in the story, and which she explicitly refrains from representing, is nonetheless actually represented in the story. Costello has never drawn on her early experience of evil in the docker's violent assault in any of her writing, but Coetzee depicts it for us in some detail; and where she refuses to re-create West's scenes of torture and death in her talk, Coetzee describes them in sufficient detail to show exactly what Costello believes should not be shown. In the act of constructing a compelling argument against the representation of such scenes, Coetzee represents them. And he thereby challenges us as readers: if we are convinced by Costello's argument, why are we still reading? And yet, if we are still reading, we confirm the accuracy of Costello's diagnosis, by manifesting exactly the same rivenness that she identifies in herself—not wanting to do what we are nevertheless not only wanting to do but doing, our very humanity driving us to imagine what we know will deprave us. So should we blame the author, as Costello does—that is, blame Coetzee; or should we blame ourselves? Either way, we discover that our relation to Coetzee mirrors that of Costello's to West, thereby enacting in our own experience the breakdown of barriers between author, character and reader that Costello presents to us within the text as morally maddening; and we find that our acts of reading are no more immune to moral critique than are Costello's. In this sense, the moral force of Coetzee's text lies in the relation it establishes between the reader and the text, which means its characters and its author—more specifically, in the questions we confront in any genuine acknowledgment of that relation (rather than any particular answers advanced by characters in the text itself), especially when the ethical substance of this text puts in question the very idea that it (like all texts) must be acknowledged as relative to, and so conditioned by, the specific qualities of its author and its readers.

In her first, more self-confident bout of self-examination, Costello offers the following simile for such literary experiences:

> There are many things that it is like, this storytelling business. One of them . . . is a bottle with a genie in it. When the storyteller opens the bottle, the genie is released into the world, and it costs all hell to get him back in again. Her position, her revised position, her position in the twilight of life: better, on the whole, that the genie stay in the bottle.
>
> The wisdom of the similitude, the wisdom of centuries (that is why she prefers to think in similitudes rather than reason things out), is that it is silent on the life the genie leads shut up in the bottle. It merely says that the world would be better off if the genie remained imprisoned.
>
> A genie or a devil. (EC, 166)

Thinking in similitudes recalls Kafka's description of Red Peter as naturally inclined to think in images. But, as is the way with similitudes, everything hangs on what is being compared to what. What, for example, is the genie? Is it the animating spirit of the events that the story recounts—in West's case, the foul events in that cellar? Or is it the recounting itself, imbued with that animating spirit and so capable of branding its audience? Or is it rather the animating spirit of storytelling as such—the imaginative capacity with which we write and read stories in the first place? Is it that the world would be better off if certain events were not narrated, certain stories not told—or rather, if the human imagination, with its genie-like capacity for fulfilling our deepest and potentially most damaging desires, were never released (as if we are being asked to imagine a world without the exercise of the imagination?).

If Costello meant either of the former alternatives, her simile could hardly be said to be silent on the life the genie leads shut up in the bottle—it is evident what sort of life is led by the people in the cellar, or their fictional counterparts—and so, according to her own account, it would not embody wisdom. If, however, she meant to compare the genie with the life of the imagination as such, then our inability to see any natural interpretation of the simile with respect to that genie's life in the bottle would simultaneously embody wisdom and confirm her comparison, by enacting the very repression of the imagination that it advocates.

But how, then, could any exercise of the literary imagination successfully enact such wisdom? It could only betray itself, and release the very genie it fears in its efforts to continue its imprisonment. And the alternative to such self-betrayal is not selective silence—a willingness to construct texts with gaps, to judge when to stay awake and when to sleep; the alternative is the complete absence of the narrative voice, the elimination of this kind of communicating passage between human beings. As the story's final sentence has it: "the corridor, it seems, is empty" (EC, 182).

Chapter Thirteen

TWO EMBODIMENTS OF THE KAFKAESQUE

THE LAST TWO LESSONS OF *Elizabeth Costello* are the only ones to have found their first public printed form in that book; so it is unsurprising that they should be among the most tightly tied to the problem-setting context of the book as a whole, as outlined in the first lesson on "Realism." More specifically, my account of those concluding portions in the present chapter is based on the assumption that they constitute two very different, and yet internally related, attempts to live up to the understanding of what it might be to be a realist in the tradition of Kafka as Costello outlines it in that first lesson—to acknowledge the distinctive inflection that his writings give to the novel's inherent interest in representing reality, without simply reiterating that inheritance.

THE IMPOSSIBLE MECHANICS OF EROS

The form of lesson 7 breaks with its predecessors in some important respects. It is much shorter than any other in the book, and it has no oral precedent—it is not a version of a text delivered by Coetzee in an academic context. Hence, it does not contain a tale of Elizabeth Costello delivering an address in an academic context. Nevertheless, like the six prior lessons, it is related to a specific academic occasion—even if in a significantly different way.

In March 2001, a symposium was held at the University of Chicago under the title of "Erotikon." Academics from a number of disciplines (philosophy, literary criticism, classics, and psychoanalysis, among others) were asked to reflect on the ways in which Eros had been represented in Western culture since the Greeks, and their debates were interwoven with poetry readings, a concert, and film viewings. A volume of papers based on these proceedings was then organized, to which various writers not present at the original event were invited to contribute; and Coetzee—who held an academic appointment at the University of Chicago—accepted an invitation to read and reflect on the volume as a whole, and then to write an epilogue for it. But the vagaries of academic publishing ensured that the collection did not appear until two years after the first appearance in print of its epilogue, as lesson 7 of *Elizabeth Costello*.[1]

It is thus only retrospectively that the reader will come to understand one motivation for the fact that this lesson, unlike any other, directly and solely articulates Elizabeth Costello's stream of consciousness, as she reflects on the contents of a book "sent her by an American friend" (EC, 183). It is thus not a story in which Costello is the protagonist, and so in which there is logical space for a distinction between protagonist and narrator; it is a tale told entirely in her voice. The same reader is similarly unable to appreciate the extent to which Coetzee has chosen to focus his thoughts on a single element of the rich and varied collection to which it is a response: a poem by Susan Mitchell entitled "Erotikon: (a commentary on *Amor and Psyche*)."[2] Viewed in either of its primary contexts, however, we can clearly see once again Costello's disposition to learn first from the poets; and the course of the meditations provoked by this particular poem taken in isolation (invoking not only a dense array of equally canonical literary reference-points—including tales and characters from Homer, Virgil, the Bible, Joyce's *Ulysses*, Holderlin, Robert Duncan, and Pindar—but also giants of science—Newton—and of philosophy—Kant, Nietzsche, and Wittgenstein) in fact sketches in the central aspects of the vast cultural universe that the excluded *Erotikon* essays unfold. Perhaps, then, it is part of Coetzee's purpose to acknowledge the extent to which Mitchell's poem (as its early place in the volume of essays suggests) crystallizes the form and content of the whole collection—as if the bricolage structure of the poem not only mimics Eros's breaking apart at the moment of sexual climax with Psyche "like . . . a bird shot in flight" (EC, 184), but also figures the intense, unsurveyable conjunctions and divergences of sense created by the interdisciplinary and interpersonal exchanges of knowledge and passion in the symposium as a whole.

Many facets of Mitchell's commentary on Apuleius's version of the Eros and Psyche story, in which Psyche cannot allow her congress with her night-time visitor to remain in darkness but rather lights a lantern and so risks driving Eros away, hang together with Costello's own obsessions. Most obviously, there is Mitchell's interest in her (our?) drive to find words for that which is dark, and should perhaps remain in darkness; and her desire to acknowledge the embeddedness of the ideal in the real—love in sex, thought in matter ("thinking drizzling off into fissures"

---

[1] The volume of essays, entitled *Erotikon: Essays on Eros, Ancient and Modern*, edited by Shadi Bartsch and Thomas Batscherer, appeared from the University of Chicago Press in 2005.

[2] It appeared first in her collection *Erotikon* (New York: HarperCollins, 2000), hereafter E. Indeed, the reader of lesson 7 is free to imagine that this is the book Costello's American friend has sent her.

[E, 53]), ideas in the body ("Antler grown from the skull, cold prong of sharpness, spicule, barb. An idea" [E, 56]). There is, further, her repeated invocation of dictionaries and mirrors; her insistence on the text's relation to author and readers, as well as to its own generic inheritance (of story, plot, and style); and her attentiveness to the sight, sound, and etymology of words—their embeddedness in matter and history, and also in one another ("*Ore* inside *core* . . . and *core* inside *score*" [E, 65]). Above all, there is Mitchell's interest in the conjunction of the possible and the impossible, understood not as the domain of nonsensical darkness but as a textual field that might be "irradiated or developed in the imagination" (E, 60). And it is onto one of these conjunctions that Costello cannot stop herself from wishing to cast a bright light: it concerns what she thinks of as more a mechanical than a metaphysical aspect of the idea of divine-human sexual encounter—"the practicalities of congress across a gap in being" (EC, 184), and more specifically those involved when goddesses condescend to men rather than when girls are visited by gods.

In other words, both the form and the content of this lesson reflect the understanding of Kafkaesque realism laid out in lesson 1. On the level of content, Costello's extended, graphic concentration on the concrete details of human-divine congress—exhibiting exactly the kind of degrading impiety towards the gods abhorred by Plato in Homer—is plainly a version of what she earlier saw as Kafka's admirable realism about his ape. For just as Kafka's fantastic premise, embedding an ape in early-twentieth-century European culture, can nevertheless be thought through with rigorous attention to the real nature of apes and the real nature of that culture, so Costello proposes rigorously to think through the true nature and consequences of an impossibility—a sexual relationship between a human being and a divine being. In inhabiting her stream of consciousness for the first time, what we are made privy to is the depth and pervasiveness of her vocation to stay awake when other fall asleep or turn away, even to the limits of intelligibility.

But this issue of content is also reflected in the nature, and so the form, of Costello's discourse. For it too embodies an impossibility: that of a fictional character engaging in direct intellectual dialogue with a real poet, and indirectly thereby with a range of equally real academics whose actual exchanges one week in Chicago are recorded in *Erotikon* (the real book that Costello's fictional [?] American friend sent her). Is such an imaginary encounter between the real and the imaginary more or less difficult to comprehend than my attempts in part 1 of this book to portray Costello and the real academics actually invited to respond to Coetzee's Tanner Lectures as engaged in actual dialogue, or to imagine a different group of equally real philosophers as the actual recipients of that invitation, or at least as being more authentically responsive to the invitation implicit in Costello's thoughts and words? Would it clarify matters to think of all three such crossings of real and fictional worlds (in Fried's terms, unintelligible and so nonabsorptive tableaus) as actually reducible to an indirect engagement between a real, Nobel Prize–winning author and various equally real academic interlocutors; or would that simply amount to an attempt to deflect ourselves from the difficult reality of our situation as readers (of Coetzee, of Costello, of this book)?

Another formal echo in this lesson of issues arising from lesson 1 is also worth noting. For Coetzee here adopts the monologic mode of narration manifest in Kafka's "Report to an Academy"; he thereby ensures that, just as in the report, his text offers no means by which its speaker might be inspected with an outsider's eye. But where Kafka's formal choice is what allows Costello to raise questions about the flexible inflexibility of words, and so about the survival of realism after our pious illusion of the word-mirror is shattered, matters are different in the present case. For Coetzee chooses to adopt a form that entirely eliminates the distance between himself as narrator and his character in a context in which the primary topic of reflection is that of men's most intimate experiences of female divinity—a kind of encounter that the tale quickly and explicitly aligns with the fecundity of poetic creativity (as Costello recalls her thwarted desire to have Robert Duncan's love-child, as if "impregnated by a passing god and left to bring up semi-divine offspring" [EC, 183]— a formulation that suggests that poems are entirely divine creations, and hence that fictional characters such as Costello herself are the divine offspring of their authors). The emphasis on goddesses condescending to men further suggests a concern with gender difference in fictional creativity—that is, with the possibilities and obstacles facing a man's attempt to imagine a woman, even entirely to inhabit her stream of consciousness.

Key themes from other earlier chapters of *Elizabeth Costello* also find a place (one might say, are reembodied or reembedded) in this new context. First, we see a further exploration of the limits of the human imagination: if we can imaginatively inhabit other modes of being, does that include the divine or not? In the course of this investigation, Costello comes to conclude that the Greek divinities are so interested in sexual congress with human beings because their mortality invests their sexuality with a quality entirely absent from such intercourse between immortals:

In the sexual ecstasies of mortals, the *frisson* of death, its contortions, its relaxings: they talk about it endlessly when they have had too much to drink— who they first got to experience it with, what it felt like. They wish they had that inimitable little quiver in their own erotic repertoire, to spice up their couplings with each other. But the price is one they are not prepared to pay. Death, annihilation: what if there is no resurrection, they wonder misgivingly? (EC, 189)

Is this last, witty rhetorical question a nod to the Viennese destroyer, Wittgenstein, who once pointed out that immortality could not answer the riddle of life, since the meaning of immortal life would be just as much in question as that of mortal life? Certainly, the distinction between endless life and the eternal life of resurrection is well drawn. And this perception of divine curiosity and ignorance in turn leads to a genuinely metaphysical one—to a vision of a universe ruled by desire:

> *Desire runs both ways: A pulls B because B pulls A, and vice versa: that is how you go about building a universe.* Or if *desire* is still too rude a word, then what of *appetency?* Appetency and chance: a powerful duo, more than powerful enough to build a cosmology on. . . . The gods and ourselves, whirled helplessly around by the ends of chance, yet pulled equally towards each other, towards not only B and C and D but towards X and Y and Z and Omega too. Not the least thing, not the last thing but is called to by love. (EC, 192)

In that concluding invocation of a cosmic algebra of desire, as much Platonic as Nietzschean, there is an echo of Costello's earlier alignment of literature with history, in terms of the chronological logic of sequences of events (from A to Z), but put to very different use. One might wonder whether we are being invited to substitute for these anonymous letters of the alphabet the names of the literary, scientific, and philosophical giants mentioned throughout the lesson—as if Costello is tempted to think of them as a cloud of heavenly bodies, a galaxy of concepts and their creators whose distinctions of disciplinary origin do not preclude a driven desire for intercourse with one another (as if the world of ideas is also one of passionate mutual impregnation across what so many want to think of as discontinuities of being—as the *Erotikon* symposium and volume alike attest). There is also a fluid transition from literary literal-mindedness about a specific encounter between a human body and that which it is not, to a far broader philosophical register—a metaphysical vision of the nature of all things. It is as if Costello is engaging in a kind of reverse engineering of Nietzsche's or Plato's philosophizing—suggesting that their claims on our attention as philosophers may in the end turn on what, if any, concrete experiences or imaginings their conceptual generalities might grow from or make possible, and whether at that concrete level they carry conviction.

Of course, that cosmic vision of appetency is not quite the end of the tale; it is not given that kind of formal weight, and so (as its implicit kinship with the kind of cosmic ecological vision advanced by Ted Hughes and criticised by Costello herself would anyway suggest) it is not straight-forwardly endorsed, even by its narrator, let alone its author. For Costello's stream of consciousness immediately provides a further, final paragraph that reframes her vision as an opening up, as the heavens are opened up by a rainbow after the rain. "Does it suffice, for old folk, to have these visions now and again, these rainbows, as a comfort, before the rain starts pelting down again? Must one be too creaky to join the dance before one can see the pattern?" (EC, 192). Yeats and Eliot thereby provide a final return to the canonical, and a sense of even this undermining of visions as itself grounded in aesthetic perception.

Costello's earlier arguments with her sister are also recalled, of course, most broadly in her continued interest in classical mythology and literature, and more specifically in her association of Greek tales of human-divine congress with the sole Christian parallel, deriving from the doctrine of the Incarnation. And here, her concern with the physical mechanics and the social context of Mary's impregnation by the Holy Spirit conjures up at least an appearance of prurience and indecency that is almost enough to make her blush as she sets it down on paper—as she imagines Mary's friends refraining (out of shame) from asking her what it was like: "*It must have been like being fucked by a whale . . . by the Leviathan*" (EC, 187).

Costello thus deliberately fails to follow the example of Mary herself, whose Magnificat is almost the only utterance she makes in the Gospels: first she questions the canonical interpretation of that song's first words, wondering whether Mary means that her soul magnifies God, or that she has been made great by and with God; and then she puts on centre-stage that which everyone in the imagined scene—Mary, her friends, especially God—want to keep offstage. In short, she indulges in the kind of obscenity that is known as blasphemy—and immediately after having newly resolved to avoid such topics.

Then again, a defence is available: for in raising the possibility of a literal or physical interpretation of the Magnificat, and in imagining in concrete detail the Christian God's relations with Mary, Costello is simply following out the logic of the doctrine of the Incarnation itself—a logic that is the most thoroughgoing kind of affirmation of the realm of matter and the senses of which religious faith has so far shown itself to be capable. In this sense, nothing real can, Christianly speaking, be considered obscene: shame and decorum are human moral values, not divine ones. Perhaps this is another respect in which Costello and her sister are spiritually as well as physically intertwined. It certainly suggests a respect in which Coetzee's realism is responsive to something within Christianity as well as to something it excludes.

WAITING AT KAFKA'S GATE

Lesson 8 of *Elizabeth Costello* bears a real but idiosyncratic relation to the embodied proceedings and performances of academic life. Coetzee delivered a version of this text as the Troy Lecture at the University of Massachusetts[3]; but he did so in the month in which *Elizabeth Costello* was published, thus unpredictably putting in question the intelligibility of the question of whether its origins are to be thought of as oral or scriptural. The lesson itself certainly contains a speech by Elizabeth Costello, or rather a number of speeches—a set of attempts on her part to provide a statement of belief, which she is told that she must provide to a board of judges, without whose approval she cannot be permitted to pass through the gate of the lesson's title. This issue—a writer's relation to cognitive claims, to those of their characters and to their own—is once again a familiar Platonic point of criticism with respect to literature; but Coetzee here gives it a decidedly literary setting—one that, as Costello notes with irritation, is essentially Kafkaesque: the whole thing is put together out of clichés, "only the superficies of Kafka: Kafka reduced and flattened to a parody" (EC, 209). How far, Coetzee seems to be asking us, can I pare down the individuality of my realist particulars and still create an impression of reality from which signification might naturally grow? In comparison to Defoe, Kafka is not so much a moderate as a minimalist realist; in comparison to Kafka, Coetzee might seem to be giving up on realism altogether, in favour of a purely postmodernist sense of ourselves as doomed to reproduce worn-out rhetorical tropes rather than penetrating to reality, or more precisely as awakening to the realization that our very idea of a reality to which our words and thoughts might aspire is itself merely one more trope (the word-mirror that is not so much shattered as revealed to be an illusion).

On the other hand, this tale can also be viewed as a reapplication of Kafka's realism of impossibilities. To be sure, the town in which Costello waits for judgement, with its brass band, peasant cleaners, and poorly dressed young couples, is exactly what one would expect of a Central European town in 1912: and the guardian at the gate, the trial, the panel of judges—each of those elements comes straight from individual Kafka stories, although not collectively from any single one. The conjunction of these two dimensions, the historical and the literary, is itself a fantasy; and our sense of conviction is further tested by introducing into that con-

[3] Cf. Laura Wright, "A Feminist-Vegetarian Defence of Elizabeth Costello," in *J. M. Coetzee and the Idea of the Public Intellectual*, ed. J. Poyner (Athens: Ohio University Press, 2006), 212.

junction the embodied soul of our old friend Costello, who is both a realistic product of early twenty-first-century Western culture and entirely fictional. The momentum of the resultant narrative is thus once again a
matter of Coetzee (just like Costello in lesson 7) rigorously thinking
through the consequences of such a conjunction. To put the matter more
from Costello's viewpoint: having previously embedded characters from
Kafka into her own talks and lectures, she now finds herself embedded as
a character in one of his tales, or more exactly as embodying a character in
a situation, both of which are familiar from Kafka's tales—the petitioner
before the gate.

How are we to understand her situation, here at the end of the rainbow,
with the gate hiding brighter, if not exactly divine, light? Costello herself
is bewildered by it, surprised at the way things develop within it; and
she also finds it profoundly irritating, if only because of its threadbare
literariness. Nonetheless, the story may still be understood as one of her
own literary exercises—a new style or form of her writing in which she
embeds herself as a character in her own tale (the style Peter Singer might
charitably be taken to have adopted); after all, she earlier described that
writing (in lesson 5) as always being a kind of writing to herself—a description that fits the previous lesson's meditative form, as if it were a
journal entry. But the tale, like Kafka's "Report," also leaves invitingly
open certain other possibilities: for example, that it is the record of a
dream, or of her experience of death or purgatory (her lifetime labour of
writing is said at one point to be over and done with). And of course, it
is, without doubt, a situation in which Coetzee has placed Costello, as if
reproducing her devotion to the Kafka model—an elaborate set of dove-
tailing commonplaces constructed precisely so as to raise all of these interpretative possibilities without settling on any.

In this sense, it both continues and radicalizes the relation Coetzee has
established between himself and Costello in the previous lessons, the one
I have been describing in terms of the (re)constitution of a crazed word-
mirror. Coetzee rings the changes on a limited range of elements distinctive of Costello's mind and milieu, endlessly finding new permutations of
his literary algebra that strain our conception of the coherence of her
character and her world, with a view to testing the limits of our willingness to accept each new Elizabeth Costello as somehow continuous with
her previous incarnations, and also somehow continuous with the real
world of real people (including Coetzee himself). Each lesson is in this
sense an essay, an experiment or trial; lesson 8 simply makes this fact
about them part of its mise-en-scène.

Costello produces three versions of her required statement of belief.
The first claims exemption from the need to have one or more beliefs that

might form the content of any such statement, on the ground that any writer, as a trader in fictions, "*maintain[s] beliefs only provisionally: fixed beliefs would stand in my way. I change beliefs as I change my habitation or my clothes, according to my needs*" (EC, 195). Recalling Cavell's sense of Costello's woundedness as having to do with her embodiedness as such, and hence with her species-specific commitment to being clothed, one might wonder what wound or trauma about the human subjection to belief and its responsibilities (primarily its responsibilities towards the truthfulness of those beliefs) is concealed behind her image of her relation to any particular set of beliefs as essentially dispensable. Given her earlier conviction of literature's ethical responsibilities, and indeed to reality as such, this initial insistence is hard to read as anything other than superficial and defensive.

The guardian anyway rejects this first version altogether, refusing even to pass it on to the board. And one can see why, given that Costello formulates it not as a statement of belief, but as a request for exemption from the requirement to produce one. Apparently, then, stating one's beliefs about the (professional, vocational) requirements of a writer is not the kind of statement of belief that is needed.

The second version—heavily revised, "revised to the limit of my powers, I venture to say" (EC, 199)—is one she is allowed to deliver to the board. In it, she describes herself as a secretary of the invisible, a taker of dictation like Czeslaw Milosz, to whom was dictated the phrase "secretary of the invisible." "It is not for me to interrogate, to judge what is given me. I merely write down the words and then test them, test their soundness, to make sure I have heard right" (EC, 199). A good secretary should have no beliefs, for in her work belief is a resistance, an obstacle. While not denying that she holds beliefs (what she calls opinions and prejudices) of all kinds about all sorts of issues, Costello claims that her ideal self is one possessed of negative capability—holding those beliefs at bay while the word which it is her function to conduct passes through her. "I have beliefs but I do not believe in them. They are not important enough to believe in. My heart is not in them. My heart and my sense of duty" (EC, 200). One might think of this as an alternative articulation of the sentiment expressed by Howard Jacobson in one of this book's epigraphs.

The board is not impressed. It questions the effect of such a stance on her own humanity and suggests (in a manner reminiscent of Costello's own beliefs as expressed in lesson 6) that holding beliefs at bay in the face of evil deeds is particularly damaging; to which Costello replies that her contribution as a writer to the humanity of others outweighs any damage done to her own, and that anyway, "beliefs are not the only ethical supports we have. We can rely on our hearts as well" (EC, 203). The board might have pointed out, but did not, that this riposte to the monster of modern Western reason in fact perpetuates the monstrous sense that truth-oriented belief is a matter of pure cognition, with the heart offering at best nonrational support. Instead, it points out that her argument fails if the invisible does not in fact use her as its secretary; and she accepts the risk of inauthenticity and failure inherent in her task, asking only that they judge her record. But the question that really tests her points out that a writer is also a human being; and that a good writer explores the complexities of human conduct and so cannot avoid making judgements upon it. And at this point Costello admits that she (like West?) is open to all voices, to those of innocent victims and to those of their murderers and violators; she will not close her ears to the latter's dictation, as long as they speak the truth; and she alone, consulting only her heart, must be the judge of that truth.

Perhaps unsurprisingly, the board refuses to pass her statement. Costello is both furious and resigned: she knows that they will take her to have expressed an inhuman faith in art and its truth, even though she thinks she knows that she lacks even that belief.

> Her books teach nothing, preach nothing; they merely spell out, as clearly as they can, how people lived in a certain time and place. More modestly put, they spell out how one person lived, one among billions, the person whom she, to herself, calls *she*, and whom others call *Elizabeth Costello*. If, in the end, she believes in her books themselves more than she believes in that person, it is belief only in the sense that a carpenter believes in a sturdy table or a cooper in a stout barrel. Her books are, she believes, better put together than she is. (EC, 207–8)

Here, the eighth lesson is putting pressure on our sense of Costello's coherence as a character, both internally and in relation to her creator. Having already shown her expressing a willingness to give words to evil in a way that she vehemently condemned in lesson 6, it now invites us to ask: if Costello's books are ultimately a record of how she lived, and so her fictional characters ultimately have no independent life or vitality, then what are we to say of Costello's autonomy from Coetzee? If, however, we see Costello's claims in this passage as a spelling out of how Coetzee thinks and lives, then we must believe, first, that Coetzee's fiction is not an exercise in teaching and preaching but in showing the embeddedness of ideas and arguments in reality, and second, that we should believe more in Costello than Coetzee.

But is Costello a genuinely sturdy character, better put together than her creator, and so more worthy of belief? Are any of her opinions and prejudices sufficiently stable to hold water, if what is rejected in lesson 6 is affirmed in lesson 8? Or is it that the only thing that needs to be sturdy about her is her vocation as a writer? That at least has not changed through all these lessons, and if she is right about what writing requires—if it requires that one not believe in one's beliefs, subordinating them to whatever voices seek to speak through one, even those of contradictory ideas—then no realistic depiction of a writer could be expected to manifest any more continuity than that. In this sense, the discontinuities of Costello at the level of belief are precisely what should invite our belief in her reality.

Whatever her frustrations, Costello finds that, if she enacts her self-description as a secretary of the invisible and turns her attention inward towards its voices, a further revision of her statement of belief becomes possible: her muse reveals what she previously thought of as an absolute limit to be only a limitation. And what prepares the ground for this possibility is what that turn of her attention first reveals—that which is literally within or inward:

> The slow thud of the blood in her ears, . . . the soft touch of the sun on her skin. That at least she does not have to invent: this dumb, faithful body that has accompanied her every step of the way, this gentle, lumbering monster that has been given to her to look after, this shadow turned to flesh that stands on two feet like a bear and laves itself continually from the inside with blood. Not only is she *in* this body, this thing which not in a thousand years could she have dreamed up, so far beyond her powers would it be, she somehow *is* this body; and all around her on the square, on this beautiful morning, these people, somehow, *are* their bodies too. (EC, 210)

This is Costello's bodily credo, her counter to Descartes and his belief that he might have dreamed up the whole of the external world, including his body: I believe that I am, that what stands before you today is I. It is the unimaginable fact of human animality, of simultaneous embeddedness and embodiedness (being in, and simply being, a body—or being and not being one's body). It is her version of Coetzee's sense of the human body as the ultimate standard of reality and truth, but in her case foregrounding the miraculousness of its sheer existence as the habitat of consciousness—its flesh continually laving itself with awareness from the inside, and so embodying the discontinuous continuity of mind and body—rather than its vulnerability to suffering.

And Costello's particular mind naturally connects the thud of her blood with that of her fellow creatures, nonhuman animals, such as the ram whose throat Odysseus cuts in Hades in order that its blood might allow him to consult the dead seer, Tiresias.

> She believes, most unquestionably, in the ram, the ram dragged by its master down to this terrible place. The ram is not just an idea, the ram is alive though

right now it is dying. If she believes in the ram, then does she believe in its blood too, this sacred liquid, sticky, dark, almost black, pumped out in gouts on to soil where nothing will grow? . . . For that, finally, is all it means to be alive: to be able to die. (EC, 211)

This ram is literary, but real: Costello can question its religious signifi-cance (and she turns to Greek rather than Christian ideas of the sacred, even though Abraham's ram must have been equally to hand), but she cannot question its concrete reality. Like Kafka's ape, Hughes's panther and the cattle she has accompanied in her imagination through our indus-trial abattoirs, Homer's ram sends a shiver of recognition down her back, a shiver of indubitable kinship—the commonality of mortal beings.

But this turns out not to be the vision, the dictation from the invisible, with which she can construct the third version of that statement. For what intervenes between this vision and her next confrontation with the board is a conversation with another dweller in the town, one who advises her that the boards ask for belief, but they will be satisfied with the effect of belief, with what she calls passion. Costello professes a lack of conviction in this guidance, but it certainly diverts her from her initial path; for when she recites the final recorded version of her statement, it draws upon what she claims to be her own early life, and it concerns not a ram but frogs— the frogs of the Dungannon River, who emerge from its dried-out mud after the torrential, drought-breaking rains.

> In the dry season they go underground, burrowing further and further from the heat of the sun until each has created a little tomb for itself. And in those tombs they die, so to speak. Their heartbeat slows, their breathing stops. They turn the colour of mud. Once again, the nights are silent.
>
> Silent until the next rains come, rapping, as it were, on thousands of tiny coffin lids. In those coffins hearts begin to beat, limbs begin to twitch that for months have been lifeless. The dead awake. As the caked mud softens, the frogs being to dig their way out, and soon their voices resound again in joyous exulta-tion beneath the vault of heaven. (EC, 216)

Is this an acknowledgment or a denial of the Christian notion of the resur-rection of the dead? Does it show that human beings can mean what those words say, or does it show that they must be meant otherwise, meant concretely and physically rather than supernaturally? If so, one might think of it as her strategy for answering a question she avoided in her first session with the board—one about her religious beliefs. Or we might see the frogs not as really resurrected bodies, but as representing beliefs that transform themselves from desiccated corpses to living beings under the refreshment of passion; or as individual words, brought back to life as their users trace them back to the originating experiences they embody (the technique Costello employs in the lesson about evil, and might be seen as employing here, with respect to the word "resurrection"); or as any and every individual thing, insofar as it is really, concretely attended to by the power of the human imagination.

The possibilities seem endless—until Costello herself explicitly excludes them: "the life cycle of the frog may sound allegorical, but to the frogs themselves it is no allegory, it is the thing itself, the only thing" (EC, 217). The point of her vision is that it rejects the very allegorical—or more generally, interpretative—possibilities that it knows it cannot deny, or avoid, raising. Costello believes in those frogs, not in something other than them of which they might be the emblem or conduit, not even life (particularly not ecological visions of life), but in the frogs themselves.

> She thinks of the frog beneath the earth, spread out as if flying, as if parachuting through the darkness. She thinks of the mud eating away at the tips of those fingers, trying to absorb them, to dissolve the soft tissue till no one can tell any longer (certainly not the frog itself, lost as it is in its cold sleep of hibernation) what is earth, what is flesh. Yes, that she can believe in: the dissolution, the return to the elements; and the converse moment she can believe in too, when the first quiver of returning life runs through the body and the limbs contract, the hands flex. She can believe in that, if she concentrates closely enough, word by word. (EC, 219–20).

The resources of figurative language and thought might legitimately be directed towards them, but only with the aim of finding a way for author and reader to inhabit the concrete reality of their mode of being. The crucial point is not the belief but its object: although her concern is first and last with what she believes, that which elicits her belief is that which not only is not capable either of believing or disbelieving in her, but that whose existence is indifferent to her belief or disbelief. What makes those frogs worthy of belief is that they "exist whether or not I tell you about them, whether or not I believe in them . . . it is because of their indiffer-ence to me that I believe in them" (EC, 217). One might say: the reality of something is shown by its ultimate independence of the domain of human belief, by the fact that it is utterly unconditioned by the existence and structure, the valencies and truth-values, of that domain.

Nevertheless, it is only from within the domain of belief that we can apprehend that something or other is real; and in the more specific case of our willingness to credit a fictional representation of reality as itself real, that point is intensified. What, then, can be the test of such belief, within its domain? Costello has a test that seems to work when she is writing, and that she applies to her new vision of the frogs: "to send out a word into the darkness and listen for what kind of sound comes back. Like a foundryman tapping a bell: is it cracked or healthy?" (EC, 219).

Her simile is not obviously consistent with the one she prefers in lesson 6, when Costello tested problematic words by searching for their experiential origin; but it fits neatly into its present context. For its glancing invocation of a newly forged bell being removed from the casing of its mould recalls the frogs in their mud tombs—but we are not supposed to be looking for allegories here, are we? Suppose, nevertheless, that we test the expression of this idea in the same way it suggests that we test all expressions of belief, that is, by concentrating on it, word by word: then the image of words as being sent out into the darkness and returning a sound leaves it unclear whether the tone that results from their contact with whatever may be out there in the darkness is a test of the words, or of that which they encounter. Is it our representations of reality, or reality itself, that is being tested, to find any cracks in its tone? I take it that Coetzee precisely wishes to keep both ways of understanding the idea in play—that he presents them as standing or falling together, even as standing and falling together. When Costello gives "the frogs a tap with her fingernail" (EC, 222), what passes the test is both the frogs themselves, in all the reality of their lifecycle, and the words that conjure them up, inviting us to participate in the reality embedded and embodied in them (like mud tombs?).

Costello later wonders, as one might expect of someone both engaged and embedded in a project of supposedly moderate realism about ideas, whether the same test might apply to more abstract terms—even, to belief itself. Can she not, must she not, ultimately test whether she believes in beliefs, or in belief, by giving the word a tap?

> The sound that *belief* returns is not as clear [as that returned by the frogs], but clear enough nevertheless. Today, at this time, in this place, she is evidently not without belief. In fact, now that she thinks of it, she lives, in a certain sense, by belief. Her mind, when she is truly herself, appears to pass from one belief to the next, pausing, balancing, then moving on. A picture comes to her of a girl crossing a stream: it comes together with a line from Keats: *Keeping steady her laden head across a brook.* She lives by belief, she works by belief, she is a creature of belief. What a relief! Should she run back and tell them, her judges, before they disrobe (and before she changes her mind)? [EC, 222]

Probably not: for as the Keatsian reference suggests, with its embodiment of the power of negative capability to which her earlier, unsuccessful statement and cross-examination referred, to picture beliefs as stepping stones across a stream and not as burdening the head of she who steps on them is not exactly to picture them as constituting one's identity and one's humanity in the way favoured by the judges. Would the words of such a picture ring true to them, when she is not even prepared to swear that they will ring true to her at another time, in another place? Would they ring true to a philosopher, who on the one hand would claim to value thought and belief only insofar as they give access to truth, but on the other finds value in a Socratic method of conversational dialogue that privileges the form of the conversation above any conclusion at which it might arrive—the journey over the destination?

These questions bring another in their train: for how does this stance of Costello's cohere with the stance she displayed in her statement about the frogs, and with her earlier statement about being a secretary of the invisible? Elements are common to all, but they recur in different contexts, and their recurrences resolutely fail to resolve into a single, overarching account of herself.

This was a point emphasized by her judges in response to the tale of the frogs, and at that time, in that place, Costello said this:

> You ask if I have changed my plea. But who am I, who is this *I*, this *you*? We change from day to day, and we also stay the same. No *I*, no *you* is more fundamental than any other. You might as well ask which is the true Elizabeth Costello: the one who made the first statement or the one who made the second. My answer is, both are true. Both. And neither. *I am an other*. Pardon me for resorting to words that are not my own, but I cannot improve upon them. You have the wrong person before you. If you think you have the right person you have the wrong person. The wrong Elizabeth Costello. (EC, 221)

As Costello immediately asks herself: is this true? The judges take it to be risibly self-contradictory, as they delight in pointing out when she claims to be able truly to characterize her own mental state ("I am not confused." . . . "But who is it who is not confused?" [EC, 221]). But a philosopher such as Sartre would regard it as an articulation of the essence of human being: he defines that way of being as a matter of being what one is not and not being what one is—of existing as a negating relation to oneself, so that the human mode of identity is nonidentity.

Embedded as we are in time, the moment in which we are consciously aware of our present state, and so seem most unified with and transparent to ourselves, is necessarily the next moment of our existence, and so can make us aware only of the state we were in but no longer are. We are embodied: but that means that those hands and facial expressions are ours, not that they are us (expressions can deceive, hands can write cheques that the bodies to which they are attached cannot cash) or that they are not us; we relate to our bodies as what we are not. We adopt projects and roles: but a waiter is always more than his commitment to his role, and his relation to that commitment is always to something that must be continued in the next moment of existence, and so to something that is never completed, a project that is always to be realized no matter how often he has already realized it. We are desiring beings: each of our desires relates us to something we lack, and beyond the satisfaction of any specific desire is the awareness that animality is a condition of dependence on that which lies outside us, that which is not us, but which must be transformed into us (ingested, consumed) if we are to continue to be. Little wonder, then, that the most fundamental desire of such finite beings is the desire to be God—an impossible desire (since finitude and infinitude are one another's opposites) for an impossible object (since God possesses distinctively human modes of being while being free from all that makes such modes of being possible). One of the difficulties of human reality, then, for Sartre, is that it is definitive of being human that one be possessed by this doubly impossible desire; for nothing is more characteristic of, nothing goes deeper with, the human mode of being than the yearning not to be human.

How do matters look from the perspective of literature rather than philosophy? Well: has not this book, with its eight lessons, presented us with eight Elizabeth Costellos, each of whom is and is not the same as every other? Do we not believe in her as a fictional character? Is each lesson, like the stepping stones, something onto which we can step, pause, balance, and move on, or perhaps a record of the steps Costello herself has taken? They have at least borne our weight up to this point, staying put rather than, or perhaps because of, ringing true; perhaps they will not, upon another reading, at another time and in another place.

But lesson 8 contains one more step. Without knowing her judges' decision, Costello returns to the gatekeeper; she has a final vision, of an old, crippled dog lying beyond her gate (a vision whose anagrammatic and literary air she distrusts, and curses) and asks him about her chances of success:

> "But as a writer," she persists—"what chance do I stand as a writer, with the special problems of a writer, the special fidelities?"
>
> *Fidelities*. Now that she has brought it out, she recognizes it as the word on which all hinges.
>
> "Do you see many people like me, people in my situation?" . . .
>
> The man behind the desk has evidently had enough of questions. He lays down his pen, folds his hands, regards her levelly. "All the time," he says. "We see people like you all the time." (EC, 224–25)

Is that because these gates, and these trials, are only for writers? Or because this gatekeeper is Kafkaesque, and so is only ever embedded in tales designed to be purgatorial to writers, or writers of a specific cast? Or is it because the fidelities upon which everything seems at present to hinge for Costello are in fact the hinge of every human life—that to step onto, pause, balance, and move on from beliefs is not the special condition of the writer but the human condition as such? Can philosophy accept any such determination of human nature as ringing true, and still acknowledge its special fidelities?

Chapter Fourteen

CONCLUSION: THREE POSTSCRIPTS

WITHIN: DRYAD

THE FINAL SECTION OF *Elizabeth Costello*—a novel that neither denies nor asserts that it is a novel, but rather declares that
the form it takes (as a novel?) is that of eight lessons—is not a
lesson, but a postscript in the form of a letter.[1] Should we, then, take it to
be part of *Elizabeth Costello*, or not? Whatever evidence in favour of
the latter answer that might be assembled by examining this postscript is
unlikely to settle the matter, since it might well be taken simply to show
that what we have is, indeed, a postscript—something at once supplementary to the primary text, and yet deemed sufficiently important or relevant
to it by the writer of that text to be included, even at the cost of violating
certain (let us say) formal requirements. Of course, any writer in the condition of modernism may well find that what appears to be a violation of
convention is the best, even the only possible, way of being true to that
which those conventions are meant to serve; and we could hardly have
expected a book that problematizes its own beginning (along with the
very idea of literary beginnings) to treat its own ending as unproblematic.
We should therefore take seriously the possibility that this apparently supplementary text could also be the heart of the matter.

The signatory of this postscript is one Elizabeth C., but apparently not
the protagonist of Coetzee's eight lessons—although that would not prevent us from seeing her as its author (whether because it constitutes a
fictional exercise composed by her, a piece of writing by her after pieces
of writing about her, or because we might think of it as signed by her soul
during its inhabitation of another body, an other who is also her). This
Elizabeth C. describes herself as the wife of Philip, Lord Chandos, who
in 1603 (in a letter composed by Hugo von Hofmannsthal in 1902) wrote
to Francis Bacon, in response to the latter's queries about the literary
paralysis into which he felt that the previously prolific Lord had fallen.
Coetzee's new Elizabeth C., having seen a copy of her husband's letter, is
now sending a letter of her own to Bacon. Coetzee is thus explicitly relat-

---

[1] It was, in addition, published separately a year before its appearance in *Elizabeth Costello*.

ing his own fictional epistle, and so the book of lessons to which it forms a postscript, to one of the founding documents of literary modernism. His parting gesture thereby returns us to the first lesson's specification of a project of moderate realism about ideas, in the context of a certain loss of assurance not only in the illusion of the literary text as a word-mirror, but also in that of words as such as capable of representing reality.

This last question is central to the original Chandos letter. Its author was obsessed with grand literary projects of various kinds (an account of Henry VIII's early years as king, of the secret wisdom of ancient Greek and Roman myth and fable, a collection of maxims and descriptions of rituals and buildings to be called "Know Thyself," and so on), each expressive of his vision of all existence as one great unity, with every creature a key to all the others. At the time of writing, however, his case has changed: "I have completely lost the ability to think or speak coherently about anything at all."[2] First, abstract words disintegrated on his tongue like rotten mushrooms, then the words of informal conversation; even the soothing harmonies of classical writers left him feeling "like someone locked in a garden full of eyeless statuary" (LC, 122). Beneath this loss of language, however, good moments of experience remain that remarkably resemble the vision of the cosmos upon which his early literary ambitions were founded: at certain unpredictable and unrepeatable moments,

> mute and sometimes inanimate beings rise up before me with such a plenitude, such a presence of love that my joyful eye finds nothing dead anywhere. Everything seems to mean something . . . : I feel a blissful and utterly eternal interplay in me and around me, and amid the to-and-fro there is nothing into which I cannot merge. Then it is as if my body consisted entirely of coded messages revealing everything to me. Or as if we could enter into a new, momentous relationship with all of existence if we began to think with our hearts. But when this strange bewitchment stops, I am unable to say anything about it; I can no more express in rational language what made up this harmony permeating me and the entire world, or how it made itself perceptible to me, than I can describe with any precision the inner movements of my intestines or the engorgement of my veins. (LC, 125)

After thus attempting to explain his paralysis, Lord Chandos ends his letter by expressing his love, gratitude, and admiration for Bacon, the foremost Englishman of his time and the one who has done most for his spirit.

One can easily see why this letter might justify its presence in the context of *Elizabeth Costello*. To begin with, there is its invocation of a pri-

---

[2] *The Lord Chandos Letter and Other Writings*, trans. J. Rotenberg (New York: New York Review Books, 2005), 121 (hereafter LC).

marily bodily human capacity to enter into the being of all kinds of entities in a way that threatens to burst the bounds of language, together with the fear that this sense of the world's utter accessibility signals the onset of madness. There is also the opposition between thinking with the heart and the language of reason, that is, between two modes of rational discourse rather than between reason and that which is beyond or beneath it. The conjunction of these two lines of thought produces a third, Costello-like similitude, comparing the impossible reality of the body's interpenetration with its external world to that of the mind's inhabitation of the body—one incomprehensible embedding mirroring another, two interlinked difficulties internal to human reality. Finally, there is Chandos's sense that it is the abstract reaches of language, those at once most distant from immediate sensory experience and most familiar to the philosophical spirit, that suffer first from a sceptical anxiety about their sense and reference; it is as if the classical monuments of philosophical thought all-too-quickly become eyeless statuary. Kant famously claimed that concepts without intuitions are empty, and intuitions without concepts are blind; von Hofmannsthal's Chandos claims rather that blindness is the fate of concepts floating free of intuition, while intuitions resistant to conceptual articulation suffer not an absence but an excess of sense and substance.

Coetzee's invention of Lady Chandos, who shares her husband's anxieties as well as his capacity for moments when soul and body are one, when his angelic vision unfolds itself, forces us to attend to some particularly troubling aspects of her husband's stance. To begin with, she is more sensitive than he—sensitive to the point of madness—to the fact that he seems perfectly capable of conveying his inexpressible vision of existence in one of the natural languages whose utter inadequacy to that task is the main burden of his letter. As she puts it:

> *Not Latin*, says my Philip—I copied the words—*not Latin nor English nor Spanish nor Italian will bear the words of my revelation.* And indeed it is so, even I who am his shadow know when I am in my raptures. Yet he writes to you, as I write to you, who are known above all men to select your words and set them in place and build your judgements as a mason builds a wall with bricks. (EC, 230)

Where Philip unself-consciously lavishes words upon that which he claims words cannot grasp, as well as upon the claims themselves, his wife constantly enacts, and constantly enacts her anxiety about having to enact, the contradiction inherent in attempting to communicate the incommunicable: "It is like a contagion, saying one thing always for another (*Like a contagion*, I say . . . ";" "Like a wayfarer (hold the figure in mind, I pray you) . . . "; and perhaps most forcefully, "words give way beneath your feet like rotting boards (*like rotting boards* I say again, I cannot help myself, not if I am to bring home to you my distress and my husband's, *bring home* I say, where is home, where is home?) (EC, 228). Why should not a Baconian word-mason simply conclude that Lord and Lady Chandos are each disproving their own claim in the making of it; for they seem able to find words that do convey with extreme force the precise contents of their vision?

But such a reversion to a view of words as perfectly capable of forming sturdy walls would leave unregistered the difference between the strategies of husband and wife (or perhaps leave unappreciated what his wife makes explicit about her husband's understanding). For Lady Chandos's mode of writing not only shows a clear awareness of the apparent paradoxicality of their situation; she shows more specifically that this paradoxicality declares the reality—the true nature—of their situation. For their joint vision of a reality beyond words can be reached only by going through words, by using words to go beyond themselves—by finding what she variously calls "the tongues of angels" or "speaking without speech"; the beyondness of reality to language is made manifest, and can only be made manifest, in forms of words that enact their own shipwreck—their simultaneous necessity and insufficiency. As Lady Chandos summarises the matter: "*Always it is not what I say but something else . . . saying one thing always for another*" (EC, 228); words are no more identical with their sense, and so with themselves, than are people (at least according to Costello in the eighth lesson). But that precisely means that the otherness of reality to language must always be its otherness to some particular utterance, that it is always and only to be revealed by saying some particular thing and then negating it—trying to capture reality in particular words that fail in their own particular way to reach what they are nonetheless specifically targeted at, aimed towards.

Denys Turner has persistently emphasized a parallel conception in the realms of religious or more precisely theological discourse, according to which negative or apophatic theology (which stresses the absolute inadequacy of language to God's nature) is seen as inextricably related to its affirmative or cataphatic opposite.[3] Insofar as God is the source of all that is, possessing in his being all the perfections he causes, then everything in creation is a potential source of imagery for the divine, and the more of it we activate in religious language the better, since only thus can we acknowledge God's superabundant variety. And yet, using language in all these ways simultaneously will inevitably lead us to speaking contradictorily about God (as male and female, light and darkness, weakness and strength); and nothing we say about him can conceivably capture his nature anyway. But that transcendence of God is best acknowledged pre-

---

[3] Cf. *The Darkness of God* (Cambridge: Cambridge University Press, 1995).

cisely by following out the consequences of attributing contradictory attributes to him; for if he is both male and female, and we know that no person can possibly be both male and female, we thereby appreciate that our idea of him as a personal God is itself a misrepresentation—a necessarily unsuccessful attempt to delineate the reality of that which is beyond delineation.

In other words, the best way to appreciate the transcendent reality of God to human language is not to fall into silence, avoiding even the assertion that nothing is assertible of Him, or to attempt some inconceivable synthesis of affirmation and negation; it is rather endlessly to employ that language in relation to him, and endlessly to experience its inevitable collapse upon itself. Theological language is thus essentially self-subverting language; the repeated collapse of its affirmations into complete disorder is its distinguishing mode of order. It is, one might say, the only way these language games should be played. And one might therefore further say that Lady Chandos has generalized this picture of religious language to encompass language as a whole, in its relation to reality.

Lady Chandos's mode of writing can therefore be seen as essentially postscriptural, insofar as that phrase folds together a certain understanding of Scripture with a certain understanding of writing as such. For it is not just that her letter is a postscript to her husband's, and so an essential supplement to it; every sentence and phrase within it attempts, impossibly, to supplement itself—endlessly adding further words and phrases to elaborate, qualify, or otherwise supplement its first attempt to say what it means, as if such supplementary writing could itself avoid the necessity for supplementation in its turn. But these supplementations are not arbitrary or accidental: each takes seriously the precise significance of the words and phrases it supplements, rigorously thinking through their implications—and so illuminating the highly specific network of associations and entailments of sense inherent in each element of language. This, one might say, is what her Sartrean vision of words as inherently nonidentical comes to: in the Wittgensteinian terms we repeatedly encountered in the first part of this book, it comes to the thought that to imagine a word is to imagine not just a language game for it but ultimately a form of life with language. For what makes a word the precise word it is has to do with its precise place in a linguistic field whose horizons are not so much fixed as endlessly to be explored. According to this vision, a word is only a word if it can be projected into circumstances other than those in which it was first encountered, and so only if it can find a home in an indefinite range of new contexts where it is necessarily conjoined with (and so modifies and is modified by) other words.

It is also important to see that, in effect, Lady Chandos's postscriptural mode of writing exemplifies what it might mean to think in images, as

Kafka claims that his ape does, and as Costello claims that her vocation as a writer demands of her. For what she is endlessly driven to supplement is the apparently unavoidable tendency of language to generate similitudes—to engender a figurative dimension of sense. And what her supplementations reveal is that this figurative dimension has a rigour and logic of its own that is the equal of the precision traditionally accorded by philosophers to the realm of propositions and inference alone, even if it is different in kind. Indeed, it is only because figurative language displays such rigour that Lady Chandos can keep faith in the capacity of language to grasp reality in its otherness, for without that rigour her words could not be thought to have a specific sense, and so could not be negated with sufficient specificity to display reality in its concrete otherness to concrete utterance.

Lady Chandos makes it clear that this vision of language's inherent paradoxicality, its fatedness to point towards that which it cannot reach, is not merely an abstract idea for her—a free-floating manner of apprehending words and world that we can evaluate purely in terms of its truth or falsity. For both she and her husband feel compelled to communicate it: they are neither of them satisfied simply with the apprehension of this vision as true, but rather experience its rapturousness as something that demands communication, and so as inherently paradoxical—a vision of the incommunicability of reality that demands that its adherents attempt to communicate it. More specifically, they experience its salvific import as something from which they require salvation. In this respect, once again, Lady Chandos makes explicit what the form of her husband's communication leaves implicit—not only the thought that they have a duty to communicate what they have come to see as a redemptive vision, but that their reception of that vision (as opposed, say to God's, who might be able to live with the whole of reality inside him) is something they suffer. Diamond would think of them as confronting an interwoven set of difficulties of reality whose perception gives them pain of a kind that threatens their sanity—pain to which they are vulnerable only because they possess the capacity that alone can relieve that pain: the power of speech. For Lady Chandos's letter—this inordinate, wounding expression of her woundedness—hopes beyond hope for a salvific response from the Francis Bacons of her world. "Save me, dear Sir, save my husband! Write! . . . Drowning, we write out of our separate fates. Save us" (EC, 229–30).

It is as if salvation is to be hoped for only from those whose vision of language and reality is utterly other to their own—as if even their vision, expressed in words that enact their own simultaneous necessity and inadequacy to it, can be properly expressed only if conjoined with a vision that opposes it. Neither vision is the whole truth about words and world, and neither is any coherent combination of the two; what rings true is rather their contradictory combination—the impossible thought that each is true only when endorsed simultaneously with its opposite, each in need of its negation to fulfil itself by acknowledging its incompleteness, each impossibly embedded in the other, as the personal fates of Philip and Elizabeth Chandos are embedded in that of Francis Bacon.

Lady Chandos's letter also brings into clearer focus two further, vital aspects of her husband's letter; both arise from her recognition of the central importance of animate rather than inanimate aspects of creation in her husband's vision. When spelling out what she wants of Bacon for her husband's sake, she says that "Words no longer reach him. . . . But fleas he will understand, the fleas and the beetles still creep past his shield, and the rats; and sometimes I his wife, yes, my Lord, sometimes I too creep through" (EC, 229–30). Her reference to the rats recalls us to perhaps the most spellbinding evocation of his capacity to merge with other beings that her husband's letter contains:

> Recently, for example, I had a generous amount of rat poison spread in the milk cellars of one of my dairy farms. I went out riding towards evening, thinking no more about the matter, as you might imagine. As I rode at a walk over deep, tilled farmland—nothing more significant in the vicinity than a startled covey of quail, the great setting sun off in the distance above the convex fields—suddenly this cellar unrolled inside me, filled with the musty death throes of the pack of rats. It was all there. The cool and musty cellar air, full of the sharp, sweetish smell of the poison, and the shrilling of the death cries echoing against mildewed walls. Those convulsed clumps of powerlessness, those desperations colliding with one another in confusion, The frantic search for ways out. The cold glares of fury when two meet at a blocked crevice. . . . My friend, do you remember Livy's wonderful description of the hours before the destruction of Alba Longa? The people wandering through the streets . . . saying goodbye to the rocks on the ground. I tell you my friend, this was in me, and Carthage in flames too; but it was more than that, it was more divine, more bestial—and it was the present the fullest, most sublime present. A mother was there, whose dying young thrashed about her. But she was not looking at those in their death agonies, or at the unyielding stone walls, but off into space, or through space into the infinite, and gnashing her teeth as she looked. (LC, 123–24)

Once again, the echoes evoked by this passage of previous elements in Coetzee's eight lessons threaten to overwhelm us. To begin with, Lord Chandos's talk of a cellar unrolling inside him evokes Costello's encounter with the hellfire of Nazi torture on the pages of West's book, and so her more general sense of literature's incomprehensible power to collapse distinctions of time and space, including the distances between one person and another (whether in Alba Longa or the next room), and between a single person's inner and outer worlds. Beyond this, there is an echo of

Costello's discussion with her son after the Gates Lecture about the idea of animals as vermin, and of the rat as an object of hatred rather than contempt, a worthy foe who will surely outlast us. Her Gates Lecture itself also articulates our commonality even with such hated nonhuman animals around the experience of death, and our whole-hearted resistance to it. Moreover, it seems to be the case for Lord Chandos, as it is for Costello, that the ability to empathise with the rats seems to occlude the ability to empathize with human beings. He sees his vision of the rats baring their teeth in the face of their fate as more divine and more bestial than any human catastrophe; the rat mother is more fully present inside him than the human victims of war and natural destruction.

Lady Chandos's letter reiterates and personalizes that sense of the mutual occlusion of nonhuman and human animals by reminding us that her husband's openness to beetles and rats does not seem to extend to his immediate family. His daughter appears only to exemplify his own conversational inadequacy, and his wife only as someone before whom he struggles to hide his emotional state. The sheer fact of Coetzee's invention of a letter from her uncovers this cost of her husband's purportedly universal empathy; and its content further suggests his blindness to her knowledge of him, indeed his blindness to her suffering of his vision— each drowning in their separate fates. And finally, Lady Chandos identifies their sexual intercourse (in which she strives to be one of the dryads or wood-nymphs of her husband's classical studies, as if to allow him to penetrate the spirit of nature in her) as the point at which she participates in his visions and he in hers, the origin of her rushes of rapture, and the occasions upon which each slips into the other's identity and essence: "Soul and body he speaks to me . . . ; into me, soul and body, he presses what are no longer words but flaming swords" (EC, 228). The bodily joy first evoked in Costello's Gates Lecture, and given a religious interpretation in her sister's remarks about the Orpean aspect of Christianity, is here aligned with a specifically sexual intercourse emphasised in the lesson on Eros: the embedding of one human body into another is here the occasion for revealing the human body's access to its distinctive fullness of being, and to other modes of embodied existence.

So, her husband's sense of his body as revealing everything to him is both true and false. It does not reveal his wife to him, even when it literally, concretely enters her body; but what his body reveals to his wife as she receives it is indeed the ultimately bodily root of their ability to perceive, and to think, with their hearts. Lord Chandos thinks of his own body primarily from without, as the object of a Baconian enterprise of understanding that might reveal the movements of his intestines or the engorgement of his veins; but he shows no sign of registering or valuing even the feel of that body from within, as her body's own cleansing blood thuds in Costello's ears before her Kafkaesque gate. The one thing with which he cannot fuse, into which he cannot infuse, his soul is his body; and so he and his wife (flesh of one another's flesh, participators in the same spirit) remain beyond one another's empathetic reach. It is from this fate of separation and isolation that Coetzee's Chandos letter aims to rescue its (and so Von Hofmannsthal's) characters; and in addressing its redemptive appeal for redemption to Lord Bacon, it also addresses us.

BETWEEN: WATERSKATER

"As a Woman Grows Older" appeared in the January 15, 2004, issue of the *New York Review of Books*, some four months after the publication of *Elizabeth Costello* and the announcement that J. M. Coetzee had been awarded the Nobel Prize for Literature.[4] Even though it is a short tale, the timing of its publication certainly demonstrated with commendable despatch that winning this prize would not herald the end of Coetzee's writing career; and since it tells of a visit Elizabeth Costello makes to her daughter Helen in Nice, during which her son John also visits, so that both might offer her the chance to live with (or rather, right next to) either of them for enhanced security in her old age, it also provided swift confirmation that one should not have interpreted (or perhaps, that one can now no longer interpret) the eighth lesson of *Elizabeth Costello* as describing either a period in purgatory or an arrival before the gates of divine judgement (what the tale would call "time after the end of time" [WGO, 14]). It thereby demonstrates that writing after writing (even when that writing is neither included within the earlier text nor included within any later one) inevitably reconstitutes the field of signification that the earlier text's unaltered particularities of detail can generate— another proof of Lady Chandos's belief in the nonidentity of words. And its content further suggests grounds for thinking of Elizabeth Costello as also not identical with herself, and as all the more credible a character because of it.

For the tale begins with Costello playing out on her interlocutor-son her incomprehension of the fact that she has, in certain respects, become the kind of old woman that she vowed years ago she would never be. On the one hand, she remains committed to that vow, and continuous with the person who made and remade it in response to her own mother's repeated deploring of the world around her; on the other hand, she does sincerely deplore both the grand sweep of history and the fine details of

---

[4] Hereafter WGO, with all page references keyed to that issue of the *New York Review of Books*.

the contemporary world it has brought about, and her untroubled identification of herself with what she calls this "deploration" is precisely what
makes her discontinuous with her earlier self. Such an amalgam of continuity and discontinuity is, of course, utterly typical of human experience;
but Costello finds it internal to this aspect of ageing that it appear incomprehensible to the one whose life it binds and separates, and so Coetzee
presents us with the possibility that human identity in time is necessarily
a form of nonidentity.

Other threads in this miniature tapestry also recall its predecessors.
There is, for example, a parade of animals, each of which is simultaneously a concrete particular and a way in which a literarily literal-minded
person keeps a grip on abstraction: so we encounter the little mongrel
who follows Costello to the grave yapping "bleak, bleak, bleak!," the
waterskater whose hunting activities on the surface of a pool trace "the
most beautiful of all words, the name of God" (WGO, 12), and the
cuckoo, who is at once a nasty bird and a singer or priest of unparalleled
excellence. And all three of these animals give dense reality to a question
that is otherwise both unmanageably abstract and unmanageably personal—the worth of art in general, and of Costello's art in particular (and
if Costello's, then surely that of Coetzee, who both is and is not her).

Costello tells her son that "the word that echoes back to me from all
quarters is 'bleak.' Her message to the world is unremittingly bleak . . . a
word that belongs to a winter landscape yet has somehow become
attached to me" (WGO, 11). She tells her daughter that she finds herself
asking what good beauty has done her—the beauty she has encountered,
but implicitly also the beauty she has at least tried to produce: "Is beauty
not just another consumable, like wine? One drinks it in, one drinks it
down, it gives one a brief, pleasing heady feeling, but what does it leave
behind? The residue of wine is, excuse the word, piss; what is the residue
of beauty?" (WGO, 12).

Rather different words echo back from her interlocutors. Her daughter
has this to say:

> What you have produced as a writer not only has a beauty of its own—a limited
> beauty, granted, it is not poetry, but beauty, nevertheless, shapeliness, clarity,
> economy—but has also changed the lives of others, made them better human
> beings, or slightly better human beings. It is not just I who say so. Other people
> say so too. . . . Not because what you write contains lessons but because it *is* a
> lesson. (WGO, 12)

Here, then, we have a new perspective on *Elizabeth Costello*'s claim (not
to contain but) to be eight lessons. But it is exactly at this point that the
waterskater comes into view; for it embodies Costello's view that Helen
is here projecting the existence of a perspective from which a quality of

an activity comes into view that cannot be seen by the agent herself. And her implication is that it is not just that there is something divine about that newly perceivable quality, but something theological about the very idea of a perspective beyond the agent from which alone it becomes visible—that its perception requires the kind of watching from a remove of which only God's eye is capable. It is hard to say whether this is an expression of humility (my perceptions are certainly not God's) or hubris (I am sceptical about the existence of such a perspective because I am already occupying the only available God's-eye view of my work, there is no creator and judger of it but me). Then again, Costello begins the tale by declaring that she has made a living out of ambivalences such as this. "Where would the art of fiction be if there were no double meanings? What would life itself be if there were only heads or tails and nothing in between?" (WGO, 11). And yet, this figure of the coin seems to suggest a fundamental difference between fiction and life itself, since if there is something between heads and tails in life then the idea of double meaning could not be enough to capture it—would in fact occlude it altogether. So can fiction represent life, or must it fail to do so? Perhaps we should be ambivalent about the matter.

One might think that Costello's exchange with her daughter has (despite the waterskater) stayed at too abstract a level for us to make literary progress; but the story shifts gear in this respect and thereby creates room for Costello's son to offer his response to his mother's doubts. For over dinner one evening, Costello stops generalizing about art and her own art and instead tells her children (not a tale, but rather a tale about) a tale she is at present writing—one in which a man unexpectedly reencounters in his workplace a young woman whom he had previously met in the role of a call-girl, in which role he had found himself making a sexual demand of her that both he and his author find shocking. According to Costello, then, this man exemplifies yet another respect in which human beings find that they are mysteries to themselves as well as to one another: "he would not have guessed he had it in him" to make such a demand on anyone. But more pertinently in the present context:

> It became his plan only when the girl herself appeared and he saw she was . . . a flower. It seemed an affront to him that all his life he should have missed it, beauty, and would probably miss it from here onward too. *A universe without justice!* He would have cried inwardly, and proceeded from there in his bitter way. (WGO, 14)

In short, Costello understands her story as one about "the humiliating of beauty, the bringing down of it"; and her children can plainly see its relation to her present, more general anxieties about the worth of art. But John responds in an unexpected way: " 'The man in the story . . . he still believes in beauty. He is under its spell. That is why he hates it and fights against it' " (WGO, 14). Both Costello and John here seem to share Diamond's sense (articulated, she found, in Milosz's poetry) that beauty is one of the fundamental difficulties of reality. But whereas the mother focuses on the possibility (both undeniably real and deeply enigmatic) of human hatred of beauty, the son sees that behind such hatred must lie an equally common and equally incomprehensible sense of its value—of the miracle of its sheer existence.

Costello remains unconvinced by her son's interpretation of her tale— more precisely, by his intuition of how this initial scenario might plausibly unfold, how even so sketchy a set of details might be seen to generate a certain field of signification. She even regrets succumbing to "the temptation to talk about stories before they are fully out of the bottle" (the bottle she first mentions in the sixth lesson of *Elizabeth Costello*). But by her own standards of evaluation, one might think that she should prefer her son's projection to her own; for her gloss on her own words moves rather quickly from the particular to the general—rather hastily transforming this particular shamefaced man into an emblem of human horror at cosmic injustice—whereas John stays with the man himself, asking only what this specific response of his really presupposes. Whether she has it in her repertoire to acknowledge this, or to act on that acknowledgment, is another matter. But perhaps the waterskater can only trace out the name of God on the surface of its pond precisely because it cannot hear God's advice about how to do it even more beautifully.

WITHOUT: CHIMAERA

Slow Man was published in 2005, and for the first third of its narrative gives no sign of having any particular connection with Elizabeth Costello, although its themes plainly bear some relation to those foregrounded in the stories and lessons in which she features.[5] It begins when a quiet, divorced, elderly man named Paul Rayment is knocked from his bicycle by a car; his right leg is so severely damaged in the impact that it is amputated above the knee. Refusing to make use of a prosthetic limb, he struggles to look after himself at home with a Zimmer frame and crutches; without any family, and reluctant to make humiliating claims on his few friends, he has to rely on the bounty of the Australian welfare state, and eventually acquires a carer or day nurse named Marijana Jokic—a Croatian with a husband and three children, for whom he quickly develops very powerful but ambiguous feelings of gratitude, affection, and benevo-

---

[5] (London: Secker and Warburg, 2005), hereafter SM.

lence, feelings that eventually lead him to declare his love for her and his desire to pay for her son's education. Marijana hears him out, then leaves the flat and fails to turn up on the ensuing days, failing also to respond to his frantically apologetic phone calls.

Up to this point, as Paul's life gradually contracts around him and he contracts like a salted slug within it, inclined immediately to retract the one genuinely heartfelt and positive action he has taken since his accident, readers will recognize many themes from *Elizabeth Costello* as well as from other Coetzee novels, and will certainly recognize the narrative voice of those eight lessons from its very first words:

> The blow catches him from the right, sharp and surprising and painful, like a bolt of electricity, lifting him up off the bicycle. *Relax!* He tells himself as he flies through the air (*flies through the air with the greatest of ease!*), and indeed he can feel his limbs go obediently slack. *Like a cat* he tells himself: *roll, then spring to your feet, ready for what comes next*. The unusual word *limber* or *limbre* is on the horizon too. (SM, 1)

That voice, which is and is not Rayment's, is always trying to find *le mot juste*, is in a position to recall etymologies and register a palimpsest of higher and lower cultural reference points, and is drawn to picture people and events in terms of nonhuman animal life. Through it, we acquire first of all a clear-eyed and unremitting focus on the body and its vulnerability to suffering. There is also a deep interest in the various ways in which a single human life can endure violent discontinuities that threaten both its unity as a life, and the mind's capacity to accommodate them. In this case, we have above all the overwhelming consequences for one person of another's momentary inattention at the wheel—the blow lifting Rayment out of his uneventful ordinary existence just as the words that represent it lift us out of our ordinary existence into the realm of the story (the bridge always already not only built but crossed). One might think of this strand of the text as a study of the very idea of an accident. On the one hand, nothing is more easily explicable, since even accidents are embedded in a perfectly intelligible causal sequence of events; but on the other hand, accidents necessarily lack significance, they mean nothing, and so the immensity of meaningful consequence they can bring in their train defies comprehension.

But this tale attempts to encompass more than one such difficulty of reality. For we also have the incomprehensible advent of passion into a passionless man's already-wounded existence; and here Rayment finds a Platonic image to express his sense of disorientation—more specifically to indicate his inability to know exactly what kind of feeling has come to inhabit him.

A memory comes back to him of the cover of a book he used to own, a popular edition of Plato. It showed a chariot drawn by two steeds, a black steed with flashing eyes and distended nostrils, representing the base appetites, and a white steed of calmer mien representing the less easily identifiable nobler passions. Standing in the chariot, gripping the reins, was a young man with a half-bared torso and a Grecian nose and a fillet around his brow, representing presumably the self, that which calls itself *I*. (SM, 53)

When it first comes to him, this image contrasts ironically with his present sense of himself, which is rather more like being in charge of "a wagon hitched to a mob of nags and drays that huff and puff, some barely pulling their weight" and all desiring to lie down once and for all in the road (SM, 53). But later, what he finds most difficult to resolve about his feelings for Marijana is the question of whether they belong more to the black or to the white steed. More precisely, elements of both black and white are undeniably there (he wants to have sex with her and to help her son to acquire a good education), but their precise relation remains obscure: is it that he is using the promise of help to get Marijana into bed, or is he rather struggling to transmute what he recognizes as an utterly inappropriate sexual impulse into a genuinely altruistic act (the truly Platonic way of thinking of the matter)? He ends the novel ensconced in his own personal chariot (or *deux-chevaux*, as someone else calls it): a recumbent bicycle made specially for him by the Jokic family, and rather more closely resembling his worn-out wagon than the original Platonic vehicle. But although he is the one who must supply the necessary horsepower to move it, it remains unclear which of his inner horses can or will be harnessed to do the work.

A third difficulty, and one that bears upon the form as well as the content of the tale, is under examination by means of Paul Rayment's lifelong interest in photography. As well as earning a living as a photographer, he has a uniquely substantial and valuable collection of photographs by the first great Australian practitioners in the medium. Rayment is deeply impressed by the capacity of photographs to transmute light into substance, to record the world itself in all its reality, and so to confront viewers with their dead ancestors in all the vital, concrete substance of their individual lives (just the enigmatic aspect of the medium that Diamond finds central to Hughes's poem about the victims of the First World War). He lost interest in the business just as the world around him woke to the enchanting possibilities of visual images that are purely digital, hence essentially malleable and unrelated to any original in the real world—"a *techne* of images without substance" that fulfils a nightmare Rayment also inherits from Plato. And a key element of the plot will turn on one of the Jokic children's inhabitation of that world of digital doctoring, and his willingness to subject one of Rayment's photographs to its manipulations.

It is Marijana who confronts him with the question of whether this technological progression was not foreshadowed in the medium of photography as such, insofar as the endless reproducibility of photographic images had already subverted the idea of a sharp distinction between original and copy in this domain. Rayment resists this implication, arguing that the reproducibility of photographic images of reality does not render each and every one of them any less images *of reality*. But neither does he ever deny the inherent mysteriousness of that fact—the fact that when we look at those images, we see nothing less than the reality that was originally before the camera that mechanically produced them. It is, for him, precisely in their loss of that paradoxical sense of internal relation to the real, in the sheer coherent frictionlessness of images unanchored to any real original, that the subsequent loss of any sense of reality as it really is must be thought to reside. But the reader is free to acknowledge that Rayment's fixation on images that can never lose their reference to their real originals also hangs together with his abhorrence of a prosthesis (something he thinks of as creating the mere appearance of a leg, as artificial as opposed to natural, and so as dishonest: "I don't want to look natural. . . . I prefer to feel natural" [SM, 59]), and thence to his general refusal to act on impulses or intentions of whose authenticity he is uncertain. It is as if Rayment experiences the whole of his life after the incomprehensible impact of the accident, both inner and outer, as utterly unmoored from its original; this is why he thinks of himself as "an after-man, like an after-image" (SM, 34)—no more than a doctored copy of himself.

The reflexive relevance of this theme forces itself upon our attention when, in chapter 13, as Rayment frantically tries to reestablish contact with his apparently offended day nurse, everything changes. For the novelist Elizabeth Costello rings his front doorbell and invites herself in. She shows herself to be surprisingly knowledgeable about the course of his life since the accident, from the very moment of the blow, and eager to offer him advice and encouragement about how to go on from his present, panic-stricken, paralysed, and hence essentially inactive condition. She seems, in fact, very impatient of his obdurate reluctance to make something, anything, of his circumstances; she wants him to push, to "push the mortal envelope" (SM, 83). One might imagine this as the advice of a concerned friend; but Rayment has never met Costello before, and the nature of her concern is not that of a friend: "You came to me, that is all I can say. You occurred to me—a man with a bad leg and no future and an unsuitable passion. That was where it started. Where we go from there I have no idea. Have you any proposal?" (SM, 85). And for the rest of the novel, Costello is an almost-constant presence in Rayment's life; living on and off in his flat, she not only offers him suggestions about how to deal with his new circumstances, but converses with all of the main characters within it, and in some cases ensures that those characters act in ways she regards as most suitable for her purposes.

How are we to understand the arrival of this unwelcome guest? Neither Rayment nor Costello is entirely sure, at the beginning of their relationship, of its nature. Costello compares herself to Doubting Thomas, wanting to explore what kind of being Rayment is: she needs to shake his hand, and feel its solidity, before she can dismiss the anxiety that "our two bodies would not just pass through each other. Naïve, of course. We are not ghosts, either of us—why should I have thought so?" (SM, 81). Once through that moment of doubt, however, she treats Rayment as a recalcitrant character in her fiction: having come to her unbidden, as a literary intuition of which she "cannot at first make sense" (SM, 85), she is having some difficulty in pursuing the possibilities he opens up for her narrative, because he shows an irritating reluctance to act—to take anything other than a profoundly passive stance to his newly reduced and transformed circumstances. In other words, the familiar realist conjunction of character and situation is simply not engendering a sufficiently interesting plot; so its author has come to confront the prime cause of that failure as she understands it, with a view to doing everything in her power to encourage him to make himself and his life sufficiently interesting for her not to abandon him (and so her initial intuition).[6]

Taken this way, *Slow Man* is a (quietly amusing) study of an author's experience of creative frustration, more precisely of the failure of an initially promising artistic inspiration—its nature, its causes, and its possible resolutions. But it aims to do so while honouring the time-honoured myth of creative writers since before Plato: their sense of their characters as having an independent reality. This is why Costello understands Rayment as coming to her rather than coming from her, and of his real personality and history as accordingly something of which she is ignorant, something that Rayment alone can reveal to her. How, then, within the

---

[6] Coetzee here engineers an overcoming of the gap that the narrator of his Nobel Lecture (entitled "He and His Man") fears must always remain between himself (a writer named Robin) and his man (whom he imagines as sending him reports of his experiences all over the world)—a gap Robin presents as analogous to that between deckhands toiling in the rigging of two ships that pass one another on opposite courses: "the seas are rough, the weather is stormy; their eyes lashed by the spray, their hands burned by the cordage, they pass each other by, too busy even to wave." If they were less busy, or the weather less stormy, could their ships have paused, lashed themselves together, and allowed the two to clasp hands? But if their business is their writing, how could they set it aside and still be in a position even to want to meet (as author to character)?

terms of that myth, might one capture the reality of the author's experience when such an independently real being fails to live up to his initial promise—stubbornly refusing to respond to his author's willingness to respond to him, to make him real by allowing his individuality to find expression in a narrative whose verisimilitude might hold the attention of readers? By presenting her attempt to stay true to her initial inspiration as if it were an attempt to discover (if necessary by force) the vital core of another person's individual existence, however deeply buried or repressed it may be.

From this perspective, many aspects of the book's apparently realistic narrative mode fall into place. The blow with which it begins is not simply the shock of an ordinary life being displaced from its own parameters; it is also the shock of a character's birth—a representation of the discontinuity between lack of inspiration and its arrival from the point of view of that into which divine breath is introduced. Before that blow, there was no Paul Rayment; and the "dead place," "the dream," "the land of whiteness" (SM, 4, 9, 13) that is the hospital is the first coherent scene of his fictional life. This is why during his transportation from the accident to the hospital something very specific comes to him: "A letter at a time, *clack clack clack*, a message is being typed on a rose-pink screen that trembles like water each time he blinks and is therefore quite likely his own inner eyelid" (SM, 3). For what is being composed is his own existence, as seen by the consciousness that inhabits this particular wounded body, coming to him as if from without, from an independently existing other.

And yet, if we read the story in these terms, it does not and cannot make sense—and for a reason that distinguishes this instance of literary nonsensicality from its closest counterpart in *Elizabeth Costello* (when, in lesson 8, Costello is inserted into the fictional world of another author). For an author and her character do not and cannot share a single world; or to put the point more exactly, the moment the author inserts herself into the world of her character, she becomes another character and so cannot intelligibly relate to her character as his author. There is, in other words, something essentially incoherent or chimerical in Costello's dual-aspect role as author and character; for it is not that we must switch between these two ways of viewing her, as we can between the duck and rabbit aspects of a duck-rabbit drawing; we must rather view her as simultaneously both duck and rabbit, author and character, and this cannot be done. For if she is able to shake her character's hand, then they are indeed inhabitants of the same fictional world, in which each is no less real than the other; but then the idea that she is the creator of that world (and so of its inhabitants) makes no sense, and her creative efforts can appear in that world only as more or less heavy-handed attempts by one person to

influence the course of another person's life—not an unfamiliar phenomenon, but certainly not a coherent embodiment of the kind of influence
that an author has over her characters and their world.

And indeed, Paul Rayment understands Costello's actions in precisely
these terms. She is a bewilderingly well-informed and persistent interferer
in his life, but ultimately just one more person whose independent reality
must be budgeted for in his thoughts and actions. And Costello's reality
in Rayment's world is underlined by the fact that she has a history within
it before her appearance at his doorstep, as of course must anyone capable
of so appearing (no one can, after all, appear from nowhere in the real
world). Accordingly, Rayment very quickly recognizes her as bearing the
name of a famous novelist, even if one who resides in Melbourne rather
than his home city of Adelaide; and he finds a selection of her books
(which includes *The House on Eccles Street*, although not *Fire and Ice*),
as well as a book about her writing, in his local library. So he draws the
obvious conclusion: she has for some reason decided that he will form
the basis for a character in her next novel, and she is impertinently sub-
jecting him to unusually close observation for that purpose. In other
words, she is not (she could not possibly be) the author of this world, but
simply an author within it—and one whose obscure remarks about his
coming to her, and about his needing to make a stronger case for himself,
are then best understood as the ramblings of a writer whom weariness,
illness, and senility have pushed to the edge of insanity.

In effect, then, Rayment resists Costello's understanding of him as ultimately fictional, by resisting any relation to her as his author—which
means by emphasizing that embeddedness in his reality without which
she would not be in a position to berate him for his irresponsibility as a
character; but Costello is no less resistant to Rayment's understanding of
her as just another real inhabitant of his (fictional) Adelaide, as is evident
in her refusal to be governed by its constraints. For despite his best efforts
to make sense of her visit as part of her eccentricity and incipient madness,
Rayment finds in her notebooks details of the fine texture of his stream
of consciousness during the days before her arrival into his life that no
one else could conceivably have access to; and this forces him to think of
himself in terms much closer to those defining her interpretation of their
relationship: "All the time he thought he was his own master he has been
in a cage like a rat, darting this way and that, yammering to himself, with
the infernal woman standing over him, observing, listening, taking notes,
recording his progress" (SM, 122). Even this image of the laboratory,
however, suggests that, within his highly controlled environment, Rayment is nevertheless free to choose which way to dart and what to yammer
to himself, and so to preserve a highly constrained sense of his own autonomy. How could he not, since he could not conceivably think of himself

as a purely fictional character without losing any intelligible relation to his own life as something that he leads, something he lives?

To be sure, the pressure of those notebooks on his sense of reality remains intense, to the point at which a further explanation of their contents occurs to him, one that balances unsteadily between the uncanny and the bathetic, but nevertheless threatens to buckle his mind.

> The greatest of all secrets may just have unveiled itself to him. There is a second world that exists side by side with the first, unsuspected. One chugs along in the first for a certain length of time; then the angel of death arrives in the person of Wayne Blight or someone like him. For an instant, for an aeon, time stops; one tumbles down a dark hole. Then, hey presto, one emerges into a second world *identical with the first*, where time resumes and the action proceeds— except that one now has Elizabeth Costello around one's neck, or someone like her. (SM, 122)

Rayment is compelled to think of himself as having died, but of course he can do so only if he postulates that there is life after death; and he thinks of this mode of being as "nothing but a trick that might as well be a trick with words" (SM, 123). Death, thus understood, is not nonexistence but a kind of fictional existence, which he pictures as inherently puny, paper-thin, insubstantial: everything is the same, but nothing is real. Here, then, Rayment arrives at a third way of interpreting the opening blow of the narrative—as representing another kind of discontinuous continuity in an individual's (deathless) existence; although his readers may rather see him as struggling desperately to find terms in which he can suffer the intimation of his own fictional status without entirely losing his grip on himself as an existing being. But whether we think of his vision as one of life-after-death-as-fictional-life or of fictional-life-as-life-after-death, Rayment's registration of its nature is both perceptive and myopic.

On the one hand, he recognizes that such a mode of life would in one sense be indistinguishable from life before death—for he sees that it is not a doctored or damaged version of that life, that life after death lacks nothing but (so to speak) existence. As Cavell (we noted earlier) argues with respect to cinematic representations of reality, all the predicates attributable to (real) life before death would continue to apply to (fictional) life after death. And indeed, the world of life after death that Rayment now imagines himself inhabiting is one in which he continues to act and to be acted upon within an independent world that he shares with others. He is, after all, still living, and so he still retains a relation to his own existence as something to be realized by him. On the other hand, Rayment nevertheless cannot avoid thinking of such a mode of life as puny and paper-thin, as if it were a kind of photocopy of the real thing, something essentially secondary in relation to an original.

But in truth, fictional people are not (certainly not necessarily) copies of real people; they can have any of the attributes real people have, and all of their inner complexity, but not by virtue of being reproductions of them. Fictional people may be part of a narrative whose realist ambitions include that of revealing something about the real world; but their capacity to convince readers to suspend their disbelief in their own reality is not a function of whether or not there is a specific individual in the real world whose existence is in any direct way a condition for the possibility of their own existence (whereas one cannot have a person in a photograph without there having been a real person before the camera that produced it). What Rayment's fantasy of his own fictionality therefore displays is an inability or unwillingness on his part to distinguish fictional people from photographic images of people. He cannot accept the possibility of representations of reality that are not reproductions of it.

Whatever one thinks of Rayment's fixation on the photographic, however, the mode of Costello's embeddedness in Rayment's world is such that it makes no sense to him. He cannot think of her as just another inhabitant of it, since what she knows about him is unknowable by anyone other than him; but neither can he coherently think of her as anything else—not his angel of death (since he cannot think of himself as utterly nonexistent) and not his author (since he cannot think of his existence as fictional, particularly since he would then be inhabiting an unintelligible fiction whose creator existed within it). But Rayment's mode of embeddedness in Costello's world is equally resistant to her understanding. To be sure, we can imagine an author such as Costello coming up with the fictional structure of *Slow Man* as a way of trying to capture her sense of a particular kind of relation in which she really does sometimes stand to her fictional creations. But in so doing, she has to acknowledge that this fictional structure is ultimately incoherent, and hence that so too must be the experience for which it seems to be the only adequate expression. For its success as a representation of that experience precisely depends upon its depicting an impossible world in which author and character can relate directly to one another.

And of course, we need to add a third perspective to this already-irresoluble conjunction of perspectives. For it is not just that Paul Rayment is presented to us as a recalcitrant character in the fictional work of Elizabeth Costello; it is also that both he and she are characters in the fictional work of J. M. Coetzee. One might say: even the world in which Costello is the creator of Paul Rayment is not the real world. There is, of course, nothing in principle incoherent in the idea of an author inventing a fictional author who herself invents fictional characters; if she did not, she would not be a very plausible depiction of an author. But the relevant fictional universes are usually neatly nested or hierarchical, with each fictional world embedded in the next fictional world up that hierarchy until the real world is encountered, and no leakages allowed between any two worlds (between fictional and fictional, or between fictional and real). As we have seen, however, Paul Rayment's world is not neatly nested within Elizabeth Costello's world; the two are rather inextricably tangled, with Costello appearing as both inhabitant and author of Rayment's world, and thereby ensuring that both she and Rayment appear to be (and not to be) inhabiting two fictional worlds at once.

So: should we say that Coetzee has created two incoherent fictional worlds, or one? Has he created two first-level fictional characters, or one first-level character and one second-level character? And is the Costello of this novel not only her own fictional depiction of herself grappling with one of her own fictional creations, but also Coetzee's fictional depiction of his own frustrating inability to create a convincingly real and alive Paul Rayment?

Coetzee hardly discourages us from thinking of *Slow Man* as another postscript to *Elizabeth Costello*, and so from including this text in our final, nonabsorptive tableau. For Costello's presence pervades two-thirds of the successor novel, and of course, her prior appearance in those eight lessons gives her character a degree of substance and a burden of history that is likely to outweigh that accumulated by Paul Rayment over the course of some eighty pages before his nemesis bursts onto the scene. Nevertheless, we must remember that until she does so, the fictional world we took ourselves to be inhabiting was indeed that of someone else— someone for all the world as unrelated to Elizabeth Costello as the protagonists of any of Coetzee's novels prior to *Elizabeth Costello*. So part of the sense of shocked hilarity occasioned by her arrival lies in our sense that, with it, two different Coetzean fictional worlds are colliding—a shock that Rayment's speedy attempts to place Costello in his own world does not entirely dissipate (in part because Costello seems never entirely to accept that embedding of herself).

It is almost as if Costello comes to Coetzee's rescue—as if her arrival allows him to transfigure a looming failure of creative inspiration into a new creative possibility, and so to find (in good modernist manner) an unrecognized fictional resource in the exhaustion of his own fictional resources, but only at the cost of making Costello appear to have definitively annexed his creative powers for the foreseeable future. It is enough to make one wonder whether Paul Rayment's fantasized images of Costello as an angel of death, or even a wild-haired, bare-breasted, whip-wielding hag with her hands at his throat (SM, 164), are displaced versions of Coetzee's sense of his own apparent subordination to the all-consuming imaginative reality of this particular character. She simply will not stop inserting herself into his imagination, and so into its worlds; and when

Paul Rayment concludes the book by saying to Costello "there are plenty of fish in the ocean, so I hear. But as for me, as for now: goodbye," it is hard not to recall that this image of the ocean of creativity was itself first uttered by the very woman from whom he wishes to declare his autonomy.

It certainly seems evident that her vision of Kafkaesque realism continues to provide the basic framework for Coetzee's modernism. For the fiction that results from his embedding of character and author in one another's worlds is aptly describable as a rigorous thinking through of the consequences of a conjunction that is no less impossible than Kafka's conjunction of ape and Western culture, or Costello's conjunction of Anchises and Aphrodite, or Coetzee's prior insertion of Costello into a Kafkaesque town and trial (or, come to that, my imaginary third symposium on the Costello of Coetzee's Tanner Lectures). But if that thinking through is sufficiently rigorous—if Costello's authorial frustration and affection is rendered as convincingly as are the frustrations and affections of the being to whom they are directed, as well as the results of their chimerical intercourse—then the fiction that emerges from this intellectual imaginative exercise (this thinking with the heart and the soul) will nevertheless be an exercise in realism. It will further the novel's venerable tradition of examining the idiosyncratic reality of individual human existence in specific circumstances by revealing how many of the apparently ineliminable conventions of literary realism can be dispensed with or violated without losing the capacity to create an impression of reality. More precisely, it will reveal how much of reality can be captured in its true nature only insofar as our representations of it reflect its resistances to representation, and so to comprehension. For it is only a Kafkaesque realism such as Coetzee's that can hope to convey an accurate impression of the various difficulties of reality, both for literature and for philosophy. And only a philosophy that is both realist and modernist—committed to achieving a lucid grasp of reality, and willing to put in question any prevailing philosophical conventions concerning that enterprise that appear at present to block or subvert its progress, including the convention that philosophical realism is no more literature's business than literary realism is any concern of philosophy's—will be capable of being properly, genuinely impressed by Coetzee's achievement.

BIBLIOGRAPHY

Anscombe, G.E.M. *Collected Philosophical Papers*, vol. 3 (Oxford: Blackwell, 1981).
———. "Modern Moral Philosophy," in *Collected Philosophical Papers*, vol. 3.
Attridge, D. *J. M. Coetzee and the Ethics of Reading* (Chicago: University of Chicago Press, 2004).
Bartsch, S., and T. Batscherer, eds., *Erotikon: Essay on Eros, Ancient and Modern* (Chicago: University of Chicago Press, 2005).
Cavell, S. *The World Viewed* (Cambridge: Harvard University Press, 1971).
———. *Must We Mean What We Say?* (Cambridge: Cambridge University Press, 1976).
———. *Disowning Knowledge: In Seven Plays of Shakespeare* (Cambridge: Cambridge University Press, 2003).
———. "Companionable Thinking," in *Wittgenstein and the Moral Life: Essays in Honour of Cora Diamond*, ed. A. Crary (Boston: MIT Press, 2007); and in *Philosophy and Animal Life*.
———. "Hamlet's Burden of Proof," in *Disowning Knowledge*.
———. "Knowing and Acknowledging," in *Must We Mean What We Say?*
Cavell, S. et al. *Philosophy and Animal Life* (New York: Columbia University Press, 2008).
Celan, P. *Poems of Paul Celan,* trans. M. Hamburger (London: Anvil Press, 1988).
Clark, S. *The Moral Status of Animals* (New York: Oxford University Press, 1977).
Coetzee, J. M. *Doubling the Point*, ed. D. Attwell (Cambridge: Harvard University Press, 1992).
———. *The Lives of Animals* (Princeton: Princeton University Press, 1999).
———. *Elizabeth Costello: Eight Lessons* (London: Secker and Warburg, 2003).
———. *Slow Man* (London: Secker and Warburg, 2005).
———. "As a Woman Grows Older," *New York Review of Books*, January 15, 2004.
———. "He and His Man," in *Nobel Lectures: 20 Years of the Nobel Prize for Literature Lectures*, ed. J. Sutherland (London: Icon Books, 2007).
Crary, A., ed. *Wittgenstein and the Moral Life: Essays in Honour of Cora Diamond* (Boston: MIT Press, 2007).
Crary, A., and S. Shieh, eds. *Reading Cavell* (London: Routledge, 2006).
Crist, E. *Images of Animals: Anthropomorphism and Animal Mind* (Philadelphia: Temple University Press, 1999).
Diamond, C. *The Realistic Spirit* (Cambridge: MIT Press, 1991).
———. "Anything But Argument?," in *The Realistic Spirit*.
———. "The Difficulty of Reality and the Difficulty of Philosophy," in *Reading Cavell*, ed. A. Crary and S. Shieh (London: Routledge, 2006).
———. "Eating Meat and Eating People," in *The Realistic Spirit*.

Diamond, C. "Realism and the Realistic Spirit," in *The Realistic Spirit*.

Dreyfus, H. *Being-in-the-World* (Cambridge: MIT Press, 1991).

Eagleton, T. *The English Novel: An Introduction* (Oxford: Blackwell, 2005).

Fried, M. "Manet's Sources," *ArtForum* 7 (March 1969).

———. *Absorption and Theatricality: Painting and Beholder in the Age of Diderot* (Chicago: University of Chicago Press, 1980).

———. *Courbet's Realism* (Chicago: University of Chicago Press, 1990).

———. *Manet's Modernism* (Chicago: University of Chicago Press, 1996).

———. *Art and Objecthood* (Chicago: University of Chicago Press, 1998).

Gaita, R., ed. *Value and Understanding: Essays for Peter Winch* (London: Routledge, 1990).

———. *Good and Evil: An Absolute Conception* (London: Macmillan, 1991).

———. *The Philosopher's Dog* (Melbourne: Text Publishing, 2002).

Gilligan, C. *In a Different Voice* (Cambridge: Harvard University Press, 1982).

Greenberg, C. *New York Painting and Sculpture 1940–70*, ed. H. Geldzahler (New York: Dutton, 1969).

Hearne, V. *Adam's Task: Calling Animals by Name* (New York: Harper Perennial, 1994).

Heidegger, M. *Being and Time*, trans. J. MacQuarrie and E. Robinson (Oxford: Blackwell, 1962).

———. *Fundamental Concepts of Metaphysics*, trans. W. McNeill and N. Walker (Bloomington: Indiana University Press, 1995).

———. *What Is Called Thinking?*, trans. J. Glenn Gray (New York: Harper and Row, 1968).

Hofmannsthal, H. von. *The Lord Chandos Letter and Other Writings*, trans. J. Rotenberg (New York: New York Review Books, 2005).

Holland, R. *Against Empiricism* (Totowa, NJ: Barnes and Noble, 1980).

———. "The Miraculous," in *Against Empiricism*.

Kafka, F. *The Complete Short Stories of Franz Kafka*, trans. W. and E. Muir, ed. N. N. Glatzer (London: Vintage, 1983).

———. "A Report to an Academy," in *Complete Short Stories*.

McDowell, J. "Comment on Stanley Cavell's 'Companionable Thinking,'" in *Wittgenstein and the Moral Life: Essays in Honour of Cora Diamond*, ed. A. Crary (Boston: MIT Press, 2007); and in *Philosophy and Animal Life*.

McMahan, J. *The Ethics of Killing* (Oxford: Oxford University Press, 2002).

Mitchell, S. *Erotikon* (New York: HarperCollins, 2000).

Moi, T. *Henrik Ibsen and the Birth of Modernism* (Oxford: Oxford University Press, 2006).

Mulhall, S. *Stanley Cavell: Philosophy's Recounting of the Ordinary* (Oxford: Oxford University Press, 1994).

———. *The Conversation of Humanity* (Charlottesville: University of Virginia Press, 2007).

Nagel, T. *Mortal Questions* (Cambridge: Cambridge University Press, 1979).

———. "What Is It Like to Be a Bat?" in *Mortal Questions*.

O'Neill, O. "Critical Review of Clark, *The Moral Status of Animals*," *Journal of Philosophy* 77 (1980).

———. "The Power of Example," *Philosophy* 61 (1986).

Parfit, D. *Reasons and Persons* (Oxford: Oxford University Press, 1984).

Pippin, R. *Henry James and Modern Moral Life* (Cambridge: Cambridge University Press, 2000).

Poyner, J. *J. M. Coetzee and the Idea of the Public Intellectual* (Athens: Ohio University Press, 2006).

Turner, D. *The Darkness of God* (Cambridge: Cambridge University Press, 1995).

Watt, I. *The Rise of the Novel* (London: Pimlico, 1957).

Wittgenstein, L. *Philosophical Investigations*, trans. G.E.M.Anscombe (Oxford: Blackwell, 1958).

Wright, L. "A Feminist-Vegetarian Defence of Elizabeth Costello," in *J. M. Coetzee and the Idea of the Public Intellectual*, ed. J. Poyner (Athens: Ohio University Press, 2006).

INDEX